HOW TO THINK LIKE
AN ECONOMIST

To my parents

HOW TO THINK LIKE AN ECONOMIST

Great Economists Who Shaped the World
and What They Can Teach Us

ROBBIE MOCHRIE

BLOOMSBURY CONTINUUM
LONDON · OXFORD · NEW YORK · NEW DELHI · SYDNEY

BLOOMSBURY CONTINUUM
Bloomsbury Publishing Plc
50 Bedford Square, London, WC1B 3DP, UK
29 Earlsfort Terrace, Dublin 2, Ireland

BLOOMSBURY, BLOOMSBURY CONTINUUM and the Diana logo are trademarks
of Bloomsbury Publishing Plc

First published in Great Britain 2024

A catalogue record for this book is available from the British Library

Library of Congress Cataloguing-in-Publication data has been applied for

ISBN: HB: 978-1-3994-0864-6; TPB: 978-1-3994-0862-2; eBook: 978-1-3994-0866-0;
ePDF: 978-1-3994-0865-3

2 4 6 8 10 9 7 5 3 1

Typeset by Deanta Global Publishing Services, Chennai, India
Printed and bound in Great Britain by CPI Group (UK) Ltd, Croydon CR0 4YY

MIX
Paper | Supporting
responsible forestry
FSC® C171272

To find out more about our authors and books visit www.bloomsbury.com
and sign up for our newsletters

CONTENTS

FOREWORD

What is the economy?

Everything useful, everything valuable and everything linking us to other people. And usually, we are unaware of it.

To understand it, we need to look at the world in a whole new way. We need to see that it is filled with *resources*. We own resources. We manage them, and use them up, but we can also create them. And we can also buy them and sell them or share them. As we look around and see resources, we will also see a complex web of relationships, which connects people and organizations too. All that is the economy.

As a first exercise in this way of thinking like an economist, consider this book as a resource. You have picked it up and started reading it. Presumably, you have chosen to spend your time in this way. A few moments ago, you decided to read this paragraph. No one compelled you to do this. And it would make no sense at all to talk about a book finding its way into your hands all by itself, opening itself up at this page and demanding that you read it.

Here are two economic questions for you to think about. Why have you chosen this book, rather than another of the millions of other books in the world? And if you bought this book, rather than simply coming across it by chance, why did you choose to spend your money on it, and not something else?

Taking that first step of seeing the world and thinking of the world as being full of resources, should make you think of plenty of other questions like those.

While resources are important, economists are much more interested in people, and the relationships between them. As with this book, people make decisions about what they will do with what they have. At its most general, the economy involves people managing resources to fulfil their desires. As an economist, I cannot tell you what you hoped that you would find in this book, which made it seem worth reading. Nor can I tell you what pleasure you have given up so that you might read it. But I will assert that you thought that it would be a good use of one of the most important resources which you have, your money, to buy this book and a good use of another very important type of resource, your time, to read it.

Continuing to think like economists, there is much more that we can say about reading this book. A mug of coffee is a resource. You use it by drinking it. A train ticket gives you the right to travel between two railway stations. You use it by making the journey. A house is a building designed so that people can live in it. In using it, not only do you have shelter and warmth, but you turn it into a home.

And this book? It's not written just to be a form of entertainment. When you have finished it, you will hopefully know more about economics and how an array of brilliant thinkers have shaped it. In some small way, that knowledge will change you. That gives us a very modern, truly economic way of thinking about people as self-managing resources. In choosing to read this book today, you might engage with the economy differently tomorrow – even if only because you have become more aware of what you are doing. We will explore what it means to think of people as self-managing in Chapters 17, 19 and 23 which review the work of Thomas Schelling, Gary Becker and George Akerlof.

The economy is a complex system within which people manage what they have and interact with other people (and what they have). Economics is then the structured study of people, as resource managers, and the system within which they manage them. That definition is deliberately vague and general. It allows the first half of the book to explain how economics gradually emerged over centuries through the ideas of people who were not simply economists. You will meet philosophers, priests, financiers, journalists and civil servants.

Go back to Athens, about 2,400 years ago, when the city was not just the leading state in the Greek-speaking quarter of the Mediterranean, but the cradle of Western civilization. Thinking about how to manage resources was a tiny part of philosophy, then a radical, new way of thinking about everything in the world and beyond it. For the ancient Greeks, how to manage external resources was less interesting than the question of how to manage ourselves. Economics therefore began as a set of arguments about the ethical behaviour of Athenian citizens.

The first major advance on that Greek approach occurred in the Islamic Caliphate more than a thousand years later. Rather than thinking about economics largely as self-management, Muslim scholars recognized the value of people being able to exchange resources. They still thought in philosophical terms – or, given that they were trying to explain the will of God, theological terms. Their approach was taken up by Christian scholars in Western Europe in the thirteenth century, who added ideas taken from Roman law about the nature of property and trade. Economics was still embedded in the analysis of individual behaviour.

It was only in 1776 that the Scottish philosopher, Adam Smith, produced the first systematic account of the economy. His book, *The Wealth of Nations*, is the common ancestor of all the ways of thinking about the economy which exist today. Its arguments had such width and depth that all economists can look back to *The Wealth of Nations* and find material which is congenial with their own idea of the economy. However, it is perhaps best to think of Smith as standing at the end of the tradition of resource management in philosophy at the point where it evolved into modern economics. A great thinker about the economy, he bridged ethics and economics.

For most of the nineteenth century, the people who wrote about the economy came to think about it after studying philosophy or, especially in Germany, history. In France, several engineers made substantial contributions to economic analysis, while in Austria-Hungary, an influential tradition of economic analysis sprang out of the law faculties of universities. As economics started to emerge as a subject in its own right, it seemed that everyone had something to say about it.

With his *Principles of Economics*, published in 1890, Alfred Marshall finally put economics on a recognizably modern footing. As a result, at the start of the twentieth century economics finally separated itself from philosophy and the humanities and developed its modern identity. Even so, in the work of psychologists, such as Daniel Kahneman and Amos Tversky, political scientists such as Herbert Simon and Lin Ostrom, and mathematicians, such as John von Neumann and John Nash, we shall see that there are academics from many other disciplines who continue to make important contributions to economics.

During the twentieth century, there were huge changes in the nature of the economy. In 1900, coal was the main source of power, cars were simply horseless carriages, and telephones a recent invention. People tended to die much younger than they do now, after working very long hours in physically demanding jobs. Very few people had university degrees. Through the twentieth century, partly because of the effects of two world wars, the USA became the world's dominant economic power.

When the structure of the economy changes, economics changes too. Adam Smith wrote in the early years of the Industrial Revolution. His analysis reflected the small scale of industry, before steam power allowed the creation of large factories. John Stuart Mill and Karl Marx were both deeply critical of the way in which the Industrial Revolution of the early nineteenth century mostly benefited factory owners, rather than their workers. Alfred Marshall continued the tradition that economics should enable an improvement in the conditions of the working class.

Finding a route out of the Great Depression of the 1930s was a massive challenge to economic thinking. The US economy, which had been the engine for economic growth across the world in the 1920s, came close to melting down. Nearly a quarter of workers became unemployed between 1930 and 1932. The English economist, John Maynard Keynes, argued that the only possible solution was for governments to spend more money.

At the core of Keynes' complex argument was a brilliant insight, which quickly gained the support of younger economists. Much of the detail of his argument was very unclear, and so economists have debated for many years about how much of Keynes' arguments should be accepted, and on what basis. But there are very few economists who would argue against the main implication of his analysis, that a country's government can play an important role in stabilizing its economy.

Keynes was much more than an academic economist. Politically active for much of his life, he was also a brilliant journalist. While he argued that government spending could have many benefits, Friedrich Hayek and Milton Friedman, who followed on from Keynes as important public intellectuals, disagreed with him on that. They went on to influence the thinking of Margaret Thatcher and Ronald Reagan, as they tried to limit the size and power of the state. Such political differences did not prevent Keynes and Hayek from admiring each other's work as economists.

In modern economics, information is perhaps the most important resource which we must manage, and many of the most important differences among economists have been about how to manage it. Adam Smith assumed that we would have enough knowledge so that the economy would be self-organizing and stable. In some ways, when Maynard Keynes reminded the world that economic stability depends upon widespread confidence, trust and hope for the future, he was looking back to Smith, and the philosophical tradition about what we can know about the economy, even as he challenged the assumption that its self-organization would always be effective.

The differences between economists were perhaps best captured by Herbert Simon, one of the greatest social scientists of the twentieth century. He argued that there are two ways of thinking about economic decision making. We can either treat people as problem solvers, who always choose the best possible actions, or else we can treat them as rule followers, who rely on procedures which are good enough.

It was natural for economists to treat people as problem solvers, especially when their analysis took a mathematical form. Economists who continue to treat people as rule followers have tended to look to psychology, and other social sciences to develop their ideas. We will see the difference towards the end of the book in a comparison of the work of Robert Lucas and George Akerlof. Lucas believed that it is always best to treat people as problem solvers. Akerlof's rule-following approach meant that people's choices would be just very slightly different, but those small differences were enough for Lucas and Akerlof to disagree substantially about the working of the economy.

That comparison also helps to explain why economic theory usually makes gradual progress. Since subtle differences in economists' thinking can have very large effects on their predictions, finding good ways of adapting economic ideas is tricky, and often takes time. In addition, the value of economic ideas is largely determined by their ability to guide economic policy. Every economist in this book has tried to apply their ideas to such practical matters.

For example, Thomas Schelling began his career by thinking about the nature of the conflict between the USA and the USSR during the Cold War, contributing substantially to the development of the doctrine of Mutually Assured Destruction. That was important in leading to the nuclear disarmament treaties of the 1970s. At the end of his career, early in the twenty-first century, he turned his attention to climate change, once again thinking about the role which governments might play in resolving this existential challenge.

We can see a very different approach to the application of theory in the work of Esther Duflo, whose work is the subject of the last chapter of the book. As a development economist, Duflo has worked with some of the poorest people in the world, trying to understand the characteristics of their economic environment which might prevent its development, so that they remain poor. In many ways, her work is a fitting end to a discussion in which Smith's *Wealth of Nations* has a central role. Duflo has argued that poverty does not simply mean a lack of money, but rather a limited ability to command economic resources. Many economic arrangements which we take for granted in richer countries have not yet emerged in poorer ones. But Duflo's work is important because she works with poor people to understand the precise nature of the barriers which they face. Then, by carrying out experiments, she can recommend small changes which might have substantial effects on well-being. This is a new way of thinking like an economist, which is proving to be very useful.

And that is perhaps the most important part of thinking like an economist: looking at the world in a particular way, not just to understand it but, by changing it, to make it better.

1

Aristotle – The Philosopher

Abundance through the practice of virtue

Athens: the cradle of Western civilization, where the greatest of the ancient Greek philosophers came together and tried to understand the world, society and what it meant to be human. The first economic thought emerged about 2,500 years ago, during the prolonged, bloody conflict of the Peloponnesian War, in which Athens and its great rival, Sparta, strove for dominance among the Greek city states.

While the Spartans eventually won the war, they left few written records, so that most of what we know about the period comes from the losing side. By the end of the fifth century BC, Athens had democratic institutions, and had become a centre of culture. Public debate and literature coalesced in the new movement of *philosophia*, or the 'love of wisdom', which flourished throughout the next century.

That movement began with the professional gadfly, Socrates, who encouraged young men to question what they thought they knew. His success in disturbing the peace meant that the Athenians found it expedient to try him on capital crimes and sentence him to death by suicide.

Socrates' pupil, Plato, was an idealist, who dreamt of the rule of a philosopher king. Believing that there might be an opportunity to put his plans into practice, he travelled to Syracuse, in Sicily, where he ended up being imprisoned and sold into slavery. Friends managed to free him.

Then we come to Plato's pupil, Aristotle, who wanted to catalogue all human experience. In Raphael's painting from the early sixteenth century, *The School of Athens*, Plato, the rational idealist, is pointing up to the sky, while Aristotle, the realist, points directly ahead to the viewer. He developed a method of argument, which was based on taking observations, and then trying to generalize from them. That led his most famous pupil, Alexander the Great, to send him specimens of flora and fauna, collected during his military campaigns. Then Alexander died, and during the subsequent political turbulence, Aristotle decided that it would be prudent to leave Athens. He died the following year.

To these three great philosophers, we should add Xenophon, an Athenian mercenary soldier, who was a contemporary of Plato, and admirer of Socrates. In later life, having been exiled from Athens, and settled in Sparta, he wrote on a wide range of topics, including economics. When Sparta was conquered by Thebes, he was exiled again, and ended his life in Corinth. This was a time when thinking was dangerous.

Xenophon's *Oikonomikos* is about the skills required to manage a household. Aristotle wrote a treatise with the same title, but only small fragments have survived. Plato has sometimes been credited as the author of *Eryxias*, a dialogue on questions of economic morality. All of them defined *oikonomia* as practical household management, but they were also interested in what it meant to manage resources ethically. They thought about how we could manage our appetites, so that we might set aside resources which would be used for the public good. Living through the first experiments with democracy, they wanted to explain how to manage communal, as well as personal, resources.

By modern day standards, classical Athens was very small. While its size varied substantially with its fortunes, we might take its population as having generally been about 150,000, more than half of whom were slaves. Slaves were often former citizens of other cities, who had been captured in war. Along with the slaves, neither women nor children had political rights, so that there were perhaps 30,000 citizens, all adult males, who were the primary audience for the philosophers' debates. In total, there might have been only 10,000 households or *oikoi*. In some ways, these were like family firms, large enough to be self-sufficient, with slaves belonging to the household producing food and clothing. Citizens, especially the titular heads of households, disdained household management, and the philosophers' thinking about the economy accepted that. While earlier literature suggested that household management should be the responsibility of wives, by the fourth century BC, women in wealthier households might also have delegated the practical management of the household to slaves. That was when Aristotle was active, and he discussed the management and manual roles which slaves took on.

In many ways, Socrates defined what it was to be a philosopher. Since all his arguments developed in his personal encounters with other people, he left no written records. What we know of him largely comes through the reconstruction of dialogues by Plato, his pupil, but also the rather gossipy stories of Xenophon, in which we perhaps see more of the man. In discussions, Socrates often started by claiming that he did not understand something which seemed quite commonplace. That drew other people into the conversation, who then had to endure persistent questioning until, tongue tied, they had to listen to Socrates' account of the matter.

Socrates did not discuss economics directly, but for Xenophon, his life was full of economic virtue. For Xenophon, households could be self-sufficient, at least so long as the citizenry practised self-restraint. In his admiration for the austerity of Spartan life, which led to his exile from Athens, Xenophon followed Socrates. He argued that in Socrates' practice of self-restraint, he freed himself to be an active citizen within the city, and to pursue loftier objectives than the everyday business of running a household. For Xenophon's Socrates, the best possible life for a citizen involved devotion to knowledge, specifically by enabling others to acquire it. The other possibility which Xenophon commended as being honourable was to become a benefactor of the city, through political activity.

After Athens lost the war with Sparta, some of Socrates' associates played a substantial role in the brief reign of Thirty Tyrants, who led what was intended to be a purgative moral cleansing of Athens. However, the Athenians revolted, and quickly restored democratic government. In the aftermath of these upheavals, Socrates was accused of corrupting the youth of the city and, for good measure, impiety. Found guilty at his trial, he was condemned to death by drinking hemlock, and died in 399 BC.

Where Socrates had intrigued and enraged the citizenry of Athens, Plato and Aristotle had long careers, which provided them with substantial opportunities to put their political philosophy into practice. Plato was about 30 when Socrates died and lived for another 50 years. During his travels through the Greek speaking world after Socrates' death, he met Dion, an uncle of Dionysius I, the king of Syracuse in Sicily, who invited Plato to train the king in philosophy. For Plato, this was an opportunity to establish his ideal of the government of a philosopher king. Neither Dionysius I, nor his son Dionysius II, turned out to have any interest in philosophy. That was how Plato came to be sold into slavery.

Aristotle, born in the city of Stagira in northern Greece in 384 BC, moved to Athens as a young man, and studied at

ARISTOTLE

Plato's Academy from about 367 BC, but established his own school, the Lyceum about 350 BC. Aristotle's father had been a physician at the court of the rapidly expanding kingdom of Macedon, and that family connection probably led to Philip II extending an invitation to Aristotle to take part in the training of his son Alexander. By 337 BC, Philip had united the Greek states under his leadership, but he was assassinated in the following year. Alexander's brief, brilliant military career ended with his death in 323 BC. By then his armies had subdued the Persian Empire, and had penetrated far into central Asia, before turning south to the Indus Valley. The vast empire collapsed almost immediately after his death.

Where Socrates debated, and Plato was a rational idealist, arguing that the observable world was derived imperfectly from an ideal world of abstract 'forms', Aristotle argued that knowledge comes from applying reason about causes of change to what we can observe. This led him to attempt a detailed explanation of all observable phenomena. The systematic study of disciplines including physics, biology, aesthetics, rhetoric, politics, and for our purposes, household management, all go back to Aristotle. Since we have lost his *Oikonomikos* volume, we must rely on passages in Book II of *Politics* and Book V of *Nicomachean Ethics* to understand Aristotle's understanding of economic relationships.

Aristotle tried to classify every object within a complex typology, in which defining the nature of an object would allow us to understand its characteristics, and its behaviour. He believed that everything existed to meet some purpose. Understanding those purposes was essential to understanding both physical and social phenomena.

For his economic analysis, it was important that Aristotle treated man as a social animal, with language necessary for the maintenance and development of social relations. By also defining man as a moral animal, who would achieve happiness through the exercise of virtue, he was effectively defining what it meant to be an Athenian citizen, able to pursue political activity as part of the exercise of virtue. Within this definition, there was an implication that the state should ensure that everyone had access to the resources needed for full human flourishing. Together, the political community and economic activity within the city should ensure the well-being of the citizenry.

It is hard to reconcile the ideas that citizens should be self-sufficient, and the habit of Greek cities forming complex alliances and fighting frequent, brutal wars to widen the area under their control. Even accepting that trade was generally directed through public authorities, the supposed self-sufficiency of households seemed to presume the ability of the city to secure resources for them, including a continuing supply of slaves. What was good for the Athenians would almost always be bad for their neighbours.

It is perhaps unsurprising in such a violent society, in which his prestige depended on a close relationship with the ruling family, that Aristotle's economic analysis should have emphasized the management of behaviour, through self-command. For his ethics, he defined virtue as tendencies which governed behaviour, and which were strengthened through their practice. A man's possession of virtue could therefore be seen in his habitual behaviour. In his political theory, there were four 'civic virtues': practical wisdom, or prudence; the delay of gratification, through temperance; courage, important since citizens were soldiers; and justice, which involves equality and fairness.

For Aristotle, the practice of *oikonomia* was especially dependent upon prudence, which could identify the mean between miserliness and extravagance, as well as temperance, which for Aristotle was the mean between self-denial and self-indulgence. (He struggled to imagine conditions under which self-denial would be problematic – we perhaps see it today in eating disorders.)

Aristotle separated virtuous *oikonomia* from *chrematistike*, the art of acquiring money. Along with the argument that households could be self-sufficient, his distinction emphasizes the extent to which economics today has moved on from its origins in classical antiquity. But for Aristotle, such money-making opportunities as there were tended to come from acquiring public contracts, for example for the supply of grain from colonies. Modern economists would recognize that in such situations, there is at least a risk of people being able to enrich themselves by controlling the supply of a scarce good. We can see in that an elaboration of Aristotle's concern that there would not be any limit to the ability to make money, which confirmed his belief that its pursuit could never lie on the path of virtue. Instead, he dismissed money-making as being suitable for people who had what he called a 'slavish disposition'.

While the moral nature of Aristotle's economic thought is most apparent in his concerns about the acquisition of riches, his enduring, practical legacy has come through the arguments which he made against charging interest on loans. We will need to place this in a wider context. The Greeks were not the only people interested in philosophical enquiry in antiquity. Jewish and Persian thought was also very rich, and early Christian theology had both Jewish and Greek roots. In the seventh century CE, Islam emerged from the Arabian peninsula, and Islamic scholars actively debated with Christian and Persian scholars when they encountered them, developing a rich body of thought. Perhaps because the Prophet Muhammad had been a merchant, Islam never shared Aristotle's antipathy towards commerce. But even in the *Qur'an*, there were arguments against taking interest on loans, whose form reflected Aristotle's analysis.

Economists have always had plenty to say about money. We value goods and services in terms of money, buying them with money. When we store money, it is part of our wealth. But that is a relatively modern understanding of the function of money. Plato's idealism allowed him to see these arguments, and he recognized that a coin was not just a lump of metal, but a token, whose value was determined by agreement among its users. He pointed to the fact that money which circulated in one city would be worthless in others, just as it would be very difficult to use Russian banknotes in a shop in the USA today.

Aristotle also had some understanding of these ideas, and he emphasized the value of a monetary system over barter arrangements, He treated money simply as coinage, struck with a stamp to confirm how much it weighed. He therefore defined money as an artificial commodity, which was sterile and incapable of natural increase. While he understood that money stored value, partly because of the nature of Greek society, and its limited social development, he did not fully understand the economic processes associated with trade. It never occurred to him that people might borrow money to buy goods, from which they would make new goods, and sell them for a profit, so that they could repay the loan, with interest just being part of the cost of doing business.

In other words, while Aristotle understood that money was a way of holding wealth, he did not realize that it could be turned into productive, wealth-creating capital. For these reasons, he concluded that asking for more than the principal amount of the loan as repayment could never be justified. Instead, he believed that any interest charge would involve an unnatural increase of the artificial commodity, money, so that it would be another form of the unbridled pursuit of gain.

These arguments were consistent with the doctrines of all the Abrahamic faith traditions, and which readily absorbed them. While Christian scholars gradually found ways to tolerate the charging of interest, that has not happened in Islamic thought. Since the middle of the twentieth century, some Muslim scholars have advocated a return to a form of banking, which would be consistent with the principles of *Shari'a*, or Islamic law. As part of their proposals, they have revived the Aristotelian arguments against the charging of interest. Islamic funds are a small proportion of all global financial investments, but one which is growing rapidly. There is plenty of debate about how fully the industry has accepted the restrictions of *Shari'a*, but it demonstrates Aristotelian ideas still being put into practice.

Writing for a social elite in a society at an early stage of economic development, with largely self-sufficient households, and restricted opportunities for exchange, Aristotle's *oikonomia* only became influential because of the breadth of his interests, and the continued importance of his school, the Lyceum, throughout classical antiquity. For many classical scholars, the very limited evidence of market-based activity at the time he was writing is sufficient to classify Aristotle's thinking about household management – and also the management of the state – purely as part of his political philosophy.

Perhaps unsurprisingly, modern economists tend to disagree. While no one would call Aristotle an economist, understanding what Aristotle had to say is a good starting point for thinking like an economist. In the 1930s, Lionel Robbins defined economics as 'the science that studies human behaviour as a relationship between ends and scarce resources which have alternative uses.' Still widely used, Robbins' definition emphasizes the breadth of economics as a discipline. For economists, as soon as classical political philosophers recognized the need to manage resources, they had to think like economists. They tended to treat economics as a branch of ethics because that was how they thought about people and society. We may find their arguments strange and incomplete and disagree with many of their conclusions. What it means to think like an economist has changed over time.

In every chapter, we will explore how great thinkers proposed new ways of thinking about the economy because they could see that, not just economic relationships, but the whole structure of society was changing. As a social science, economics makes no claim to contain absolute truths. Its theories instead reflect the societies from which they developed. Greeks tended to believe that they could meet their material needs by leading austere lives and calling that the pursuit of virtue. For Athenian citizens, it was perfectly natural to spend the income which they might otherwise have saved, or devoted to a life of luxury, on philosophical enquiry, and engagement in the governance of their city. It was also perfectly natural to acquire the resources of a neighbouring city by defeating it in a war. In that social setting, Aristotle did not have to pay much attention to understanding what we now consider to be the core economic activities such as buying and selling, or trade.

Aristotle's way of thinking about scientific and ethical enquiry remained influential for centuries, and for almost a thousand years, his philosophy was taken as the original source text by Muslim and Christian scholars, who only gradually modified his arguments. That meant that his statements on economics were often treated as being authoritative. Beginning from practical resource management, his economic analysis reflected his virtue ethics. Believing that it was impossible to pursue wealth, and virtue, he concentrated on how people might use their wealth to promote the common good. In doing so, he set out an approach to economics, which may be valuable as we grapple with the challenges of controlling climate change, a matter in which the pursuit of public virtue seems inevitable.

2

Thomas Aquinas – The Angelic Doctor

How can a merchant enter the kingdom of heaven?

In the second half of the thirteenth century, the 'Dumb Ox', Thomas Aquinas, painstakingly brought together Aristotle's virtue ethics, early Christian doctrine and Roman commercial law into an authoritative statement of economic theology.

His answer to the question above: do not exploit the needs of others, but do not sacrifice your own.

After Aristotle died, his school, the Lyceum, kept going for nearly 800 years until Christian authorities, certain that pagan philosophy was against God's will for the world, shut it down. For the next thousand years, philosophy and economics sat within religious thought.

After the fall of Rome, Greek-speaking Constantinople became the capital of a new empire, which controlled the Eastern Mediterranean, with Christianity its official religion. Within a century of the revelations of the Prophet, Muhammad, Muslim armies had established the Caliphate, which stretched through Arabia, north to Baghdad, then west through North Africa, and finally into Spain, where Cordoba became an important city in the Emirate of Andalusia. As Western Europe emerged from its Dark Ages, it started to rebuild its economic and social relationships with the Eastern Roman Empire and the Caliphate.

That led to many wars, such as the Crusades, but also trade in goods, and in ideas. By the beginning of the thirteenth century, 600 years after the first wave of Muslim expansion, Jerusalem was firmly under Turkish control. Constantinople, sacked in 1204 by Venetian armies during the Fourth Crusade, had lost most of its power, Christendom had split between its Orthodox and Catholic traditions, and at the western end of the Mediterranean, Spanish princes were gradually expanding their territories, while Norman kings had taken control of Sicily.

As they spread, early Christian and Muslim teachers encountered sophisticated Greek and Persian thought. Believing that they had the revelation of God, religious teachers debated with scholars from older traditions, absorbing many of their ideas. We are interested in the debates between Muslim scholars, and Greek Christians, who had already adopted many of Aristotle's ideas, including his belief that the main economic problem was to manage desires to ensure sufficiency. Wealth and Christian virtue did not easily sit together.

Islam was different. Trade had an important place in Arab culture. For Islamic scholars the challenge was to define conditions under which trade might promote virtue. Where Aristotle had emphasized the importance of prudence and temperance, to understand the exchange of goods and services, Muslim scholars added justice to the necessary virtues of commerce.

In the second half of the twelfth century, Cordoba, famed for its religious tolerance, with Muslims, Jews and Christians living together, was a flourishing centre for these philosophical debates. Maimonides, a Jewish writer, produced the *Guide for the Perplexed*, which set out to reconcile Aristotelian thought and Judaism. The Muslim scholar Ibn Rush'd also produced a detailed guide to Aristotle's thought. He became known as

Averröes when his work was translated into Latin, the language of the church across Western Europe. His commentaries gave Christian thinkers in Western Europe their first exposure to the detail of Aristotle's philosophy. That led to its translation into Latin for the first time. More than 1,500 years after Aristotle's death, these scholars came to his work with fresh eyes, bringing a new interpretation to what were already ancient texts.

By the early thirteenth century, responding to the way in which society was changing in Western Europe through urbanization, population growth and trade, St Dominic and St Francis founded religious orders, with the intention that they would preach the Gospel in urban centres, while relying on their hearers (and adherents) for material support. That marked a change from the practice of contemplative orders, which operated in monastic communities in the countryside.

Sustained economic and social development led to demand for a new economic theology. As emphasized by the question at the start of the chapter, lay people wanted guidance about how to manage resources without falling into the sin of avarice. The Dominicans and Franciscans responded to this challenge by adapting the arguments of Muslim scholars.

As well as contending with Islam, Western Christianity also faced emerging religious movements in the thirteenth century. Partly because of the huge success of Dan Brown's book, *The Da Vinci Code*, the Cathars have become the best known of these. Led by lay people, these new groups claimed to be able to offer entry to heaven in a much simpler way than the Catholic Church. Papal armies crushed what the Church judged to be heresy – with the result that we know little about the Cathars other than what can be gleaned from records of their trials for heresy.

In this period of uncertainty about the nature of legitimate Christian doctrine, the Franciscan Order came under attack. St Francis had insisted upon his followers' complete renunciation of property on the basis that Christ had commanded all his priests to be materially poor. In 1279 to ensure that it complied with this evangelical command, the Franciscan Order renounced all rights of ownership over the land and buildings which it used, placing them under the trusteeship of the Pope, as Christ's representative on Earth. In 1318, the Church's hierarchy decided that the Franciscan teaching about poverty was heretical, ended the arrangements for the management of property, and executed the most radical Franciscans. Religious orthodoxy extended to economic arrangements.

Rather as in classical Athens, medieval economic theology addressed the social elite. The priests who developed these arguments were often academics in the emerging universities, but some were confessors, who provided religious guidance to wealthy individuals. So that it could speak effectively to changes in society, the Church needed to develop its own economic theology. Incorporating new ideas of economic justice, and setting new limits to what was acceptable, took time.

Born into a noble family in southern Italy around about 1225, Thomas Aquinas joined the Dominican Order, probably against the wishes of his family, trained in Cologne and Paris, and then, during the 20 years before his death in 1274, produced a stream of commentaries and teaching material, which culminated in the massive *Summa Theologiae*, which he left unfinished at his death. Rather like Aristotle, Aquinas has a dominant place in intellectual history partly because of the volume and width of his work. He began the *Summa Theologiae* by asking what we can know about God, and the whole of his creation, but in the Second Part of the *Summa*, he discussed the motivation of behaviour, the importance of free will and the emotions, the nature of the virtues (and hence of sin), divine law, the Christian virtues of faith, hope and love, and all four of Aristotle's civic virtues (prudence, temperance, fortitude and justice).

The last section of the Second Part, what is often called the *Treatise on Law and Justice*, is a clear summary of what was understood about economic relationships after Christianity absorbed Aristotle's ideas. Applying arguments about justice to trade and the exchange of goods, it explained how Christians could manage their material wealth so that buyers and sellers would be satisfied with the outcome of transactions. Explaining the exchange of resources within a framework of virtue ethics, it introduced elements of a recognizable economic analysis.

Aquinas's teacher, Albertus Magnus, had already written in detail about how to find a just price when buying and selling. He argued that there were two possibilities. In the first, there would be many similar transactions, and the just price would be typical of the prices agreed in these transactions. This reasoning anticipates the law of one price in modern economics – so long as there is perfect information in a market, and many buyers and sellers, all transactions should take place at a unique price. Any seller wanting more than that price will be unable to find buyers. Any buyer refusing to pay it will not be able to buy anything.

If the transaction is unusual, Albertus Magnus proposed that the buyer and seller will need to agree upon a price. He proposed that in the event of disagreement, they should consult a valuation expert, quite possibly a priest, who would set a price. We can relate this to the practice today of including a clause in the contract for the future sale of an asset which stipulates that when the parties disagree, they will allow an external body to settle the matter by binding arbitration.

To this, Aquinas added the principle of voluntary exchange. Whether there is a market price for the transaction, or negotiation over the price, both sides must agree voluntarily to the transaction taking place. Then the discipline of competition will apply when the goods being exchanged are standardized, and there are many similar transactions providing a sound reference. Expert valuation will be useful where the goods are unique.

At the beginning of the fourteenth century, John Duns Scotus, one of the most eloquent and penetrating thinkers of this period, went further, realizing that we exchange goods because of differences in our valuation of them. He did not use the modern terminology, but he would have understood the idea that the free exchange of resources creates economic value by ensuring that they end up in the hands of the people who value them most. He effectively argued that when a buyer and a seller negotiate, they act justly by sharing the value which is created in exchange. He argued that sellers will not generally insist on the highest price which buyers are willing to pay. That was important, because for Aquinas and his contemporaries, difficult cases in which the seller seemed to have economic power, and so could choose what price to charge, were important for understanding the nature of justice.

In an important example, Aquinas considered the ethical challenge of whether it would be justifiable for a merchant reaching a city under siege, which he knew was about to be relieved, to set a higher price for his goods, even though he could be confident that there would be abundant supplies on the next day.

Aquinas concluded that the merchant had several justifications for charging the higher price. First, reaching a city under siege was likely to involve risks. The journey could have been costly, or physically demanding. Navigating a safe route might have required exceptional skill. Aquinas concluded that these were valid reasons for charging a higher price. Secondly, it was important that the merchant knew that the high price would only last for a short time. Only by setting the high price today could the merchant realize the returns which came from being the sole supplier. Refusing to accept the higher price would involve acting against his own interests.

For Aquinas, achieving justice in exchange was a matter of self-restraint in situations in which a merchant could exploit buyers. As well as need, he noted that people's ignorance or gullibility might lead them to accept a price only because they were not fully informed. He argued that sellers only act justly when they disclose all relevant information. This is still an important principle in commercial law. A contract can be struck down if there has been a failure to disclose relevant information.

Justice works both ways, though, and that explains the conclusion that the merchant should not sacrifice his own economic interests to benefit the buyers, for that would turn the exchange into an act of charity. This important distinction lies behind the more modern idea that markets work well because everyone is looking out for their own interest. Aquinas, along with other scholars of the thirteenth and fourteenth centuries, did not go quite that far. They recognized the importance of justice in trade, even while they wanted to promote other types of social activity, such as giving alms to the poor, in which other virtues, such as love, would guide our actions.

In discussing justice in exchange, Aquinas emphasized commutative justice, which involved the giving of equal values. He also argued that there was an important role for distributive justice. This had its roots in the idea that there would be a natural distribution of people's worth within an economy, which he tended to associate with the social roles into which people were born or appointed. For example, he believed that kings should be able to display magnificence and magnanimity. He applied the same arguments to bishops, the appointed rulers of the church. Magnificence and magnanimity were classical virtues, with generosity of spirit being essential to such social roles. Aquinas linked them to charity, and the voluntary sharing of resources, so that the rules which governed these activities would be different from the rules of exchange.

Such arguments do not really make sense today, when we expect that economic status ultimately depends on our ability to create resources which other people value. People are paid salaries which reflect the value of the role which they fill for their employers, not their age, or their gender, or even their family status. Aquinas's distributive justice seems problematic, as it involved acceptance of gross inequalities in society, which generally flowed from the ability to use the threat of violence to secure economic power.

The Franciscans and Dominicans often disagreed on matters of economics, which is hardly surprising given the Franciscan practice that they could not own (but only use) material goods. We can see in Aquinas's understanding of property much which tempered his arguments about distributive justice. Since we live in God's creation, there are no absolute ownership rights. Instead, they are conditional on their wise use, so that in principle, the community might take ownership of unused assets.

For economic purposes, and for the practice of justice as a virtue, property rights prevented expropriation by force. But with property rights conditional on use, scholars debated the applicability of the traditional 'law of necessity'. Extending the claim that we should never act against our own interests, they argued that we should not allow ourselves to suffer harm through inaction. It followed that a poor man, unable to buy bread, would be acting justly in stealing the bread he needed to survive. The necessity would be the result of the avarice of his richer neighbours, who had not been moved by charitable impulses to meet the need.

This is the founding principle of Catholic Social Teaching, which was initiated with the Papal Bull *De Rerum Novarum* in 1891. In the ordinary business of life, involving the production and exchange of resources, we can act as if we own property outright. But when it comes to the consumption of resources, we must be mindful that their distribution ensures that they are being used well. There is no virtue in poverty – and there should be no poverty in a virtuous society.

Although they accepted that trade benefited society, did not simply enrich the merchant class, and was not motivated by an insatiable desire to make money, theologians in the thirteenth century were very reluctant to set aside the traditional teaching which prevented interest on loans. They started to accommodate it by adapting arguments which Muslim scholars had developed, which permitted profit sharing in partnerships.

For his arguments about the legitimacy of trade finance, Aquinas drew on the Roman law of partnership, rather than Islamic principles. He appears to have been familiar with the types of partnership which were frequently used for the financing of shipborne trade, in which some partners' participation was entirely financial. He proposed that financial partners who shared in the risks associated with shipping should be entitled to share in the profits (and the losses) of the partnership.

Following on from that analysis of the practical elements of trade, Aquinas demonstrated that money and capital are distinct concepts. Following Aristotle, he treated money purely as coinage, and so a store of wealth, a medium of exchange, and a means of payment. Unlike Aristotle, he argued that within business ventures, money finances the purchase of goods, which can then be transformed, even if only by shipping them to a different country, so that the final products can be sold to make a profit.

The distinction is important. Aquinas recognized that without money being available as the capital to finance trade, it would not proceed. By insisting on risk-sharing as a prerequisite for a return on investment, he treated such finance as a form of what we now call equity finance, rather than debt finance. Sharing in profits, financial partners were direct investors in trading expeditions, and exposed to risk.

This made it easy for him to argue against the charging of interest, because his analysis had no role for banks. Go back to the just price argument that we can accept the market price as being just when there are many transactions. That was not really the case with financial agreements in the thirteenth century. Apart from trade finance, there were few opportunities. Borrowing tended to reflect necessity – and so was perhaps best met by charity. A lender with considerable economic power could easily exploit the needs of borrowers. Foregoing interest would then be just.

After Aquinas, the next major advance in thinking about finance and the economy was to accept that fixed interest on loans could be legitimate. It took more than three centuries before theologians began to concur that there were ethical arguments for charging interest. The Swiss Reformer, John Calvin, writing in the middle of the sixteenth century, was among the first to do so, and even he expressed regret about his accommodation of what had become an increasingly common practice.

Even more than Aristotle, Aquinas's economics addressed moral questions, with his arguments directed towards the wealthier members of society. Where Aristotle argued that virtue came from managing appetites, and engaging in the life of the mind, and the city, Aquinas placed trade at the centre of his economic analysis, setting out how by acting justly, we can take care of the interests of other people, without foregoing our own.

3

Adam Smith – The Founder

In praise of the invisible hand

The eighteenth-century Scottish philosopher, Adam Smith, made economics possible. Looking back to earlier thinkers, he explained how society depends on the cultivation of virtue. Looking forward, he understood much about how economic relationships would develop, but he also gave economists their way of thinking about the management of resources. A keen observer of human behaviour, he was never happier than when he retired to his family home in Kirkcaldy, where he lived with his mother, and worked through his ideas during long walks by the Firth of Forth.

From thinking about the Scholastic economic theology of medieval Paris, we leap to radical developments in political philosophy during the Scottish Enlightenment of the second half of the eighteenth century. By that time, recognizably modern European states had emerged, with their centralized governments enjoying political authority over the whole of their territories. After Western Christendom had fractured in the sixteenth century, Europe had been gripped by civil and religious conflicts until well into the seventeenth century. In the worst of these, the Thirty Years War, approximately one third of the population of Central Europe died between 1618 and

1648, largely from disease and malnutrition. Once both sides were exhausted, the war ended in stalemate. Across Europe, the eighteenth-century Enlightenment movement was an attempt to ensure that nothing similar would happen again.

By the middle of the eighteenth century, rivalries among European powers had spilled out into Asia and North America, with Spain, Great Britain and France fighting wars as they sought to build global empires. When Great Britain prevailed, securing its control of India and the Eastern seaboard of North America, the French responded by supporting the British North American colonies in the War of Independence. The economic damage caused to France by the loss of overseas possessions was an important contributor to the French Revolution.

Four months before the American colonies declared their independence, Adam Smith had published *The Wealth of Nations*. He argued that the colonies should either be relieved of tax burdens, or else made part of Great Britain. Presciently, he also predicted that the colonists would win any war. No doubt that helped to make the book's initial reputation, but it is much more than a commentary on the politics of the time. Taking the idea that people were the best judges of their own interests, Smith built his system on the principle of economic freedom. He knew that public institutions were important, but he treated them as guarantors of personal liberty, and enablers of economic virtue. All modern economics flows from the ideas of this great, liberal political philosopher.

The posthumous son of a tax collector, he was born in Kirkcaldy, a small Scottish town, in 1723. His pious mother raised him, and they remained close for most of his life. In 1740, on graduating from the University of Glasgow, he went to Oxford to study theology, as preparation for entering the priesthood of the Anglican Church. From *The Wealth of Nations*, we know that Smith did not enjoy that experience, believing that Oxford academics, who enjoyed substantial incomes from the large endowments of their colleges, did not have any incentive to teach well. Deciding against entering holy orders, he turned to the study of moral philosophy.

Returning to Scotland in 1746, he arrived in Edinburgh to find the university closed. In the previous year, the city had surrendered to the Jacobite army of Prince Charles Edward Stuart, whose family claimed the British throne. After defeating the rebels at Culloden, in the last battle fought on British soil, the government proceeded to pacify those areas which were considered to have been Jacobite strongholds. It reinforced the garrison in Edinburgh Castle, and shut most of the city's institutions, including the university. That gave Smith an opportunity to begin his career as a public intellectual, giving lectures on rhetoric.

Those lectures meant that Smith was a participant in the Scottish Enlightenment almost from its beginning. Partly a response to the Jacobite rebellion, Scottish thinkers wanted to design civil institutions which would be sufficiently strong and flexible so that change would happen through political debate, rather than violence. That required a new toleration of differences in political and religious beliefs.

The career of Smith's friend, the great philosopher David Hume, demonstrates how this took effect slowly. In the 1750s, there were attempts to try him for heresy in religious courts. While those failed, the closest that Hume came to the professorial position which he so richly deserved was in becoming the librarian of the Faculty of Advocates. His public reputation as the 'Great Infidel' made him a catch at genteel dinner parties in Edinburgh, as well as literary salons in Paris, but it also ensured that he could only be a visitor to the groves of academe.

Smith's Edinburgh lectures were a stepping stone to his appointment as Professor of Ethics (and then of Moral Philosophy) at the University of Glasgow after the death in

1746 of his former teacher, Francis Hutcheson. Hutcheson had introduced John Locke's liberal, rationalist philosophy to Scottish undergraduates. While Smith's teaching lacked Hutcheson's vigour, he built on his predecessor's material, and poured his ideas into the two books for which he is now remembered, *Theory of Moral Sentiments*, published in 1759, and *The Wealth of Nations*. The hallmark of Smith's approach was care and precision, and although he promised a third book, on jurisprudence, for many years, it never appeared. We have some idea of its plan and contents from the detailed lecture notes taken by a student in 1762. Smith's lectures also covered aesthetics, the origins of language and the philosophy of science. He first used the term 'invisible hand', famous from its use in *The Wealth of Nations*, to capture the way in which economic activity is self-organizing, in his *History of Astronomy*. Probably written as he worked on *Theory of Moral Sentiments*, this was an exploration of how we develop knowledge.

Smith was not an economist. He was a philosopher, who worked in the tradition of virtue ethics, although in a very different way from Aristotle or Aquinas. As a result, Smith considered *Theory of Moral Sentiments* to be more important than *The Wealth of Nations*. He argued that since humans are social animals, we feel sympathy for others. Smith's sympathy is not empathy – being aware of the feelings which others have – but literally 'feeling together', which relies on an imaginative projection into the state of mind of other people. To explain how sympathy works, he used a vivid example of what we would feel if we saw someone else's arm being cut off with a sword.

Invoking sympathy meant that he did not need to invoke God as the motivation for people's behaviour and social order. Instead, he argued that we use our capacity for sympathy to feel how an internal 'impartial spectator' would respond to our actions. Through such introspective analysis, we tend to choose actions which will win the approbation of other people, not just the people with whom we engage directly, but also actual observers. For Smith, our concern about the promotion of our reputations would enable us to act virtuously.

Perhaps this captured Smith's own tendency for internal dialogue, but he seemed to imagine the impartial spectator taking on a role very similar to a medieval confessor. Where Albertus Magnus suggested that merchants who could not agree on the price of a good might seek the advice of an expert, Smith believed that was unnecessary because we carry our expert around with us, providing counsel and judgement.

Smith's arguments are inherently optimistic. He had great confidence in people's ability to act for the benefit of society. Although he believed that moral education was important for that to happen, he relied on our desire for the approval of others to guide our behaviour. He realized that it would be very easy for us to be influenced by the opinions of the upper classes and the wealthy. Almost certainly, he would have been appalled by celebrity culture and the rise of social media influencers.

It was perhaps a natural bias for a philosopher to argue that we will want to be considered virtuous, and so consider how to be seen to follow the path of virtue. The argument was certainly in keeping with the times. As a young man, the eminently practical Benjamin Franklin, whom Smith met both in France and Scotland, developed such a practice of considering what would win social approval before taking actions. Hume provided a very similar explanation of what guides behaviour to Smith, with his argument that our 'passions' or desires motivate us to act; and that 'reason' or rationality can only play a supportive role in directing our actions to satisfy our passions.

Where Aristotle had emphasized prudence and temperance, and Aquinas had thought about justice as being important for economic behaviour, in *Theory of Moral Sentiments*, Smith argued that it was impossible to identify a dominant virtue, but then clearly placed most emphasis on temperance. For

Smith, acting in our true interests meant being willing to defer pleasures. Widespread temperance in society was necessary for the emergence of high levels of trust, and cooperation among people. Anticipating the economic arguments of *The Wealth of Nations*, temperance enabled saving, the formation of capital, and the development of industry. Those processes would increase national wealth and people's incomes.

The sunny optimism which underlies *Theory of Moral Sentiments* only faltered when Smith examined Bernard Mandeville's arguments in *The Fable of the Bees* that public virtue depends on private vice. Smith had no time for the argument that prosperity depends on greed. He argued strongly that greed would lead to false dealing, which would be corrosive of trust, reducing the opportunities for commerce. Here, we see Smith going back to the slightly earlier claims of the French jurist, Montesquieu, about 'doux commerce' having a civilizing effect on people.

Like Aquinas, Smith realized the importance of self-interest, motivating the argument of *The Wealth of Nations* by claiming, 'It is not from the benevolence of the butcher, the brewer, or the baker that we expect our dinner, but from their regard to their own self-interest. We address ourselves not to their humanity but to their self-love, and never talk to them of our own necessities, but of their advantages.' Balancing self-interest and social awareness, Smith transformed Aquinas's principle that we should be aware of the needs of others, without sacrificing our own interests.

The reputation which *Theory of Moral Sentiments* won for Smith led to his appointment as tutor to the young Duke of Buccleuch, whom Smith accompanied to France between 1764 and 1766. Soon bored by his charge's lack of intellectual curiosity, he began to plan *The Wealth of Nations* in detail, meeting some of the country's leading thinkers on economic matters, notably François Quesnay and Anne-Robert-Jacques Turgot, the leading thinkers of the physiocratic approach to economics. They believed that wealth emerged from the produce of land, and that manufacturing transformed resources, rather than creating new products. They also developed the idea, which is central to *The Wealth of Nations*, that without saving, there could not be investment.

The physiocrats were never a coherent group. Other than opposition to the prevailing, mercantilist approach to the management of commerce, little united them. Mercantilist doctrine had emerged over the preceding century and was based on the claim that the wealth of nations could be measured by their holdings of bullion. This led to arguments for the protection of domestic industry from foreign competition. Treating trade almost as an extension of warfare, mercantilist advice was intended to ensure that the value of exports would be greater than the value of imports. It envisaged a substantial element of state management of the economy, with large companies dominating trade. That made mercantilism a justification for the concentration of economic power in the hands of wealthy elites. On becoming finance minister to Louis XVI in 1774, Turgot attempted to apply physiocratic principles to the reform and stabilization of the French government's finances. Seen as attacking the privileges of the nobility, opposition to his plans led to his dismissal from office in 1776.

Having absorbed the physiocrats' ideas, Smith returned to Scotland, and retired to his family home in Kirkcaldy, where he drafted *The Wealth of Nations*. Working in almost complete isolation, even putting off visits from David Hume, he reflected on the nature of economic relationships. Building on the arguments in *Theory of Moral Sentiments*, he argued that our economic behaviour is motivated by self-interest, but that this turns out to be beneficial for society. In concluding that the economy was largely self-regulating, he explained how its operation could display structure and order, as if the distribution of resources was managed by the same invisible hand, which he had invoked in his analysis of astronomy. That led him to concur with the physiocrats that government should not try to manage the economy.

In his analysis of economic value, though, Smith disagreed with the physiocrats. Instead of insisting on the primacy of land, he considered that the market value of goods must reflect the costs of producing them. He defined costs in general terms as the payments made to hire land, labour and capital. He contrasted the cost of production with the use value derived from consumption of goods. With exchange being entirely voluntary, he concluded that prices had to compensate sellers for the costs which they incur in bringing goods to market, while buyers would need to derive greater use value from their purchases than they had paid for them.

Such ideas were familiar from Aquinas's economic theology. Smith put them in a much more general context. *The Wealth of Nations* opens with the example of a pin factory, introduced to explain the idea that having people perform just one stage of a manufacturing process, using machinery, can be much more efficient than having a single worker perform each stage of it. In such examples, Smith assumed that businesses are very small, and that they would compete with other, similar businesses. In 1776, that was perfectly reasonable. James Watt had patented his separate condenser in 1769 but only produced the first prototype of his steam engine in 1776, so when Smith was writing, factories relied on water for power. They were more typically workshops than the dark, satanic mills of William Blake's romantic imagination. In describing an economy in which competition among businesses was commonplace, *The Wealth of Nations* reflected the economic organization of the society in which it was written.

Smith's thinking about competitive markets remains important. Much of modern economics is built on his realization that as we pursue our self-interest, our competitors restrain our ability to do that. We cannot set prices which are higher than our competitors' and expect to make many sales, especially if everyone is fully informed about economic conditions. Our high prices will not seem like good value. Arguing against mercantilist ideas, he demonstrated how allowing the concentration of economic power, and diluting competition, had proven harmful for society.

His trenchant criticism of mercantilist economic management continued in his analysis of money. In the eighteenth century, the emerging private banks issued their own notes, backed by their reserves of gold and silver. Smith thought about metal coinage as tokens of agreed value, but he was wary about treating bank notes as money, preferring to treat them as a convenient way of claiming the right to the underlying metallic coinage. That understanding explains why he devoted the central part of *The Wealth of Nations* to explaining the changing value of silver over time.

We can see the physiocratic influence in his use of the value of grain as his preferred measure of constant value, which he associated with the wages of unskilled labour. In this account we see Smith at his best, marshalling historical data to produce a convincing narrative. He followed the history of the price of silver with an account of the 'opulence of different nations', in which he concentrated on the development of agriculture and industry across Europe, once again drawing on physiocratic ideas, as he emphasized that the rapid development of industry in Europe did not fit well with his narrative.

Having examined the nature of money, Smith could discuss the nature of capital. Building on arguments from *Theory of Moral Sentiments* that temperance and justice promote fair dealing, trust, cooperation and ultimately saving and investment, he argued that investment leads to capital formation, which is necessary for social and economic development. He dispensed with the mercantilist argument that a country's wealth was its stock of bullion, arguing instead that it was to be found in its capital, which could be used to produce goods. That led Smith to distinguish between productive and unproductive labour, depending on whether the output would be part of the capital stock, and allow the future production of capital and consumption goods, rather than being consumed immediately.

All this was a preliminary to a sturdy defence of free trade, and a discussion of the role of the state. While some economists want to treat Smith purely as a champion of unfettered individualism, he was certain that public action was necessary for the efficient working of markets. For example, he believed that the state needed to have a monopoly of the use of force, to ensure the defence of the state. Supportive of the struggle of the American colonists to achieve independence, he believed that such a monopoly required the consent of citizens.

He also argued that justice had to be administered by the state, so that the courts would be open to all. He gave examples of public works, such as roads, or lighthouses, where private contractors would be unable to generate the revenue needed to cover the costs. Lastly, consistent with his association of wealth with capital, he argued that there was a need for public support of education, so that workers would be more productive. In that, he anticipated ideas which would only be developed fully two centuries later. From there, the book concludes with an examination of public finance, written as historical scholarship, but including an account of how best to manage taxation.

The Wealth of Nations was not just the founding document of modern economics. Smith's reflections on the functioning of economic institutions in the second half of the eighteenth century gave the study of the economy a structure which later writers adopted. The questions which he raised threw up problems which are still important today. Like the Roman god, Janus, with his two faces, Smith went back to the tradition of virtue ethics. By recasting the economic philosophy of Aristotle and Aquinas in a completely new way, he established the necessary structure for the study of industrializing economies.

4

Robert Malthus and David Ricardo – The Realist and the Theorist

So many people, so little land – and no profits?

No one did more to justify Thomas Carlyle's sneer that economics is the 'dismal science' than Robert Malthus. He made his reputation with his 1798 *Essay on the Principle of Population*, in which he argued that the working class would always be poor, receiving wages which would usually be just enough for them to survive. He intended the *Essay* to be a corrective for the arguments of the political scientist, William Godwin, that human nature was perfectible, and social progress inevitable. That also made Malthus a critic of Adam Smith, who also suffered from the seemingly incurable optimism which was common among eighteenth-century intellectuals.

We remember Malthus only for his *Essay*. His other economic ideas became the raw material for his friend, David Ricardo. This brilliantly successful financier discovered *The Wealth of Nations* while on a visit to Bath in 1799 when he was 27. After retiring from his work in the City of London in 1815, and setting himself up as a country gentleman, he turned to writing *Principles of Political Economy and Taxation*. In the few years remaining to him – he died in 1823 – Ricardo established a new way of thinking about the economy, whose influence continues to be felt today.

As the second son of an upper middle-class family, Malthus's route into economics was quite different from Ricardo's. He studied mathematics at Cambridge, obtaining a first-class degree. That led to his ordination as a priest in the Church of England, that common path for second sons, familiar from the novels of his contemporary, Jane Austen. On becoming the rector of Walesby in Lincolnshire in 1803, his increased income allowed him to resign his fellowship at Jesus College in Cambridge and marry. In 1805, he became a professor of history and political economy at Haileybury College, which trained boys for entry into the service of the East India Company. For most of the nineteenth century, economic analysis took the form of political economy, with its emphasis on understanding the distribution of national wealth. This appointment as a professor of political economy made Malthus the first professional political economist in England.

His education made it natural for Malthus to give a mathematical framing to the ethical problem in the *Essay*. His presentation was quite simple, but by relying on mathematical ideas, Malthus introduced a new, formal way of thinking about the economy. Ricardo would go on to develop that approach.

The *Essay* starts from the fact that food production requires inputs of both land and labour. Malthus was willing to accept that both workers and land will become more productive over time. His most important assumption was that since workers have children, they produce more workers, as well as food. He also assumed that a larger workforce would produce more food. Should there be more than enough food to meet workers' needs, Malthus proposed that either workers would have more children, or else more of their children would survive to adulthood. The important point was that surplus food would lead to a growing population. By a similar argument, a shortage of food would lead to higher death rates, or fewer births, and a falling population.

Malthus formalized this argument by assuming that it is natural for population to increase by a constant percentage rate. As an example of this, he cited evidence from the USA indicating that the population there had doubled every 25 years. He then suggested that in every period, the production of food would increase by a fixed amount.

Suppose that the population were to double each period, following a sequence such as 2, 4, 8, 16. If food supply were to increase by four in each period, we might have a sequence such as 4, 8, 12, 16. Across those four periods, food supply per person would have fallen in half. Population would eventually outstrip the food supply.

From the fact that this did not happen (with any regularity) in Europe, where population growth appeared to be much slower than in the USA, Malthus concluded that there must be checks on population, which prevent its explosive growth. He defined the positive checks of disease, famine and war, over which people would not have any control. He also suggested that people could anticipate the positive checks by implementing preventive checks, and so voluntarily restrict the growth of population. The possibility of preventive checks also allowed him to suggest that there could be a socially determined subsistence level, which would be higher than the level required for bare, physical subsistence.

In best Enlightenment style, Malthus's argument started from the 'passion between the sexes', which he took as being the ultimate cause of procreation. Rather like Smith appealing to temperance, Malthus argued that practices such as chastity, late marriage and abstinence from sexual relations within marriage would reduce the birth rate, and therefore the rate of population increase. To strengthen his argument, after the first edition of the *Essay* came out, he and his brother travelled through Scandinavia and Russia, seeking evidence of the operation of positive and preventive checks. His studies informed the later versions of the *Essay*, which expanded substantially in size and scope through to the sixth edition, published in 1826.

As part of that process, he outlined policies which governments should adopt to improve public morals. He argued against public action to limit the operation of positive checks, such as the Poor Laws in England, which provided (very limited) public support for people who were unable to support themselves. For Malthus, funding to relieve poverty would cause population growth. The number of poor people would therefore grow, with more of them dependent on the public purse.

Such arguments led to the notorious claim in the 6th edition of the *Essay*, 'The infant is, comparatively speaking, of little value to the society, as others will immediately supply its place.' But Malthus was thinking of the situation of illegitimate children, whose parents abandoned them – an act which Malthus considered to be criminally negligent. Malthus mildly noted that such children, treated as objects of charity, often died within a year. This was scarcely surprising. In the early nineteenth century, nearly half of all children died before the age of five. As a priest, Malthus would have baptized, and buried, many.

Believing that public policy should encourage the adoption of preventive checks, Malthus proposed that the clergy of the United Kingdom should be required to provide moral education for people who wanted to be married. In this, he drew on the experience of his travels across Scandinavia, where the clergy of the Lutheran national churches were effectively civil servants, with their regular parochial visitations intended to encourage the spread of Christian morality. Smith also considered this an important role for the clergy of an established church.

Set aside the moral arguments, and Malthus's ideas are important today because of his emphasis on the fragility, and transience, of economic growth. As we struggle to manage climate change, and plan the transition to net zero, arguments with Malthusian overtones have become popular. Without suitable preventive action, we may face increasing positive checks.

In addition, economic historians use 'Malthusian models' as a way of thinking about the structure of society until the eighteenth century, when sustained economic growth began in parts of northwest Europe. Perhaps we might expect Malthus, developing his ideas at the end of the eighteenth century, to have been aware of the continued expansion of the economy. However, even in Great Britain, then the richest country in Europe, wages did not rise persistently until the middle of the nineteenth century. Malthus would have required incredible prescience to have seen so far into the future.

Even his friend, David Ricardo, a much greater, and more original thinker, lacked such prescience. Retiring from business and having published some economic pamphlets on questions of economic policy, Ricardo could easily have retired to his country estate. Instead, urged by his friends, especially James Mill, whose son John Stuart Mill became one of the greatest economists and philosophers of the nineteenth century, Ricardo began to draft *Principles of Political Economy and Taxation*. Certainly, without Mill's persistent coaching, Ricardo would not have finished it. A hard taskmaster, Mill's determination that Ricardo should complete his work was exactly what this diffident author needed.

Lacking Smith's interest in constructing persuasive, comprehensive arguments, Ricardo spent less than two years writing *Principles*. Partly for that reason, it has always had the reputation of being a difficult book to read. Some of its twentieth-century editors took the liberty of re-ordering the text to try to make it more readable. To some extent, though, it was almost inevitable that the text would be challenging for readers because Ricardo was trying to do something entirely novel. *Principles* was much more than an update of *The Wealth of Nations* with a few new ideas. Instead, throughout the book Ricardo explored new economic concepts and new ways of thinking about the economy. To write it, he even had to find the terminology he needed to explain the purpose and method of economic research.

The complexity of the task which Ricardo took on helps to explain why Smith's reputation is so much greater than his, certainly among the public. For many professional economists, though, Ricardo has had at least as much influence on the thinking of economists as Smith. For example, some of his ideas, especially his analysis of international trade, continue to appear in introductory classes, and throughout the twentieth century, economists paid homage to his ideas by using them as the basis of mathematical models. Trying to do that with Smith's narrative accounts, and detailed historical analysis, is impossible.

As well as borrowing Malthus's idea that wages would always be close to the subsistence level, he used Malthus's theory that the rent on land was simply a charge for the use of a scarce resource. Then, arguing that capital only had value because of the work which had previously been done on raw materials, Ricardo argued that labour was the ultimate source of all economic value. This 'labour theory' differed from Smith's 'adding up' theory, in which the rents paid to use land, the interest paid to use capital, and the wages paid to workers were distinct costs of production, and the sale value of a good was simply the costs associated with producing it.

Ricardo's reimagining of the nature of value allowed him to concentrate on the theory of income distribution. Writing during the Industrial Revolution, against the backdrop of political disputes between landed and commercial interests, Ricardo told Malthus that understanding how much of the value of output would be paid to workers, to landowners and to the owners of capital, was the central problem of political economy.

Ricardo argued that over a long enough period, the rate of profit on capital would fall to zero. In this long-run state, a good's value would consist of the wages needed to produce it, and the rent of land used in production. Given the assumptions which he needed to generate this result, Ricardo knew that his argument only applied exactly in certain special cases. However, his argument that there would be a falling rate of profit remained important in political economy for much of the nineteenth century.

The example with which Ricardo was most satisfied is often called the 'corn model'. Land, labour and capital are all necessary inputs for arable farming. By providing capital, renting land and hiring workers, farmers would manage production. Ricardo assumed that farmers would use labour and capital in fixed proportions, and with the same intensity across all land being used, even though he assumed that land varied in its quality. He assumed farmers would use the most fertile land when they started production, bringing more land under cultivation as they needed to expand output.

Applying Malthus's population model, wages would be at the subsistence level, and so farmers could not push them lower. Applying Malthus's theory of rent, Ricardo argued that the rent paid for any piece of land would be equal to the difference between the quantity of wheat which a farmer could produce from it and the quantity produced on the least productive piece of land on which crops were growing. That was what these economists meant by saying that rents were charges for access to fertile land. It followed that farmers' profits would then be the difference between the amount of grain produced on the least productive land and the wages (in terms of output) paid to the workers producing it.

Ricardo then argued that farmers would continue to use more land until they could no longer make any profits. That would happen when some farmer was growing crops on land whose yield was just enough to pay workers their wages. That farmer could not earn any profits, and the land would yield no rent. Across the farming industry, the rate of profit would be zero, wages would be just enough for workers to survive, and landowners would collect the whole of the surplus from production in the form of rents. Ricardo showed that in this process, as the share of capital fell to zero, the shares of value claimed by rents and wages would increase.

With the corn model, Ricardo took the first, tentative steps in developing economic theory, and his approach dominated political economy for the remainder of the nineteenth century. Had Ricardo concentrated on the questions of how much land would be used, and how much grain would be produced when the rate of profit fell to zero, then he would have anticipated the economics of the late nineteenth century. As it was, by arguing that farmers would continue to rent land until they could not make profits from doing so, he established the structure for a type of argument which economists still use today.

We can also see how Ricardo developed a very different type of analysis from Smith by exploring differences in their accounts of international trade. Both were convinced of the merits of free trade. However, to debunk the mercantilist argument that national wealth required a trade surplus, and the accumulation of bullion, Smith turned to his knowledge of the historical development of international trade. His theoretical analysis of trade was quite simple, and largely borrowed from his good friend, David Hume.

Hume had argued that if two countries produce two goods, with each of them having an 'advantage' from being able to produce one at lower cost, then if each country specialized in the production of the good which it could produce at lower cost, both countries could be better off. Such specialization would mean that more of both goods would be produced. Trade would then allow consumption of both goods to increase in both countries.

Ricardo moved beyond that, in a brief example of how cloth and wine might be traded by England and Portugal. To make his point, he began, gallantly, by assuming that the Portuguese economy was more productive than the English one, so that in a year, Portuguese workers would produce more wine, and more cloth, than English workers. In Hume's terms, Portugal had the advantage in both products. Ricardo argued that trade could still be beneficial, so long as the Portuguese advantages in wine and cloth production were different.

Given the difference in climates between the two countries, we might reasonably expect that Portuguese workers would be much more productive than their English counterparts in winemaking. For trade to be beneficial, it was only necessary that there was a smaller difference in workers' productivity in cloth production. Then we might say that Portugal had the comparative advantage in winemaking, and England had the comparative advantage in cloth production.

We can now apply Hume's argument in this more general setting. Assume that the Portuguese decided to specialize in winemaking. Producing less cloth and more wine, they could increase their consumption of wine and export the rest of the increased output to England. At the same time, with the shift from winemaking to cloth production in England, more cloth could be used in England, and exports to Portugal would increase. Through such trade, the Portuguese and the English could consume more wine, and use more cloth. Both would be better off.

Many students will see a version of this argument in the first economics course which they take because it sets out quite elegantly the fundamentals of how to think like an economist. Economists admire Smith, but they are really Ricardians.

For Ricardo, there were many political implications of economic arguments. Seeking to influence public debate, Ricardo was elected to parliament in 1818, effectively by buying an Irish seat in the House of Commons. That gave him a public platform from which he could argue for political and economic reform. At the time, the Corn Laws, which restricted imports of cheaper foreign grain into Great Britain, were the focus for intense debates between landowners, who benefited from higher rents, and manufacturers, who believed higher prices of grain forced up wages, so that they were subsidizing landowners. Ricardo was firmly on the side of the manufacturers in wanting free trade. With Britain having the most productive capital stock in the world, he believed that the country should specialize in manufacturing, allowing other countries, such as the USA, which had the comparative advantage in agriculture, to specialize in the production of agricultural commodities.

At first, his deep knowledge of economics and public finance gained him a respectful hearing in debates. But he was soon decried as a 'prophet without honour', and dismissed as a theorist (and crank), who might just as well have arrived from another planet. It may be that by delivering careful, but unwelcome, analysis to parliamentarians, Ricardo was the first true economist.

With his principle of population and his theory of rent, Malthus made it possible for Ricardo to develop a new type of political economy. Like Ricardo, Malthus wrote a book with the title *Principles of Political Economy*, but this never had anything like the influence of the *Essay on the Principle of Population*. Ricardo was simply more systematic, and more thorough. Ricardo's *Principles (of Political Economy)*, especially the corn model, became the bedrock of nineteenth-century political economy. While that model is no longer used, much of Ricardo's terminology, many of his concepts, and his style of argument continue to be essential for thinking like an economist.

5

John Stuart Mill – The Classical Liberal

Can work ever be rewarding?

Forget economics for a moment. To understand John Stuart Mill's life, and his way of thinking about the economy, we need to know about his relationships with his father, and his wife, Harriet Taylor. While his father trained him how to think, Taylor encouraged him to think about what needed to be done so that everyone would benefit from the processes of industrialization which swept through European economies in the nineteenth century.

We have already met John Stuart Mill's father, James, as he coached Ricardo through writing *Principles of Political Economy and Taxation*. That was an offshoot of James Mill's role as the organizer of the circle of 'Philosophical Radicals'. This group had formed around the political philosopher, Jeremy Bentham, remembered for his development of utilitarian ethics, which have had a substantial influence upon economists. Committed to the exploration of liberal, secular, utilitarian thought, James Mill wanted his children's education to be a rigorous grounding in Bentham's philosophy.

Never wealthy, he called his oldest child John Stuart after a landowner who had provided important financial support at the start of his career. Fortunately for James Mill's plans, the boy turned out to be precocious. Scarcely out of infancy, John Stuart began to study the classics. Able to translate Plato by the age of eight, he also had to master mathematics, philosophy and, ultimately, political economy. With Bentham's active participation, James Mill shaped his son's intellect unsparingly, training him to accept the utilitarian premise that every action should be chosen to maximize the well-being of society.

Perhaps the plan was not so different from parents sending their children to lessons in Mandarin when they are four years old. However, in this plan, James Mill largely ignored his son's feelings, and even his autonomy as an individual (an especially interesting oversight, given the Philosophical Radicals' strong opposition to slavery). The result was perhaps predictable. At the age of 20, John Stuart went into a period of low mood. Instead of turning to public service, he discovered romantic poetry, and through that, love, as reliable sources of happiness, eventually concluding that he could not achieve happiness self-consciously.

In 1830, while he was 23, he met Harriet Taylor. She was then the 21-year-old wife of John Taylor, who ran a pharmaceutical wholesale business. The relationship between Mill and Harriet Taylor quickly flourished, and while John Taylor was willing to overlook this to some extent, staying at his club during the evenings, his patience ran out in 1834, when he insisted upon his wife setting up her own home.

His close relationship with Taylor provided Mill with the inner resources needed for his father's extraordinary efforts to bear fruit. After his youthful reaction against being force fed ideas, he became one of the leading public intellectuals of the middle nineteenth century. Primarily a philosopher, he addressed the moral and ethical questions which emerged in the economic system of Britain in the mid-nineteenth century.

The world's leading industrial power, it was also well on the way to acquiring its global empire.

Mill played a substantial role in the imperial project. Like his father, he rose to the position of Examiner of Correspondence in the East India Company, the private company which managed British interests in India until 1858, when the government decided that it needed to rule the country directly. A remnant of the mercantile system, and notorious for its corruption in the eighteenth century, by the middle of the nineteenth century, the company was an anachronism. The Mills understood this, even as they oversaw the company's relations with the princely states, which were formally independent of British rule. Their work did much to improve the governance of India.

Mill kept his work for the company separate from his intellectual endeavours. These flourished in the 1840s, with the production of the first editions of *A System of Logic* in 1843, and *Principles of Political Economy* in 1848. His books became the standard introductions to those subjects for the remainder of the nineteenth century and were the foundation on which he built his other work. Today, Mill is probably best known among economists for the essays *On Liberty*, published in 1859, and *Utilitarianism*, from 1861, in which he set out the liberal political philosophy taken for granted in much of modern economics.

His ability to make complex ideas interesting, and to engage a wide audience in discussion of complex matters of social and economic policy also made Mill a successful journalist, who wrote frequently for the Liberal supporting *Morning Chronicle*. It was entirely natural that he should put aside his work on *Principles of Political Economy* in 1845, when disease destroyed the Irish potato crop, and the Great Famine began. In a powerful series of editorials, Mill argued for immediate, large-scale public relief. That brought him into dispute with the Malthusians, for whom the famine was simply the operation of a positive check. Strongly opposing all public relief on principle, Nassau Senior, the Professor of Economics at Oxford, simply dismissed one million deaths as 'not enough to do any good'.

For Mill, political repression was the ultimate cause of the famine. He followed Ricardo in taking aim at the political interests of the landed gentry who dominated the Tory government at Westminster, noting that Ireland was experiencing famine when Britain was the wealthiest country in the world. He argued that in bringing Ireland into the United Kingdom, Britain had established an aristocratic regime, in which the rural population had the status of cotters (peasant farmers). That meant that they had to work hard on large estates in return for the most meagre subsistence. Mill argued that Irish property law retarded people's moral capacity, and that substantial land reform would stimulate a social and moral transformation, the diffusion of commercial virtues, and individual economic autonomy. No doubt those were all worthy objectives, but they could not address the pressing problems of relief of hunger.

Mill also argued that the government should buy, and then improve the fertility of at least 4,000 square miles of land, which could then be given to 'peasant' proprietors. That was still a long-term plan, which would not address the immediate needs of a starving population. Indeed, to some extent Mill largely agreed with his opponents because he opposed extensive outdoor relief – what we would now call the payment of social benefits. Breaking the famine ultimately required increased food supplies. Repeal of the Corn Laws in 1846 enabled the importation of cheap grain from Europe, but by then, the famine had claimed perhaps a million lives, and caused the migration of another million people.

In 1848, a year of political revolutions across Europe, Mill completed the first edition of his *Principles of Political Economy*. By the time the seventh edition appeared in 1871, Germany and Italy had become unified nation states, and the second Industrial Revolution was beginning. Railway networks had replaced canals, reinforced concrete was allowing cities to rise upwards to the sky, advances in engineering and industrial chemistry had transformed the scale of manufacturing, and oil and electric power were starting to replace coal and steam engines. Businesses could deploy capital on a vast scale, Smith's pin factory example had become an interesting curiosity. There was also deep-seated economic inequality. In the USA, Reconstruction was giving way to the Gilded Age. Mill developed his political economy to address the needs of industrial society.

Drawing on the ideas which Malthus and Ricardo – and indeed his father – had developed in the previous generation, Mill's *Principles* was a masterly account of classical political economy. He combined the fluency of Smith's historical analysis with the rigour of Ricardo's theoretical analysis. Drawing on ideas from all the social sciences, he considered many questions of public policy, believing that to be more useful than developing theory. Synthesizing the work of the preceding generation, he was always generous in giving credit to his predecessors, but modestly self-effacing about his own contributions.

Mill gave a central place to Ricardo's three-sector model of the distribution of income, in which rents reflected the fixed supply of land. Politically more radical than Ricardo, Mill argued that since rents did not reflect returns to skill, or effort or risk, then except to the extent that they were a return on capital investment intended to increase output, they should be taxed. The land would still be in scarce supply, so that the tax would simply divert rents from landowners to the public purse. Such taxation would have no effect on productive economic activity.

In applying Ricardo's theoretical insights in this way, Mill's approach was very similar to Smith's. They both believed that concentration of political power would affect economic power, and the distribution of income. Partly through Taylor, Mill met many of the early socialists and discussed their ideas in detail. While sympathetic to their objectives, his political liberalism led him to reject their proposals for the common ownership of property and utopian socialist experiments, such as the establishment of communes. Instead, he believed that reforms of education and property law were a more realistic route to transforming the economic standing of the working classes.

Believing that too much of the prosperity which had come with industry had benefited a relatively small class of business owners and professionals, he proposed that there should be limits on bequests as well as taxation of land. Turning to the working classes, Mill argued that organization, education and economic competition would have important beneficial effects. Recognizing that competition among workers for jobs could hold wages down to subsistence levels, he advocated the formation of trade unions to reduce that competition. Building on Smith's analysis, he argued that universal education would increase workers' moral autonomy, enabling them to take on more productive roles in organizations.

The organization of the working class would reduce the imbalance in economic power which they faced when dealing with employers. Perhaps sharing Smith's optimism, Mill argued that competition among producers would exert downward pressure on the prices of goods, while competition among employers who faced effective trade unions would bid up wages.

We can easily trace Mill's interest in improving the condition of the working class back to the education which his father gave him, but also Harriet Taylor. Planning the publication of *Principles of Political Economy*, Mill had proposed a fulsome dedication to Harriet Taylor as an effective co-author. However, John Taylor vetoed that. For some reason, in the version inserted into copies circulated privately to friends, there was no mention of her having such a role.

Towards the end of his life, Mill claimed in his *Autobiography* that his sympathetic treatment of early socialist movements, especially co-operativism, were largely the result of Taylor's promptings. However, none of Mill's (male) friends accepted his description of their working practices. They could not discern evidence of the co-authorship, which Mill alleged was the result of their constant discussion and refinement of ideas.

By the time that *Principles* appeared, the Taylors had lived separately for nearly 15 years, with Harriet Taylor returning to the marital home only to nurse her dying husband in 1849. Remember that Mill's *Principles* first appeared in 1848, the year after Charlotte Brontë published *Jane Eyre* under the pseudonym, Currer Bell. At the time, there was no clear path for Mrs Taylor to be acknowledged as Mill's partner, either in work or in life.

Widowed, Taylor was finally able to marry Mill in 1851, but they both suffered from tuberculosis, and Taylor died in 1858, while they were living in Avignon. Mill kept a house there for the last 15 years of his life and is also buried there. Assessing Taylor's influence on Mill is difficult. During her life, she published nothing separately from him, but Mill was very clear that Taylor should be considered the author of the essay, *The Enfranchisement of Women*.

Claiming that reform of education and property law would benefit society was hardly novel. However, in arguing that there should be complete equality between the sexes, Mill broke new ground. Almost certainly, this is where we see Taylor's influence on Mill's thinking most clearly. His policy proposals went well beyond his advocacy of women's right to vote when he was an MP in the 1860s. He emphasized the importance of equal property rights at a time when women could not own property separately from their husbands – a reason that many widows would choose not to remarry. He also emphasized that women had the ability to benefit from education, and that they should be able to join the professions. He foresaw substantial social benefits from breaking down such systematic discrimination. Once again, though, we see him arguing for the reform of property rights and education to break down the concentration of economic power.

Had he lived to see its publication, James Mill might well have considered that *Principles* demonstrated the efficacy of his educational programme. The Philosophical Radicals had developed a strongly egalitarian form of political liberalism. They also developed the utilitarian approach to ethical behaviour. Arguing that actions produce pleasure, or pain, they proposed that we should choose the actions which maximize the total pleasure. While they believed that people are concerned for the well-being of others, they disagreed with Smith that it would be possible to rely on the sympathy of political leaders to promote justice. Instead, they argued that only democratic government could align the interests of statesmen with those of the people. We can see their emphasis on aggregate well-being in Mill's proposals for land reform, property rights, education and the organization of the working class.

As a liberal, Mill argued for freedom of belief, action and association, subject to the principle that actions should not cause harm. Consistent with his version of utilitarianism, he argued that society has an interest in any action which might have effects on others' happiness. Here, he introduced the 'harm principle'. A society which prevents only those actions which will tend to cause others to experience pain would promote the 'general happiness'. For Mill, the only form of public intervention consistent with personal liberty was the prevention of possible harm.

His political economy sprang from those philosophical and psychological roots. Like Smith, he emphasized the role of economic competition, which he specifically exempted from the harm principle. If we produce the same type of goods, but I undercut you and, as a result, obtain your customers and force you to close your business, I have not harmed you. Business ventures require us to take risks, to make judgements and to operate in a sea of uncertainty. Neither you, nor I, can be certain of a return on the skill, effort and knowledge which we apply to our ventures. It may simply be chance which offers me the opportunity to undercut you. We cannot therefore say that the harm which you have experienced is the result of my actions. Rather, it is the outcome of all the actions which take place in this market.

We can read Mill's *Principles* as the final, complete statement of classical political economy. Alternatively, we should be aware that as he repeatedly revised the book over more than 20 years, he began to explore some problems which were inherent in its theoretical structure. The final edition was still grounded in the ideas of Smith and Ricardo, but it pointed clearly to the more modern economics which emerged in the last third of the nineteenth century.

We can see this in his changing treatment of the wages fund doctrine, which had developed shortly after Ricardo's death. The wages fund was supposed to be the part of the revenues which a business earned from its current production, which it set aside to pay wages in future. This reflected the way in which the political economists thought about how money flowed through a business. They believed that there would be fixed capital, often held as machinery, but also circulating capital, needed to meet payments. The wages fund was part of that circulating capital.

Economists had argued that it was possible that this wages fund might increase over time, especially if workers were able to form trade unions and take strike action. As part of his analysis of how the working class could organize themselves, Mill argued in the first edition of *Principles of Political Economy* that in certain trades, bargaining seemed to have increased wages. Concerned that these higher wages would have a depressive effect on the wages of other workers, Mill eventually concluded, with typical optimism, that in the long-run, higher wage rates would be sustained through preventive checks. Unlike Malthus, he predicted that wages could stay well above the (physical) subsistence level.

By 1870, Mill had changed his mind about the wages fund argument. Reviewing William Thornton's book, *On Labour*, Mill accepted that employers only hire as much labour as they need to produce their planned output. He realized that they would treat falling wages as a windfall. Unless the fall in wages led them to change their production plans, employers' demand for labour would stay the same, and their total wage bill would shrink. Without any wages fund to distribute, younger economists had begun to treat wages purely as a cost of production. That effectively undermined the three-sector model of distribution, which had been central to political economy, and also the labour theory of value. Mill gave this work his blessing.

Even as he acknowledged its shortcomings, Mill continued to work within the classical tradition of political economy, which Smith had established. Malthus questioned the possibility that society could be perfect, and Mill accommodated his concern that social policy should be mindful of the dangers of a rapidly increasing population. Mill's father, a devoted disciple of Bentham, helped to establish a utilitarian framework for political analysis, and supported Ricardo as he invented new methods of economic analysis. A very capable analytic philosopher, John

Stuart Mill built on those foundations through the width of his reading, his even-handed presentation of problems, and his awareness that on matters of political economy, there would rarely be any easy answers. He placed political economy within the context of social philosophy, intending that it should be a tool for social reform rather than for political revolution. For that, we turn to Karl Marx.

6

Karl Marx – The Communist Visionary

Prophesying that capitalism will destroy itself

If only Karl had made capital, instead of just writing about it.
More than once, in letters to his friend, collaborator, editor and
source of financial support, Friedrich Engels, the great socialist,
Karl Marx, ruefully recalled his mother passing this judgement
on his career.

He died in obscurity in London in 1883, having published
only the first of the three volumes of his masterwork, *Das
Kapital*, leaving it to Engels to edit and publish the remainder.
Within 20 years of his death, his version of revolutionary
socialism had swept through intellectual circles in German-
speaking countries, supplanting the earlier, utopian thought,
with which Mill had engaged.

Marx shared Smith's belief that it was possible to establish
a unified science of humanity, which would go well beyond
economics, incorporating philosophy, politics, history,
geography and anthropology. Where Smith ordered the
destruction of all his unpublished work, Marx's notebooks and
manuscripts have been mined by devotees for insights into the
system which the master had constructed. That was the result
of some of his adherents leading the Russian Revolution which

established the Soviet Union. From the 1920s until 1990, Marxist thought became the foundation of a distinctively Soviet social science. Every thought which he committed to paper has been published, translated into all major languages, and debated carefully. His economic thinking is just one part of his broad approach to the social sciences.

The son of a lawyer, who had converted from Judaism to Christianity, Marx completed studies in law, theology and philosophy, and obtained his doctorate from the University of Jena in 1841. Soon a newspaper editor, he quickly became well known for his attacks on both the Prussian government, and other socialists, whom he often treated as being insufficiently committed to real struggle. As a result, he was frequently in conflict with the authorities, and so during the 1840s, he moved between Paris, Brussels and Cologne, continuing to edit radical newspapers, but also devoting himself to detailed study of what he quickly named classical political economy – Smith's system, as developed by Ricardo.

During the wave of political revolutions which spread across Europe in 1848, Marx and Engels wrote *The Communist Manifesto*, urging the working classes to revolt. In the subsequent wave of political repression, Marx concluded that it was better to leave continental Europe, and so he settled in London. Ensconced in the British Library, he read, and wrote, although he broke off from his research quite frequently, sometimes to earn money through journalism, and sometimes to engage in revolutionary politics. From about 1857, he devoted himself to systematic research, but while he collected, and ordered materials, he was rarely satisfied that his arguments were ready for print. The publication of an introduction, *Critique of Political Economy*, in 1859, was followed by the publication of the first volume of *Das Kapital* in 1867.

Marx questioned the permanence and reality of social relationships. A Marxian analysis of Marx might conclude that his work was largely determined by the environment in which he was working. This avowed atheist presented us with a world history in which labour had fallen from something akin to a state of grace, was enduring hardships, and finally, in the Communist Revolution, would find its true purpose as social relationships were restored to their ideal form. Even as he had rejected the narratives of the Abrahamic faith traditions, his thinking echoed the systematic theology of the nineteenth century, as well as romanticism, and evolutionary theory. It may be tempting to place Marx beyond the flow of bourgeois political economy, but his arguments were largely a reinterpretation of his predecessors' work, which he shaped into his justification for the eventual establishment of communism as the final stage of economic development.

In this gargantuan effort, he relied upon his interpretation of Georg Wilhelm Friedrich Hegel's systematic philosophy. He predicted boldly that social development will certainly end in communism, with all assets then being held in common. He was much vaguer about the details of the process. Mottos such as the 'dictatorship of the proletariat', and 'from each according to their ability, to each according to their need', are memorable, but they did not emerge naturally from the dense analysis of *Das Kapital*. Since his death, revolutionary governments which have been committed to Marxist programmes have implemented socialism by binding Smith's invisible hand. They have emphasized state ownership of capital, and state control of enterprises, with output and prices being set within the government bureaucracy. Such state socialism has now largely vanished, but Marx's work remains. It is often troubling, and may be wilfully obscure, but it is always profound.

We have seen that through the first half of the nineteenth century, writers on political economy engaged with Smith's system. Ricardo and Mill had argued for political reform, with Mill imagining an economy in which competition harnessed to social reform would eventually eradicate poverty among the working class. Marx and Engels took a completely different approach.

Engels, sent to England so that he might be less of an embarrassment to his bourgeois family, had assessed *The Condition of the Working Class in England* in the early 1840s. Drawing upon close observation of working-class districts, carried out while he represented his family's business interests in Manchester, he presented evidence of the systematic exploitation of workers. At this time, Manchester was a centre of radical liberalism, most famously propagated by the campaigners for free trade, Richard Cobden and John Bright. *Manchesterismus* became a by-word in Germany for a small state liberalism, which placed excessive trust in the operation of markets. Marx's response to this bourgeois liberalism, suited to the property-owning democracy of Great Britain had much more of a theoretical orientation than Engels'. To that extent, we must think of him as following on from Ricardo, rather than Smith.

We might also think of Marx as being like the painters in the Renaissance, who carefully dissected bodies so that they could understand what they could see in a new way and depict it more precisely in their art. Marx worked like an anatomist on the economy and society as he searched for his new reality. Accept Marx's arguments, and we should treat other social scientists as chasing illusions, with their senses misdirecting them.

Rather than starting from a blank page, Marx adapted Smith's historicism, and Ricardo's labour theory of value. In the grand sweep of Marxian history, capitalism was simply one stage in the development of society. He understood political economy as having emerged from within capitalism without sufficient reflection on the extent to which it only applied to a capitalist society. That was why the political economists' senses were misdirecting them – they had failed to realize the extent to which they were observing specific types of social relationships, so that their analysis was grounded in the mundane reality of the nineteenth century. Focused on detail, they produced miniatures compared with Marx's vast canvas.

Marx did not reject political economy. Instead, he used it as raw material, which he fed into his own theories. Ricardo's labour theory of value was especially important. Like Smith, Marx wanted to explain not only how society had developed, but how it would develop. Where Smith had generally been optimistic, believing that rational debate would improve society, Marx was convinced that the structure of a capitalist economy kept the working class in poverty, and that capitalism would develop over time in such a way that it would inevitably destroy itself, giving way to socialism as the precursor of communism.

Before Marx, political economy had examined the processes of production of goods. Ricardo had developed a theory of the distribution of income across social classes. Theories of value explained the market value, needed for buying and selling, and use value, for when goods were consumed. Framing the economic problem in Hegelian terms, Marx argued that there was a unity to the processes which determined the level of production, the distribution of income, the extent of buying and selling, and the process of consumption. He placed production at the centre of all of these, arguing that without production, there could not be any distribution. He also noted that production could only take place after an earlier allocation of resources, which was in turn the result of previous rounds of production. For Marx, all economic relations were complex, and developed gradually over time. His political economy did not stick to what he called the analysis of material conditions, but quickly became idealistic and abstract.

Marx's version of the labour theory of value therefore began from speculation about the close relationship between production and consumption in primitive agriculture, and then considered how the nature of production and the ownership of resources might have changed over time, ending with the claim that the nature of production in the capitalist economy of the nineteenth century had given capitalists the ability to exploit the working classes.

This version of history therefore began with the assertion that the head of a family of peasants, which had to rely on the produce of a small landholding to meet its material needs, might allocate the family's working time to a variety of activities, with the fruits of their labours then being shared. Add slaves, and we would have something quite like the Greek *oikos*. (Given this starting point, Marx would presumably have embraced the anthropological research which has since demonstrated the extent to which communal sharing of outputs have often been part of hunter-gatherer societies, with the move to agricultural subsistence considered to have reduced individual well-being, although it allowed for population growth.)

As the economy developed from this rudimentary state, households stopped being self-sufficient, and so they started to exchange products with each other. For Marx, this began to create problems for the economy. Since he believed that only labour was productive, he argued that we should concentrate on the underlying exchange of labour time (and effort) which went into production, rather than what we see happening – the exchange of products.

In effect, he argued that since production required labour time, we should really commission each other to produce goods, hiring workers' time, skill and effort. But that was not the path followed in the historical development of economic relationships. Instead, Marx argued that products had acquired a dual nature, becoming commodities. Commodities differed from products because of their exchange values, which allowed them to be bought and sold in markets. Marx also recognized that after their purchase, traded commodities were still essentially products, so that they retained their use value.

Explaining the emergence of commodities was important for his system because it provided a new explanation of the difference between the use value and the market value of commodities.

Now, to explain the difference between use and exchange values, Marx believed that he needed to have an economy in which payments were made in money. Building on traditional explanations of the emergence of money and metallic currency, he argued that we should not think of money being valuable just because it could buy goods and services. The exchange value for any commodity was the amount of money for which it could be sold. For Marx, that money represented the abstract labour necessarily embodied in the commodity brought to the market.

This abstract labour was not simply the actual labour used in production, but the amount of labour which would be used by a capitalist who was skilled in managing production by economizing on the use of labour. In addition, this abstract labour was effort used in production, shorn of skill and risk taking, capturing the features of manual labour of the industrial age, after the division of labour had turned many jobs into repetitive routines, and capital accumulation had increased the scale of production. It represented labour as Marx saw it at the time when he wrote, at the end of the Industrial Revolution, with the 'capitalist mode of production' predominant.

Thinking of money as representing abstract labour, Marx also restated the definition of money. Instead of defining money as a medium of exchange, in which all prices could be stated, Marx called it a 'medium of circulation' for all commodities. He argued that people offer to sell commodities, and then use the sale proceeds to buy other commodities. That money-commodity-money cycle might seem entirely innocuous and nothing more than a general description of economic relations, but it allowed Marx to claim that capitalism involved a different form of circulation, which would begin with money. That money would be used to buy commodities. After an increase in the value of those commodities, they could be sold for more money.

Think of a merchant who buys goods in one country, and then ships them to another one, profiting from the difference in prices. In such an example, Marx's money-commodity-(more) money circulation might still seem innocuous, and strictly, he did not see the problem as being in such money-driven circulation by itself, so much as the way in which it took place in a capitalist economy.

For Marx, the defining characteristic of the capitalist class was an insatiable desire for money. To try and satisfy that desire, capitalists would use money as circulating capital, which they would use to buy commodities, transform them, and then sell for a higher price.

We now need to think about the role of workers in this system. We have got as far as talking about how products become commodities when they are bought and sold. In that process, workers lost control of the sale of what they produced. A little like Mill, Marx looked at the form of property rights, and noted that workers tended to have contracts in which they were paid wages. They exchanged time, effort and skill for money. In Marx's theory, that made labour another commodity. Marx called this process 'the alienation of labour' because workers lost control of the sale of their output to its final users, and their work became another commodity. This played a critical role in his account of the structure of the capitalist economies of the nineteenth century.

Go back to capitalists using their money as circulating capital. Almost none of the commodities which they purchase would be at all productive. They would sit in a store, perhaps decaying slowly, until people came into the factory, and worked on them, transforming them, and increasing their value. Without that time, effort and skill – the commoditized labour of the workforce – the capitalist could not sell commodities for more than their original cost. That led Marx to redefine profit. It was no longer a return on capital but 'surplus value', which measured the value which workers created in the production process, but which capitalists were able to keep for themselves. The higher the rate of surplus value, the greater the extent of capitalist exploitation.

Marx could of course rely on the Malthusian argument about population to argue that in this system, there would always be downward pressure on wages. Arguing that competition among capitalists would lead to labour-saving innovation, he argued that even with workers organized through trade unions, a 'reserve army of the unemployed' would keep wages low, increasing the rate of surplus value. Within a capitalist economy, the working class became the unwilling servants of capital.

Marx sometimes treated capitalists as if they were purely financial investors, taking their returns without the exertion of any effort. Yet the mention of innovation confirms that Marx understood that the nature of capitalism would change constantly. He had developed a philosophical framework, in which capital and labour stood in a complex relationship, in which each affected the nature of the other.

We now come to the core of Marx's critique of capitalism. Instead of money enabling the circulation of commodities, the nature of production had changed so that money, transformed into commodities, would generate more money, benefiting capitalists. For Marx, capital was 'dead labour', and he compared it to a vampire, which needed live labour to thrive. Indeed, while labour had become commoditized, by calling capital 'self-expanding value', he treated it almost as a malign entity. The work of economics was then to contain its influence, which would require the elimination of the capitalist class.

The insatiability of capitalists' desires would force them to compete against each other in often desperate efforts to increase their capital. Marx predicted that such competition would cause capitalism to expand globally through imperialist conquest and colonization, until it became the dominant mode of production everywhere. For Marx, competition among capitalists spurred innovation, drove down the rate of profit, destroyed jobs, and ensured that there would always be a reserve army of the unemployed keeping wages low. He foresaw a series of increasingly severe crises in capitalism, with wealth becoming more and more concentrated.

For Marx, capitalist accumulation was a pathology of the economy. Instead of being condemned as a vice, Aristotelian *chrematistike* had become central to the functioning of the economy. Where Aristotle had looked to the development of individual character to overcome this vice, Marx believed that the crises of capitalism would eventually lead organized labour to undertake a socialist revolution.

These arguments made Marx the most political of economists in the nineteenth century. While Ricardo and Mill had both become MPs and had argued for a wide variety of economic and social reforms, both were liberals, and so were content to work within the constraints of the British political system. When young, Marx's commitment to revolutionary action forced him to move repeatedly, until he arrived in Britain, which tolerated his activities. In his lifetime, Marx's scientific socialism amounted to little more than a theory which allowed working-class movements to justify a revolution by the disenfranchised, but socialist movements across Europe quickly adopted Marx's scientific socialism after his death. Yet while he reimagined classical political economy, arguing that it had assumed the inevitability of capitalism, he largely accepted that it should explain the distribution of income across social classes. When Marx died, younger economists had turned away from Ricardo's labour theories of value, and asked what would happen if capital, by itself, was productive.

7

William Stanley Jevons, Carl Menger and Léon Walras – Three Quiet Revolutionaries

Finding value at the margin

While Marx was still preaching political revolution, an intellectual revolution began, which turned political economy into economics. There was no gunfire, and no one dragged classical political economists off to re-education camps, but by 1900, economists had largely dispensed with Ricardo's labour theory of value and the analysis of the distribution of income. Their new way of thinking about prices and value is still widely used in economics today.

For example, in their theory of wage determination, these economists played down Malthus's principle of population, and the inevitability of wages remaining at subsistence levels. Instead, they argued that since wages were the cost of hiring workers' time, they should be treated as a price, and set at a level which would balance the willingness of people to work, and organizations' need for workers. In this new economics, if there was unemployment, with people looking for work, but unable to find it, then wages would fall until everyone wanting to work could do so.

Mill had started to push economics in this direction. We have already seen that towards the end of his life, he gave up on the classical wages fund doctrine, accepting instead that wages should be treated simply as a part of organizations' costs of production. That shattered the integrity of the classical theory of income distribution and gave younger economists the freedom to develop new ideas about what determines the level of wages.

As one of the best philosophers of his time, Mill was also aware that because political economy needed the concepts of use and exchange value, it was imperfect. In his utilitarian analysis, he argued that whatever was useful was also valuable, but in his political economy, he continued to associate exchange value with the costs of production. He argued that the separation of value in use from market value had no important effects on the operation of the theory of political economy. For the new economists, that was definitely not the case, and their theory inextricably linked value and prices.

In 1870, it was by no means clear that the development of economics would take this form. Classical political economy had largely been an English tradition. It had survived the emergence of the first industrial societies, waves of urbanization and migration, and the rise of European empires. The economics which replaced it also had English roots. In contrast, the French approach to economics had largely developed in engineering schools, so it concentrated on analysis of the structure of industry. In Germany, historians led study of the economy. They emphasized the importance of observation for drawing inferences about regularities in economic behaviour. The German historical school also influenced the American institutionalists, who emphasized the role of economic relationships and remained important well into the twentieth century. Lastly, there were socialists of many ideological hues, who, like Marx, were important critics of bourgeois society, and thus of political economy.

In a way, this chapter treats three great economists almost as set designers, who came on to the stage after the dramatic climax of the first act, with the development of scientific socialism, and reset the scenery for the start of the next act. They had an important role but were never in the spotlight. But their designs were very adaptable, so that other economists were able to build on them. In the competition between the economic traditions which existed in 1870, their ideas have come to dominate our thinking about the economy. When we talk about the supply and demand for a good, or the role of the business cycle in explaining levels of unemployment and inflation, we are drawing on this way of thinking about the economy.

These set designers were the Englishman, William Stanley Jevons; the Austrian, Carl Menger; and the Frenchman, Léon Walras. All three developed innovative approaches to economic analysis in the early 1870s, independently of each other. As a result, despite the similarities in their thinking, each one had a distinctive legacy.

Jevons studied chemistry at University College London in the early 1850s. Leaving without a degree, he worked in Australia setting up the mint, where he developed interests in philosophy and economics. Returning to the UK, he tried to work as an independent journalist, before becoming a tutor at Owens College in Manchester, which later became part of the University of Manchester. He eventually returned to University College London, where he was a professor from 1876–1880. Resigning to have more time to pursue his research, he drowned in 1882, while still in the early stages of drafting his *Principles of Economics*. His most important book, *Theory of Political Economy*, from 1871, attacked the tradition of classical political economy quite intemperately, proposing the alternative that economic value is not created in the production process, but rather through the ability of goods to generate utility for their users. He argued that we needed to think of the supply of labour as the result of balance between the pain of effort, and the pleasure of its reward with wages.

While Jevons was working on *Political Economy*, Carl Menger was training as a lawyer in Vienna. There were no departments of economics in Austrian universities, and study of the discipline had come to rest within their law faculties, so when Menger sought to become an academic, it was quite natural that his *habilitation* thesis, written to demonstrate that he had the skills needed to take up an academic position, should be on economics. Published in 1871, as *Grundsätze der Volkswirstschaftslehre* (*Principles of Economics*), it won him a professorship at the University of Vienna. His book initiated a specifically Austrian tradition of economic theory. Steeped in the Aristotelian tradition, Menger's approach was both inductive, and introspective, working step by step through very careful definitions. He was perhaps the first economist to think about the importance of scarcity as the basis of value to explain the prices of goods.

The last of the three, Léon Walras, trained as an engineer, but never practised that art. Promising his father that he would study economics seriously, he passed through many very different jobs, then worked as a journalist, before he made a deep impression on a Swiss politician with his understanding of the economics of public finance. That led to his appointment in 1870 as the first Professor of Economics at the University of Lausanne.

Compared with Menger and Jevons, Walras had a very substantial direct effect on the development of economics, but only after his death. In life, he worked in relative obscurity. His fame depended largely on the relatively brief book, *Éléments d'économie politique pure*, published in 1874. This set out a new way of thinking about the economy, the theory of general equilibrium, which treated the economy as a set of interconnected markets.

In the general equilibrium of an economy, the prices of goods are set so that there is just enough of each good brought to market to meet the demand for it. In Walras's approach, Smith's invisible hand is a virtual puppet-master, animating and ordering the whole economy. The mathematical structure of a general equilibrium system is necessarily very complex, and Walras never managed to obtain a complete solution. It was only in the 1930s that economists developed the mathematical tools needed to confirm his intuition about the nature, and stability, of a general equilibrium.

By the time that Walras linked his own work with Jevons' and Menger's, Jevons had drowned, knowing of Walras's work, but not Menger's. Walras pointed out that they had all placed consumer well-being at the centre of their analysis. All three had emphasized the importance of scarcity, which is the starting point of modern economic analysis. Scarcity occurs whenever our wants outstrip our ability to meet them.

It then follows that to buy more of one good, perhaps apples, we must decide to buy less of another good, say pears. We can then define the opportunity cost of an apple as the number of pears which we give up so that we can consume another apple. It also follows that with scarce resources, prices are opportunity costs of goods expressed in terms of money, so that the opportunity cost of any good will be its own price divided by the price of an alternative.

This way of thinking about scarcity led Jevons, Menger and Walras to develop arguments which demonstrated a fundamental economic result, that people who want to maximize their utility should allocate their spending across different goods, so that the additional benefit – or marginal utility – derived from a small increase in expenditure on any good would be equal. Anyone whose choices do not satisfy this equi-marginal principle could change the mix of goods being purchased and increase the utility which they derive from consumption.

In this type of analysis, it was natural to think about the effects of small changes in the way in which resources were used. For example, someone visiting a grocery store might decide to experiment by buying a little more fruit, and a little less bread. A business might plan to increase its output very slightly by buying a new machine, rather than by asking a few of its staff to work longer hours. Thinking about these sorts of changes in the balance of expenditure naturally led to discussion of how people might substitute consumption of one good (fruit) for another (bread) as prices changed. That led to the development of a theory of the determinants of the demand for a good, couched in a new terminology.

It took longer for economists to develop the theory of the supply of a good, for which the problem turned out to be how to balance the use of workers and machinery so that businesses maximized their profits. In the marginalist approach, rather than capital and labour being assets owned by different social classes, they became commodities needed in production. The classical analysis had assumed that production required fixed inputs, with businesses setting the price of their output so that they recovered the costs of hiring the resources needed for production. In the marginal analysis of businesses' output decisions, they could decide how much capital and labour to hire and choose the profit-maximizing combination.

But this is looking ahead. As Jevons, Menger and Walras developed their ideas, the span of their analysis, compared with that of Mill, or Marx, or even Smith, was quite modest. For example, they had nothing like Ricardo's three-sector model to explain how the distribution of income would change over time. But the new economics, a science of individual decision making, rather than the communal management of resources, had the internal consistency that classical political economy lacked. It could afford to by-pass the problems of distribution which had pre-occupied earlier economists because it seemed to offer new ways of understanding the structure of the economy.

This approach has come to be known as neo-classical economics. Thorstein Veblen, the most creative of the American institutionalist economists, invented the term to tie together, and dismiss, this new way of thinking about the economy, which to him seemed to be little more than an attempt to revive the classical tradition by analysing exchange, rather than social relationships.

At this early stage of the development of neo-classical economics, it was quite easy for Veblen to point to the extent to which the approach seemed to be a small variation in the classical approach. There was nothing novel in the idea of the margin. For example, in his numerical examples, Ricardo had discussed how the distribution of income would change as production of wheat increased. His marginal unit was simply the last strip of land which was brought into cultivation, and the marginal value of that land was the amount of wheat which it produced.

In addition, marginal analysis built on Mill's insight that what was useful would be valuable and set out principles for measuring that value. Arguably, the new economics simply took ideas which had already been used in classical political economy and reformulated them. While the idea of the margin might already have been familiar from classical political economy, its use in neo-classical economics, and the introduction of the substitution principle, ensured that it was used in very different ways.

As an example of how such analysis could quickly clarify earlier thinking, consider the resolution of the diamond–water paradox. Smith had noted that while water is necessary for life, it is generally freely available, while diamonds are prized even though they have few uses beyond ornamentation and storing value. The total value of water can be immense, but that value is associated with a small fraction of what we use: water for rehydration of a hospital patient, for example. Usually, when we turn on a tap, we place a small value on the water. A low price does not mean that we do not value a good. Instead, we should think of it as having a low price because it is generally abundant. It is only the rarity of diamonds which makes them valuable.

Turning to methods of analysis, neo-classical economics adopted Mill's utilitarian principles. It was natural to assume that people wanted to maximize the utility derived from consumption, or that organizations wanted to maximize the profits which they made from production. As soon as we mention optimization and think about the possibility of making small changes in resource use, the use of mathematical analysis seems almost inevitable. This is where we see that Jevons, Menger and even Walras were set designers rather than leading actors. They cleared the way for others to apply those methods of analysis, but they made little progress in applying mathematics to economics.

While Walras could see that their analysis shared general principles, there were many differences in their approaches. The idea of increasing the use of mathematics in economic analysis was appealing both to Walras and Jevons, but not for Menger. Trained in law and classical philosophy, he formulated his ideas of the economy in response to the arguments of the German historical school. For the members of that school of thought, the method of economics was careful documentary analysis. Economic theory would then emerge by induction as a set of principles which could explain regularities in observed behaviour.

For Menger, and the Austrian School, economics was largely theoretical, but it involved complex reasoning about human behaviour. Menger's approach drew on the Aristotelian and Scholastic approach, in which we can understand the properties of an object if we first classify its nature. He defined goods in terms of their possession of properties which would tend towards the satisfaction of (human) needs – an essentially utilitarian understanding – but he then argued that people must also understand both that consumption might satisfy needs, and that they can manage the use of the good. From its beginning, the Austrian tradition has been very interested in understanding what information people have, and how they might use it.

This approach naturally lends itself to philosophically grounded economic theory. For example, from the definitions of goods, and the purpose of economic activity, we can define a market as a system for allocating goods to the people, and organizations, who place the most value on them. We can also define the role of organizations as being to transform goods, such as labour and capital inputs, which can only meet needs indirectly, into goods which can be consumed to meet needs directly. Such ideas were certainly implicit within classical economics, but Menger's explicit formulation of them has been important for much modern thinking about how the structure of the economy emerges.

The novelty of Walras's analysis also came through abstract theorization, but he emphasized the formal logic of optimization much more than either Menger or Jevons. In Walras's general equilibrium framework, inputs into production processes would somehow combine to produce final goods. Indeed, within the Walrasian approach, there is no need for organizations to emerge to undertake the production of goods. In return for payment, people rent out factors of production. That allows the production of a variety of goods, which people will then purchase.

The general equilibrium in a Walrasian system consists of the market prices for each factor of production, and each good, chosen so that the quantity of each good brought to the market equals the quantity which is sought in the market. A well-known way of putting this is that for every good, in the general equilibrium, supply equals demand.

This means that all factors of production are fully employed – so that, for example, there will not be any workers looking for jobs, but also, there will not be producers who are looking for more workers. On the consumption side, there will not be any wasted production – all output will be purchased – and no one willing to buy a good at its market price will be unable to do so.

There are many other, rather more technical conditions, which must hold in a general equilibrium. When they are satisfied, the invisible hand has done its work perfectly. All resources will be used efficiently, and no planner could improve upon its work.

In their very different approaches, Jevons, Menger and Walras became quiet revolutionaries. To observers in 1870, socialism and historical analysis might have seemed much richer approaches. But the conceptual structure of neo-classical economics quickly led to the development of an analytical framework, which could be applied to any problem involving management of finite resources. Veblen was correct to link classical and neo-classical thought, but wrong to think of neo-classical thought largely as an attempt to revive a failing tradition. It was an engine of enquiry, and the first chief engineer was the Cambridge economist, Alfred Marshall.

8

Alfred Marshall – The Frail Master Craftsman

A complete anatomy of the economy

Alfred Marshall *enjoyed* bad health, sometimes using his supposed frailty for his personal benefit. A bout of serious illness in early middle-age led him to worry for the rest of his life that effort might exhaust him. Seeming frailty allowed him to organize his domestic arrangements around his needs. Yet that never stopped him from packing his bags and wandering for hundreds of miles through the Alps almost every summer. Nor did it prevent him achieving his ambition of building a Cambridge School in economics.

Jevons was arguably the first person to understand the importance of marginal analysis. While his work had announced new possibilities, his early death cleared the way for Marshall to provide the first comprehensive account of recognizably modern economic principles, completing the transition from political economy to economics.

From his admission to Cambridge as an undergraduate student in 1861, Marshall's career reflected his determination to achieve great success. His father, William, a clerk in the Bank of England, had obtained a place at Merchant Taylors' School for his son, anticipating that Alfred, under his stern tutelage, would qualify for a scholarship at St John's College, Oxford, where he would have read classics as preparation for entry into the Anglican priesthood.

On leaving school, the young man rebelled, borrowed money from an uncle and, winning a scholarship, went to St John's College, in Cambridge University, to study mathematics. In 1865, he graduated second in his class – Lord Rayleigh, who in 1904 won the Nobel Prize for Physics, outdid him. His achievement secured him a Fellowship at St John's College.

His professional association with Cambridge lasted for the rest of his life. Marriage in 1877 required him to resign his Fellowship, and he found a position as the Principal of University College, Bristol, which had been established by two colleges of Oxford University as part of the expansion of higher education in England. It was while he was in Bristol that he fell seriously ill, and in 1881, he stepped aside as Principal. After several months of convalescence in Palermo, he returned to Bristol simply as Professor of Political Economy. From there, in quick succession, he moved to Balliol College in Oxford University as a lecturer in political economy, and then returned to Cambridge as Professor of Political Economy in 1885. From that post, held until retirement in 1908, he would become the dominant figure in economics in Britain.

Marshall had seen an undergraduate degree in mathematics as preparation for the priesthood, much as it had been for Malthus. Throughout the 1860s, he retained some sense of vocation, but with his exposure to debating clubs at Cambridge as a young fellow, and specifically through being a member of the group in which the philosopher Henry Sidgwick had a central role, he ended up wrestling with the extent to which religious faith was reasonable. As part of that process, his studies in moral sciences shifted from metaphysics into epistemology, then ethics, and ultimately, as his confidence in Christian doctrine faded, and he sought practical applications for his philosophical enquiries, political economy. Having lost his religious vocation, Marshall seems to have found a similar purpose in his economic studies. As a young man, he purchased an oil painting of a workman, which he set above his fireplace. Marshall claimed to have kept it close by him during his initial studies of economics, using it as a reminder that he was to 'fit men like that for heaven', and not simply to be a 'mere thinker'.

This gradual approach to the study of economics through a thorough grounding in both mathematics and ethics explains how Marshall was well suited for the task of turning political economy into recognizably modern economics. He had technical skill, so could easily build on Ricardo's arithmetic examples, and Mill's exposition of economic processes. He could also engage with the traditional ethical basis of economic argument, while creating the new problem-solving techniques which it needed to become an autonomous discipline, and finally separate from ethics.

It was probably in 1866 that Marshall began to study Mill's *Principles of Political Economy* carefully. While he later claimed that he had explored Mill's evolutionary analysis using differential equations, there is little evidence of that in his private papers. Instead, he gradually widened his reading of economics after spending most of 1868 in Dresden, where he improved his knowledge of German, and read philosophy. A later visit to Germany in 1870–71 brought him into contact with the work of Wilhelm Georg Friedrich Roscher and the German historical school, as well as socialist thinkers.

It might then seem that as the marginal revolution began in 1870, Marshall had the skills and the knowledge needed to formulate his vision for economics. Had he been more like Jevons, he would have published his initial ideas in the 1870s. Walras wrote to Marshall in 1874, urging him to publish. Instead, Marshall prevaricated.

Marshall was like Smith in preferring to wait and pull together ideas until he was satisfied with his analysis. Also, like Smith, he gradually pruned back his original plans for publication, although his plans never extended beyond economics. The result is that, more than Smith, Marshall's lasting reputation depends on one book, *Principles of Economics*, which became the standard introduction to the subject from its eventual publication in 1890, until it was overtaken by Paul Samuelson's *Economics* in the 1950s.

Walras was certainly correct that Marshall could easily have written useful books before *Principles of Economics* came out. For example, he spent a legacy from the uncle who had previously supported his undergraduate education on touring the USA in 1875, visiting factories, talking with industrialists, and building up an appreciation of how a young country might build its industrial base from behind trade barriers. His conclusions then found their way into a draft text. Marshall's reluctance to publish worried Henry Sidgwick, who feared that his colleague would lose the recognition which the originality of his insights deserved. To forestall that risk, Sidgwick had two chapters from the draft manuscript published privately in 1877, as *Pure Theory of Foreign Trade*, and *Pure Theory of Domestic Values*. Many of the ideas found their way into Part V of *Principles*, which, for Marshall, was its core.

Then, on his marriage to Mary Paley – the first woman to complete the Moral Sciences programme at Cambridge, and one of the first Fellows of Newnham College – he took over from her the writing of a short book on *Economics of Industry*. Remarkably, by Marshall's exacting standards, the book appeared in relatively short order in 1879. Moving to Bristol, the administrative load of running a new college, and illness, contributed to Marshall finding little time to order his thoughts for future publication until his convalescence in Palermo. With his anxiety about exhausting himself through overwork, that began his pattern of spending the summer working on the book every year in the 1880s, until finally, in 1889, he could send it to the printers.

Marshall began *Principles of Economics* by claiming that the purpose of economics was to improve the well-being of the great mass of the working population, of whom his 'patron saint' was a representative. This was more than a nod to Malthusian population dynamics, or even acceptance that economics needed a theory of distribution. Marshall's vision for economics was not all that far from Mill's moral science. Especially in the 1890s, he regularly met with trade union leaders to understand better the needs of the working classes.

Principles of Economics began by introducing the fundamental terminology of his economics, before analysing wants and demands, the nature of production, and the structure of industry, starting from the assumption of free enterprise in competition. He discussed the economic theory required to understand the operation of markets very carefully. First, he examined the markets for goods which people consume, where he emphasized the role of marginal utility in establishing demand. He then discussed markets for the inputs required to produce goods. That led to him developing an argument that businesses would change their output in response to changes in both the market price and costs of production. He dismissed the claim of critics that this was just a way of reconciling the ideas of Mill and Jevons, believing that his investigations had led to a more complete theory of the relative importance of demand and cost factors over time. Finally, returning to his claim about the ultimate objectives of economics, he concluded *Principles* with an exploration of the distribution of incomes, which concentrated on wage setting, and then explained the income of capital and land.

The claim that he had appropriated parts of Mill's and Jevons' arguments reflected the way in which he followed Jevons in using marginal utility to analyse the demand for a good, and Mill's treatment of the costs of production to analyse the supply of a good. However, in analysing how businesses would set their profit maximizing output, Marshall used marginal analysis to argue they would choose the level of output so that further expansion would no longer increase profits. He also demonstrated that neither Mill nor Jevons could have been entirely consistent in their arguments. Lastly, he argued that demand factors would be important in determining how prices would respond immediately to a change in market conditions, but that over time, businesses would adapt their production processes, so that cost factors would become more important in determining prices, and the quantities traded.

There are notable similarities between the contents page of *Principles* and the syllabus of introductory courses in economics, which universities currently offer to students of other disciplines. That reflects the way in which the economic theory which students meet in such courses is often a descendant of Marshall's diagrammatic approach, which allowed him to explore the possible effects of changes in one factor in an otherwise unchanging economic environment. His main objective in this approach was to understand what affects the market price at which a good will be bought and sold, and the quantity which will be bought and sold. His ability to integrate diagrams into *Principles* reflected the formal mathematics which underpinned his arguments.

Given Marshall's belief that economics had the capacity to transform society, it was natural that he planned *Principles* to be more than an introduction to the new body of economic theory. In 1886, in his inaugural lecture at Cambridge, he referred to the discipline, 'not as a body of concrete truths, but an engine for the discovery of concrete truths'. This was a very different conception of economics from Walras's general equilibrium theory, with its complex analysis of inter-linked markets, in which the whole economy could be in equilibrium. Although Marshall had the technical capacity to develop such an approach, that never appealed to him because of his doubts about whether formal mathematical arguments could ever be fruitful in exploring the 'ordinary business of life'.

Indeed, Marshall was sceptical about the value of mathematical economics, believing that some of his pupils had too much confidence in what they could achieve with formal arguments. In a letter to A. L. Bowley, Marshall claimed that unless mathematical arguments could also be set out in everyday language, they did not contain any useful economic knowledge. His advice to Bowley concluded with the suggestion that it was important to 'burn the mathematics' especially if it turned out to have no clear value as economic argument.

His reticence about the use of mathematics reflected his belief that good economics would be like biology. The motto *natura non facit saltum* – nature doesn't jump – appeared on the title page of *Principles*. Marshall's arrival at Cambridge in 1861 coincided with passionate debates over Charles Darwin's evolutionary theory, from which he took that motto. The theory of evolution through natural selection was important during his struggles with his faith, but it also led him to conclude that the study of markets and firms needed a similar type of theory.

Readers of the book may not find much in it to demonstrate how Marshall used those ideas. He explained structural change in the economy with his discussion of differences in behaviour in the short-run and the long-run, terms which are rather loosely defined, but which led readers to think through how they might be applied in specific situations. Marshall was also interested in understanding why industries emerged in specific locations, and at a particular time, why they would flourish, and why they eventually decline. These ideas developed into the concept of 'industrial districts'. His rather tentative explanation was that businesses in an industry often might cluster together first to ensure access to resources, and then remain in those locations as relevant skills and knowledge become concentrated in specific towns and cities.

Given that Marshall and Smith worked in very similar ways, it is natural to compare *Principles of Economics* and *The Wealth of Nations*. Both ended up with a highly polished surface, reflecting the care with which Smith and Marshall developed their arguments. With *Principles*, it is very easy to miss the extent to which Marshall carefully placed sophisticated ideas in the text. He also never claimed to have originated ideas, presenting his new interpretation of economics as if it was already widely accepted.

As with *Theory of Moral Sentiments*, Marshall advertised *Principles* as volume one, projecting for many years a second book. When he finally published *Industry and Trade* in 1919, reviewers found that it was exhaustive in its descriptions, but rather dated in its quite rudimentary analysis. By then an old man, and experiencing substantial cognitive decline, Marshall had simply waited too long to publish many of his ideas. His final book, *Money, Credit and Commerce*, came out in 1923, the year before his death. It too was a collection of older ideas, some developed half a century before. It may be that Mary Paley Marshall had to take the lead in organizing and editing the material.

Publishing so little, Marshall secured his reputation through his teaching. When he arrived at Cambridge, the teaching of political economy took place in the history and moral science degrees. In 1903, Marshall finally achieved his long-term ambition of establishing an economics degree. His 'Cambridge School' emerged quite fitfully but was built largely on the oral tradition of his teaching.

Think of Marshall as a master craftsman equipping his apprentices for admission to an economists' guild. The structure of teaching at Cambridge in the late nineteenth century, which involved students meeting their tutor individually, enabled this approach. Marshall did much of his teaching at his home, Balliol Croft, which had been built for him and his wife after he became Professor of Political Economy. In supervision sessions, his students had to defend arguments which they had developed in essays. Mary Paley Marshall provided the student with tea and cake, while her husband carried out his questioning perched on a stool. The inquisition over, the student would depart with books, and an essay, by then heavily annotated. Little by little, he built up a cadre of former students in academic posts across England, ensuring that British economics would have a Marshallian flavour.

He was unrelenting in his determination to establish a school of economic thought, subordinating personal relationships to that ambition. However, he simply failed to see how his wife, Mary Paley, could have been a partner in his intellectual enquiries. They had met in the mid-1870s because he was supportive of the development of Newnham College. After they married, Marshall used her as a lecturer in political economy for women students while he was in Bristol. Despite all that, throughout his life, he opposed mixed sex education, and so played a prominent role in the successful campaign in 1896–7 against allowing women to complete their studies at Cambridge by graduating with degrees.

Perhaps that explains why it never occurred to him that his wife could have been a capable reader, and critic, of *Principles*. Instead, he only allowed her to undertake very simple research tasks to support its preparation. After Marshall's death, as the executor of his estate, Mary Paley created a new role for herself as the honorary librarian of the newly founded Marshall Library, remaining active in that role until the late 1930s. Some Cambridge economists thought that her widowhood gave her a new lease of life.

Marshall's insistence on it being his school of economics might also explain his dismissal of Jevons' achievements.

Like Mill, Marshall generally made a rule of treating all his predecessors' contributions to the development of economics generously. When it came to Jevons, he stated that economists of the late nineteenth century owed more to Jevons than to almost anyone else. Nonetheless, he also claimed that the development of *Principles* owed very little to Jevons' work on utility as the basis of demand. Instead, Marshall cited Mill, and several writers from the first half of the nineteenth century, such as Ricardo, Antoine Augustin Cournot, Jules Dupuit and Johann Heinrich von Thünen as having been important influences.

Marshall may have been entirely accurate in his recollection of his intellectual development. Jevons was only eight years older than Marshall. He developed his arguments about the role of marginal utility in the 1860s, with his first publication around 1866. But that was precisely when Marshall began to study economics seriously. As early as 1872, when Marshall reviewed Jevons' *Theory of Political Economy*, he claimed to have found little which was novel in it. Fearing that he might have been unfair, Marshall even discussed that review with his former student, Herbert Foxwell, who had become a colleague of Jevons and who was also working on demand theory.

Much later, Foxwell would also experience the effects of Marshall's determination to develop the Cambridge School in his image. A candidate to succeed Marshall as Professor of Political Economy in 1908, he found that his old teacher was perfectly capable of putting to one side the claims of four decades of friendship, as he manoeuvred Arthur Pigou into the role instead. Bruised by the experience, Foxwell was never reconciled with Marshall.

With his fear of ill-health, and an apparently instrumental approach to relationships, Marshall succeeded largely through his ability to build paternalistic relationships with many of his best students. In the *Principles*, he set out to write for 'men of affairs', and to seek the widest possible readership, rather than to write simply for his academic peers – a very different ambition from Walras. He banished the formal mathematical analysis to a technical appendix. Claiming a degree of continuity with Mill, he defined much of the modern structure of economics. That careful analysis inspired many followers on both sides of the Atlantic, especially, as we shall see much later, in the University of Chicago.

9

Joseph Schumpeter – Creator and Destroyer

What makes a great performance in economics?

'As a young man, I set out to be the greatest lover in Vienna, the greatest horseman in Austria, and the greatest economist in the world.' With a store of such aphorisms, 'Schumpy', always a showman, both entertained and scandalized students and colleagues at Harvard in the 1930s. Several endings to that well-attested aphorism exist – the most common on the web being, 'Alas, for the illusions of youth, as a horseman, I was never quite first-rate.' As well as his hoard of stories, colleagues and students at Harvard recalled him bringing a new approach to economic analysis from the old world of Europe. His deeply felt influence on his students and younger colleagues was exactly the reason that Frank Taussig, the head of Harvard's economics department, had repeatedly sought to recruit him from 1925, until he finally arrived in 1932.

Schumpeter's career spanned some of the great turning points in the history of economics. Born in 1883, he became the youngest professor in Austria-Hungary in 1911, just before World War I destroyed the country. He worked in Europe during the 1920s, while the continent struggled to recover from the effects of war. When he arrived in the USA, the country was in the depths of the Great Depression. He remained there during World War II, dying in 1950.

He was born in Triesch, in Moravia, in 1883, (now Trest, in the Czech Republic), into a family of German-speaking mill owners. On his father's death when he was only four years old, his mother remarried, and relocated to Vienna. There, Schumpeter completed his secondary schooling at an elite *Gymnasium* before studying law and political economy at the University of Vienna. From there, he travelled to England, where he met Marshall. The meeting was not a great success. Schumpeter blithely ignored the older man's warnings about becoming excessively attached to theory. He also visited Walras in 1908 and presented him with a copy of his first book, which was on the history of economic thought. Unfortunately, Walras seemed unable to accept that such a young man could have written so well, and so repeatedly asked Schumpeter to pass on his gratitude to his father.

Schumpeter had thought very seriously about both the history and method of economics. In the book which he showed to Walras, he had compared the development of the Historical School in Germany, and the Austrian School. Ever since Menger's work had first appeared, there had been ongoing debates between German and Austrian economists about how best to establish our knowledge of the economy. While the historical approach imputed causal links from data specific to a time and place, Menger's 'exact theory' proposed that the urge to satisfy needs was the ultimate motivation for human action. That led Menger, and the members of his Austrian School, to be doubtful about the use of data within economic analysis.

Attempting to bring this debate to a conclusion, Schumpeter proposed that while German and Austrian economists had adopted different modes of analysis, they had a shared understanding of the nature of economic relations, so that history and theory were ultimately complementary. History could provide evidence, against which theory might be judged.

It seemed to Schumpeter that the differences between the dynamic analysis of both Germans and Austrians and the static analysis of English economics were much more substantial. He believed that English economics only analysed how the final state of the economy would change as circumstances changed. Think of Marshall's approach of allowing one factor affecting a market to change at a time. For Schumpeter, the dynamic analysis of German-speaking economists allowed discussion of how the new state of the economy would gradually emerge. Throughout his career, he used dynamic analysis in his own work, and was sceptical about the value of static analysis. An Anglophile, he believed that English economists had failed to live up to their potential.

On his visit to England, Schumpeter married Gladys Seaver, who was perhaps 12 years older than him – that is how little we know about her. He then found a job as a lawyer in Cairo, and from there took up an academic position in Czernowitz (now Chernivtsi, in Ukraine). He had left Seaver in Cairo, although she reappeared briefly in 1924, when he married for a second time, bigamously.

By the time that Schumpeter became a professor, the Austrian School had developed well beyond Menger's initial formulation, largely through the work of his pupils, Friedrich von Wieser and Eugen von Böhm-Bawerk. Through von Wieser, the school had developed its analysis of marginal utility and demand, and from von Böhm-Bawerk, it had acquired a theory of capital. Schumpeter used their ideas as building blocks for his dynamic analysis, first set out in 1911 in *Theorie der wirtschaftlichen Entwicklung* (translated into English in 1934, as *Theory of Economic Development*), in which economic development took place through invention and innovation.

In this book, Schumpeter first presented the dynamic economic analysis for which he is best known. Sharing Marshall's objective of explaining how the economy would change over time, he took a very different approach. Schumpeter would later criticize Marshall's belief that economic analysis should be biological in form. While that might at first seem surprising, given that Schumpeter was one of the founders of evolutionary economics, and that they agreed that entrepreneurial activity is necessary for economic development, Schumpeter's dynamic analysis was very different from Marshall's static analysis.

Influenced by Darwinian theory and believing that intense competition was the usual situation in economics, Marshall imagined entrepreneurial activity to involve responding intelligently to environmental constraints. His understanding of economic development was essentially ecological. Entrepreneurship was integral to it, but it was almost a social function, and in his discussion, it was largely impersonal.

For Schumpeter, working within the Austrian tradition, it was much more natural to think about entrepreneurs as having agency, so that they would think about how they could best use resources in new ways to meet human needs. In that way, he argued that the economy would evolve. There were no guarantees that entrepreneurs would succeed, so they inevitably had to bear risks. Many people could think of new ways of meeting needs. They would need managerial skills to coordinate other resources, and Schumpeter emphasized the importance of process innovation, in which businesses would implement new, more efficient ways of meeting existing needs.

Drawing on capital theory, Schumpeter argued that entrepreneurs would also need access to resources, and in an industrial economy, that would mean raising capital from investors. Entrepreneurs had to be able to explain credibly to potential investors how they would obtain returns. Rather than evolving because of changes which were largely external to the economy, in Schumpeter's analysis, change was the result of human agency, with the impersonal forces of competition simply determining which of the changes would turn out to be evolutionarily fit, and so survive. When the next generation of entrepreneurs proposed further innovations, their ideas would be shaped by earlier innovations. Schumpeter's vision of economic development might seem to owe more to Marx than Marshall.

With Schumpeter, there was always something other than economics going on – often a woman. During World War I, as Austria-Hungary finally collapsed, he became fascinated by politics. In 1919, he became a youthful right-wing finance minister in a left-wing government, which was trying to manage Austria after its shattering defeat in the war. Vienna was then one of the leading centres of Marxist thought. Along with other Austrian economists, Schumpeter's admiration for the complex system of Marxian analysis perhaps enabled him to join such a government. He may also have thought that he could be a policy entrepreneur and imagined that it would be possible for him to operate independently of his colleagues.

That political naïveté and the inevitable policy differences with his colleagues led to his forced resignation within a matter of months. He then acquired a banking licence, and so became the President of Biedermann Bank in Vienna in 1921. When the bank collapsed in murky circumstances in 1924, he was left with very large debts. To pay them off, he went back into academia, as Professor of Economic Theory at the University of Bonn, but he also had to take on commissions to write about economics and banking.

Given Schumpeter's personal circumstances, it is perhaps surprising that he wrote anything after 1925. First, his mother died, and then, in the following week, his young wife, Anna, died in childbirth, along with their baby. Schumpeter never recovered properly from those blows. He went into a period of deep depression, which continued after his third marriage in 1937, at least until the end of World War II. In his personal papers, there is also plenty of evidence of very odd habits, including copying out the entries in his wife's diaries, and the maintenance of what became almost a personal cult, in which he turned increasingly to his dead wife and mother, whom he styled *die Hasen* (the hares), for their intercession in the struggles of his life. However, one of the ways in which he tried to manage his mental state was by working to the limits of his physical capacity.

After his wife's death, Schumpeter's first attempt to revive his career was an analysis of money and credit cycles. He planned to make a major contribution to economic theory and also address the challenges facing the European economies. Unfortunately, he was not the only economist with such a plan. John Maynard Keynes produced his *Treatise on Money*, in 1930. Although Schumpeter was in the last stages of preparing his own book on *Money and Currency*, he immediately shelved the project. After his death, the manuscript was still in his papers, and was published as *Das Wesen des Geldes* in 1970.

Despite the move to Harvard, in the 1930s his ambition to be the world's greatest economist seemed to have been denied. Still suffering from depression, he spent the decade working himself into a state of exhaustion as he struggled to complete a monumental study of business cycles, which he believed would provide an explanation for the Great Depression. For this, Schumpeter argued that there were three different types of cycle: an inventory cycle, in which businesses would build up and run down stocks over a three-year period; a credit cycle, which lasted about nine years, driven by variation in banks' willingness to lend; and the much longer cycle of technological innovation, which had been proposed in the 1920s by the Soviet economist, Nikolai Kondratiev. Schumpeter's explanation of the Great Depression was that there was a confluence in the downswings of these cycles in the early 1930s.

Once again, Maynard Keynes beat him to the prize. His *General Theory of Employment, Interest and Money*, published in 1936, quickly won the support of many, younger economists, including those at Harvard. It appalled Schumpeter. Reviewing it for the *Journal of the American Statistical Association*, he began by alleging that the book contained theory only to justify policy prescriptions, and that rather than being a general analysis, it 'expresses forcefully the attitude of a decaying civilization'. It concluded with broad hints that Keynes' conclusions could easily be refuted by any knowledge of European history.

In 1937, Schumpeter married for the third time. His wife, Elizabeth Boody, was herself a professional economist. Already divorced, she entered the relationship, aware that she would need to be housekeeper, business manager and nurse. Independently wealthy, she managed their household, allowing Schumpeter almost complete peace. She provided research assistance and read his work critically as she typed it. Like Marshall, Schumpeter ended up personally dependent on a strong, capable woman. Without Boody's companionship, and the supportive environment which she created at their home, depression and overwork might easily have killed him.

Almost immediately, Schumpeter was able to complete *Business Cycles*, which finally appeared in 1939. Its carefully marshalled evidence and exhaustive arguments had almost no effect on economics. The book was received politely – Ragnar Frisch, the great Norwegian mathematical economist, who would become one of the first winners of the Nobel Memorial Prize in 1969, remarked that it would be pleasant to read something which was not about the war.

With Boody's support, Schumpeter continued to work through the 1940s, during which he completed *Capitalism, Socialism and Democracy* and most of *History of Economic Analysis*. While Boody worked on the *History* after Schumpeter's death in 1950 to prepare it for publication, she was suffering from breast cancer, and died in 1953, so that the final publication in 1954 served as a memorial to them both. Scrupulously honest, she had carefully kept all his papers, which is one reason why we know so much about his inner life.

Capitalism, Socialism and Democracy, which first appeared in 1943, built on his theory of economic development. It was to be his most successful book, with its third edition published in 1950; but Schumpeter claimed to have despised it. He seems to have treated it as something of a 'pot boiler', which had failed to plumb the depths of theory. The showman always courted the applause of academia, rather than the money of the *hoi polloi*.

It introduced the now famous idea that innovation involves creative destruction. He argued that innovations affect production processes, and the resources used to produce the goods and services which people consume. Thinking of the value of goods used in production processes as being determined by the value of the goods which they produce, Schumpeter argued that creative destruction occurs when process and quality innovations make existing processes redundant. Factories using an old technology will start to make losses, and face closure. While innovation is creative, elsewhere in the economy it will have destructive effects.

Posed by Schumpeter, the answer to the rhetorical question in *Capitalism, Socialism and Democracy*: 'Can capitalism survive? ... I do not think it can,' may simply seem to be deliberately provocative. Remember, though, that he was deeply conservative, and that led him to mistrust President Franklin Roosevelt, whom he saw as a demagogue, who had forced the USA into a European war, where he would enable Winston Churchill and Joseph Stalin to destroy the German nation. (This complex man fully shared in the cultural anti-Semitism prevalent in his generation. Elizabeth Boody, a specialist in Asian trade and politics, was suspected of

Japanese sympathies. An FBI investigation into them both found no evidence of wrongdoing.)

He wrote *Capitalism, Socialism and Democracy* during the global crisis of World War II, in which governments everywhere had to direct economic activity. Partly because of the reorientation of economic activity required for the war effort, large organizations, with their specialized research and development divisions, were better placed to engage in innovation than individual entrepreneurs. Schumpeter believed that innovation had become a bureaucratic process, and that through persistent innovation, increasing returns would be internal to the organization. Large organizations would therefore always be able to undercut smaller competitors, and so would acquire substantial market power. He concluded that through democratic socialism, with the public owning enterprises and directing their activities, it would be possible for the benefits of economic development to be distributed justly.

With his *History of Economic Analysis*, Schumpeter brought his career to a close by thinking about the development of economics. It is a heady brew. He had worked on it over the last 15 years of his life, and it was a unique attempt to survey the whole development of economics. Almost certainly, Schumpeter, who had completed his schooling in a Viennese *Gymnasium*, read a greater proportion of economic theory as it had developed from ancient Greece through to the 1940s – and in the original languages – than anyone before or since.

Since the book was still incomplete at his death, in the published version we perhaps see rather more of how Schumpeter – and Boody as his editor – worked through the ideas than if there had been the final text. But coursing through the 1,200 pages of this draft are crisp, emphatically final judgements. We may disagree with them, but it is difficult not to marvel at the sage's erudition. Using one of Schumpeter's favourite terms, it was a truly outstanding performance.

By 'performance', Schumpeter meant sustained excellence in developing a theoretical framework. For that reason, he considered Walrasian general equilibrium to have been the greatest achievement of economics. Marx's historical determinism also scored highly as performance. Mill came close to achieving a great performance, but he had rushed his work, spending only two years on it, instead of the ten which Schumpeter believed that the *Principles of Political Economy* had deserved. He saw Smith largely as a compiler of facts, who had impeded the progress of economics. Treating Smith as an economic philosopher, Schumpeter placed him at the end of the pre-history of political economy, rather than having been its founder. Marshall's performance was the most disappointing. As well as his reliance on static theory, Schumpeter criticized his belief that economics had the moral purpose of transforming the working class, his desire to be widely read, and his wary use of mathematics.

His assessment of Marshall's weaknesses makes it even more interesting that Schumpeter had something of a blind spot when it came to mathematics. Yet Taussig had wanted to hire him to strengthen Harvard's teaching of mathematical economics. Schumpeter enthusiastically developed a course, and taught it for two years, before passing it on to Wassily Leontief, whose substantial contributions to the theory of economic development won him the Nobel Memorial Prize in 1973. (He also trained four Nobel laureates, three of whom, Paul Samuelson, Thomas Schelling and Robert Solow appear in later chapters.) Schumpeter appeared to be quite relaxed about passing this course on to one of the colleagues he cheerfully acknowledged to be a 'young genius'.

'Performance' suggests something of the stage. Schumpeter enjoyed shocking people as he entertained them. It was perhaps a convenient persona, especially in the 1920s and 1930s, when depression led to him writing at a Marshallian pace, while working almost entirely on his own. Some reviewers of *Business Cycles* thought it remarkable that one man could produce so much detailed work. 'Performance' was also similar in nature to 'creative destruction', as Schumpeter found when his students flocked to the bookshops to buy Maynard Keynes' *General Theory*. And perhaps that helps to explain why 'the greatest economist' shook the discipline, but never entered its mainstream.

10

John Maynard Keynes – The Last Amateur

Treating the economy as a unified system to create a new role for government

In May 1919, John Maynard Keynes decided to resign from the British government's delegation to the Versailles Peace Congress. The Congress, set up at the end of World War I, was dominated by the victors, Britain, France and the USA, with the British and French governments determined to 'Make Germany Pay'. After working in the UK Treasury throughout the war, Keynes was perhaps Britain's leading expert on international finance. He was convinced that the peace terms being imposed on Germany would seriously damage the economies of continental Europe, and possibly lead to another war. Driven by furious indignation, he set a target of writing 1,000 words per day, seven days per week, so that his polemical book, *The Economic Consequences of the Peace*, could be published at the end of 1919. An immediate, global success, it established Keynes as a major public intellectual. He was a new type of economist, who would forge a new economics. About half of the rest of this book will be about how other great economists have responded to his thinking.

When Keynes wrote *Economic Consequences*, Schumpeter was Austria's finance minister. Writing an obituary of Keynes in 1946, he praised it unreservedly: 'The feat was one of moral courage. But the book is a master-piece – packed with practical wisdom that never lacks depth; pitilessly logical yet never cold; genuinely humane but nowhere sentimental; meeting all facts without vain regrets but also without hopelessness: it is sound advice added to sound analysis.'

Writing *Economic Consequences* for the public, and so quickly, showed how different Keynes would be from Marshall and Schumpeter. In the years of economic turmoil in the 1920s, and through the Great Depression of the 1930s, a stream of pamphlets and newspaper articles flowed from his desk, making policy proposals.

From 1909 until his death in 1946, Keynes was a Fellow of King's College, Cambridge. But he was also a historian, a philosopher, a mathematician, a publisher, a civil servant, a connoisseur of the arts, the builder of a theatre, an administrator of public funding for the arts, a private investor, a financial adviser and investment manager, an adviser to governments (and sometimes their representative in international negotiations), a journalist, and a political activist in the Liberal Party of Herbert Henry Asquith and David Lloyd George. Typically fitting in a couple of days per week in Cambridge around his many other activities, he was the last amateur, appearing to disdain effort, even as he worked himself to exhaustion.

Determination to change the world fuelled the writing of *Economic Consequences*. That determination was also important when he came to write his greatest work, *The General Theory of Employment, Income and Money*, in the depths of the Great Depression. When it was finally published in 1936, postgraduate students in the USA clubbed together to place a bulk order directly with the publishers so that they could read it as quickly as possible. By the end of World War II, those young economists had started to teach a new, Keynesian economics.

Maynard Keynes – he dropped 'John' while at school – was the oldest child of one of Marshall's first students, John Neville Keynes, who fretted endlessly about ensuring that Maynard would be able to make a name for himself. He prepared his son for a King's Scholarship at Eton, which led directly to a university scholarship at King's College in Cambridge University. There, like Marshall, Maynard Keynes completed an undergraduate degree in mathematics.

He then went into a year of postgraduate studies at Cambridge, attending some of Marshall's lectures in 1905 – having read the *Principles of Economics* in preparation. Putting off the decision about whether to become an academic, he joined the civil service, working in the India Office in 1907–08. He told his father that the position appealed to him largely because of its prestige. Working on currency reform, he quickly became an expert on monetary economics and financial institutions.

While at the India Office, he kept his links with Cambridge, working on a Fellowship Dissertation on probability theory, for which his examiner was the analytical philosopher, Alfred North Whitehead. On completing the dissertation in late 1908, he could easily have become a philosopher, but instead he chose to teach economics. Pigou offered Keynes £100 per year for lecturing, in the same sort of private arrangement as Marshall had made on occasion to give young men time to establish their careers. And so, in early 1909, Keynes gave his first lectures (on money, credit and prices). The arrangement with Pigou was soon superfluous. He was elected as a Fellow of King's College in March 1909.

Keynes and Marshall were both Cambridge maths graduates, and economists, but they had completely different personalities. Keynes was a consummate networker, quickly recruited into the 'Apostles', a discussion club for students, but with life membership, so that at many meetings, university staff would be present. When he was an undergraduate, the Society – as its members generally called it – was in thrall to the philosopher, G. E. Moore, who argued that moral goodness required the pursuit of truth, love and beauty.

For Keynes, always practical, Moore's philosophy found expression in a lifelong belief that personal relationships were more important than authority, or tradition, as well as a deep interest in creative arts. He quickly formed long-lasting friendships with the writer Lytton Strachey and the artist Duncan Grant. They provided Keynes with introductions to Vanessa Bell (who became Grant's partner in work and life) and her sister Virginia Woolf. Grant, Bell and Woolf, along with the art critic, Roger Fry, then became central figures in the circle of artists and writers known as the Bloomsbury Group. Keynes, the great networker, was counted among this group. He leased a house in Gordon Square, next to the Bells and Strachey. Keynes ran a publishing house for the group before World War I, and managed investments for its members afterwards. Until he was wealthy enough to buy the lease of Tilton House on the Sussex Downs, he used Charleston, the Bells' country house, which was only a mile away from Tilton, whenever he needed peace to write.

When World War I broke out, Keynes' expertise in international finance led Lloyd George, while Chancellor of the Exchequer, to recruit him as an adviser. That became the position in the Treasury from which he resigned to write *Economic Consequences*. By 1920, aged 36, he had a secure academic position, a proven record as a policy adviser, a substantial public reputation, and had embarked on his career in investment, picking up the first of many directorships of investment companies.

World War I had destroyed three empires: Czarist Russia, the German Reich and Austria-Hungary. Great Britain, with its global empire, survived intact, but at great cost. Keynes' work, securing finance for the Allies during the war, was a precursor of his efforts to influence British government policy throughout the 1920s and 1930s as the country struggled to rebuild its economy given its diminished standing in the world.

Through the 1920s, unemployment in Britain stayed above 10 per cent. Rapid price increases during the war had forced the country to abandon the gold standard, under which the value of sterling was fixed in terms of gold, while the exchange rate with the US was fixed at $4.86 per pound. To restore Britain's standing in international trade, the government wanted to return to the gold standard. It fell to Winston Churchill, as Chancellor of the Exchequer, to do this in 1925. Keynes dashed off another polemic, *Economic Consequences of Mr Churchill*. He argued that the higher value of sterling would force export-led industries, notably coal mining, to cut wages. Churchill was forced to provide mine owners with substantial subsidies, but the industrial unrest which Keynes had predicted led to the General Strike in May 1926.

By this time, Keynes' passion for dance had led to his marriage to the Russian ballerina, Lydia Lopokova. Their obvious devotion for each other – when apart, they wrote to each other daily – quickly overcame the puzzlement of his Bloomsbury friends at what seemed to them an unlikely match. Keynes' biographers have also struggled to explain it. Perhaps we should simply accept *Vogue*'s description of the wedding in its August 1925 issue, as 'a delightful symbol of the dependence upon each other of art and science'.

By the late 1920s, Keynes had begun to argue that the government needed to develop policies which would address Britain's economic problems by encouraging investment in productive capacity. As we have seen with Schumpeter's work on business cycles, other economists had also developed theories which explained fluctuations in output and unemployment, largely through changes in the level of investment.

To develop the arguments in his *Treatise on Money*, published in 1930, Keynes imbibed the work of the Swedish economist Knut Wicksell, who had died in 1926. Wicksell had argued that investment depended on banks making loans to businesses, noting that when banks make loans, they are issuing new money. When the economy is growing, that new money will push the price level up. Seeing that output is selling for higher prices, firms will believe there are more opportunities to make profits, and plan to invest more. (A recession would then result from a low level of investment.) From such arguments, Keynes proposed that if the government instructed the Bank of England to lower interest rates, then firms would see that they could borrow cheaply enough to make profits, increasing investment, starting the expansion process which Wicksell had envisaged.

When *Treatise on Money* finally appeared in 1930, Keynes' arguments no longer seemed completely convincing, even to him. Before the May 1929 General Election, he had written the pamphlet, *Can Lloyd George Do It?* with Hubert Henderson. They argued for direct government spending to enable the economy's recovery, and so the pamphlet marked a new shift in Keynes' thinking, leading him to become increasingly critical of the position of successive governments, often called the 'Treasury View', that the route to economic recovery lay in a balanced budget, and 'sound money'.

The Wall Street Crash of late 1929, and the onset of the Great Depression, also affected Keynes' thinking. By 1932, amid a wave of bank failures, unemployment in the USA reached 25 per cent. Great Britain had again left the gold standard in 1931, and the value of sterling had fallen by 20 per cent. Around the world, governments were retreating behind tariff barriers to protect their domestic industries, often while threatening to default on their debts. And with the rise of Fascism, political disorder gripped Europe. Keynes concluded that this was more than the downswing of a business cycle, and that he needed a completely new way of thinking about the economy.

That came in *The General Theory of Employment, Interest and Money*, which sparked an intellectual revolution. Instead of concentrating on the behaviour of markets, Keynes divided the economy into functional sectors, such as households, industry and government. He argued that money would flow between those sectors as income and expenditure. Keynes realized that households would not spend all the income which they received but would instead deposit some of it with banks. In turn, banks would make money available to firms, who could borrow to fund investment expenditure, effectively buying goods from other firms to make more goods in future.

Keynes then asked what would happen if households decided to save more than firms want to invest. He concluded that their savings would pile up in banks. Fewer goods would be produced than before, and profits would fall, so firms would have to pay lower wages and dividends. The economy would shrink, and it would keep shrinking until household savings and business investment were equal. Here we have the first part of Keynes' explanation of the Great Depression. In almost every economy, the savings-investment channel had become blocked, leading to persistent unemployment because across the economy there was not enough demand for firms' output.

As a professional investor, Keynes knew that investors form beliefs about the future through intuition. Calling them 'animal spirits' he emphasized their fundamentally psychological nature. He also understood the importance of investors being able to predict what other investors would do, suggesting that they would tend to have a herd mentality. That allowed him to explain the blockage of the savings-investment channel as resulting from a loss of confidence across investors. In effect, he claimed that in the 1930s, the world had experienced a wave of pessimism, with beliefs justified by, but also causing, all that was happening.

In 1936, many reviewers, like Schumpeter, seemed unconvinced that this was any sort of 'general theory', reading the book much more as a 'tract for the times'. Keynes' ideas were not fully formed. His arguments were often confusing. There were places where he caricatured opposing ideas, so that he could demolish them more easily. Accept all that, and there was still an eloquent challenge to the 'Treasury View' that governments should patiently wait for the recovery to start.

We can also read *The General Theory* as a brilliant argument about the agency of governments in times of crisis. Even if shifting animal spirits depress demand in the rest of the economy, governments should be able to take a longer view. They can act in the interests of society by providing more public services, and spending more on goods and services produced in the private sector. Given the way in which spending and investment would ripple through the economy, Keynes argued that only a modest increase in government spending was required to spark a recovery.

While writing *The General Theory*, Keynes became seriously unwell. The ultimate cause went back 20 years, when, shortly after joining the Treasury during World War I, he had contracted peritonitis. With hospitals full of injured soldiers, his doctors had to operate on him on his kitchen table. Complications of the illness had affected his heart. In 1936, immediately after *The General Theory* came out in print, he was placed under strict medical supervision. With diet and exercise overseen by Lopokova, recovery took more than two years. By that time, the economic policy debate had moved on, and he turned his attention once more to the question of war finance. Even before rejoining the Treasury in 1940, he was campaigning, with the pamphlet *How to Pay for the War* arguing for a substantial increase in taxation, especially of wealth.

Once back in the Treasury, Keynes proposed other ways to finance the war, quickly developing a scheme by which British assets overseas might either be sold to raise funds, or else be pledged as security against loans issued in sterling. He also became a representative of the British government in a wide range of negotiations with the USA, covering international trade arrangements and the finance of post-war reconstruction. Created Lord Keynes, and taking a seat in the House of Lords in 1943, he was the lead negotiator for Britain in the formation of the IMF and the World Bank and, in 1945, of the 'American loan' which enabled Britain to embark on post-war reconstruction.

Given Keynes' stupendous energy and range of talents, there is much which we need to miss out. He was a fearless speculator, who often seemed to risk his wealth – but always came good eventually. From the mid-1920s, as Bursar, he had control of King's College's finance, and through shrewd investments, made it one of the wealthiest Cambridge colleges. He used his access to finance to promote the Cambridge Arts Theatre in the 1930s, overseeing its construction, and supporting Lopokova as she put together the new theatre's first season. He was appointed the chair of the Council for the Encouragement of Music and Arts in 1940, and subsequently the first chairman of the Arts Council of Great Britain.

Where Schumpeter had joked that he had formed the intention of becoming the world's greatest economist, Keynes outdid him. At least in part, that reflected differences in their way of working. While Schumpeter rarely had collaborators, Keynes was adept at finding younger academics with whom he could build fruitful working relationships. In the 1920s, the obvious examples would be Dennis Robertson on monetary theory, Frank Ramsey on probability theory, and Hubert Henderson on the development of an active government policy. By the 1930s, his associates became known as the Cambridge Circle. They included Piero Sraffa, Richard Kahn, and Joan and

Austin Robinson, and helped to shape, and promote, the ideas of *The General Theory*.

Keynes and Schumpeter were both much more than academics, and we have seen how some of Keynes' many other activities informed the development of his economics. Up until about 1923, he was entirely orthodox in his teaching. In middle age, as the European economies, and then the US economy became mired in the Great Depression, he concluded that we needed to change how we think about the economy. *The General Theory* appalled Schumpeter, perhaps for almost the same reasons that it delighted younger economists. Keynes classed the economics of Marshall, and Pigou, Marshall's successor in Cambridge and his own teacher, as 'classical'. With supreme self-confidence, he announced the book as the first account of a new form of economic analysis, which we now call macroeconomics. As Pigou noted, no one before Keynes had attempted to understand the behaviour of the entire economic system at an aggregate level.

Perhaps Keynes did this self-consciously. For much of the last 30 years of his life, he carefully kept almost every paper which passed over his desk, and his secretaries kept copies of all his correspondence. He seemed to be aware that he was living a great life. Becoming an economic revolutionary was just part of that. If that makes him sound like Marx, Keynes remained resolutely bourgeois and politically liberal. Living that great life, he lacked the time – and perhaps the inclination – to explain the ideas in *The General Theory* in detail. Dying while in government service, he could safely bequeath that challenge to his many followers.

11

Friedrich Hayek – A Very Different Type of Liberal

Treating the economy as an organism, not a machine.

In *Treatise on Money*, Keynes cheerfully admitted that he could scarcely read German. In contrast, Lionel Robbins, who graduated from the London School of Economics in 1923, and became a professor there only six years later, was fluent in the language. That meant that he understood that Keynes had simplified Wicksell's theories to make the case for active government policy. Moreover, he knew exactly to whom the LSE should turn to challenge Keynes: the Viennese economist, Friedrich Hayek.

Hayek had trained in the Austrian law and economics tradition. He was born into a family of academics (the philosopher Ludwig Wittgenstein was a distant relation), and many of his family, including his father and brothers, chose careers in the natural and life sciences. Indeed, Hayek had originally intended to study psychology, but war service in northern Italy, during which he contracted malaria, interrupted his studies. After World War I, he found few opportunities in Vienna for advanced study of psychology. Eventually, believing that this would offer him more secure career prospects, he turned to economics. In the latter part of his career, Hayek would return to his early interest in psychology, thinking about the structure of the economy in organic, or ecological terms.

Other economists quickly recognized his talent. He joined a seminar group, run by von Wieser, which brought together socialists such as Rudolf Hilferding and Otto Neurath, as well as the pugnacious liberal, Ludwig von Mises. At von Wieser's suggestion, Hayek began working for von Mises in the Austrian Institute for Business Cycle Research. He quickly abandoned his youthful, social democratic leanings, instead embracing the classical liberalism which would define his political economy. His commitment to the traditional explanation of economic fluctuations, based on the fluctuations in the availability of credit, first caught Robbins' attention.

In 1930, at the start of the Great Depression, Ramsay MacDonald, Britain's first Labour Prime Minister, had established an Economic Advisory Council. Inevitably Keynes, the consummate networker, was a member. He talked the Prime Minister into appointing him to chair a committee of academic economists, the others being Hubert Henderson, Arthur Pigou and Josiah Stamp. Wanting to include a representative of the LSE, Keynes invited Robbins to join them, which he did. But they fell out over Keynes' proposals for additional government spending. Robbins ended up writing his own report which was deeply critical of Keynes' recommendations for public works and tariff barriers. Hayek seemed to be a natural ally in this debate.

Hayek arrived in London in January 1931, and gave a series of lectures on credit cycles, which were published later in the year as *Prices and Production*. Hayek's biographer, Bruce Caldwell, has joked that the incomprehensibility of the lectures ensured the LSE's subsequent job offer. Immediately, Robbins, as editor of *Economica*, also gave Hayek the job of reviewing Keynes' *Treatise on Money.*

If Hayek's review was harsh, as Robbins wanted, Keynes' public response was savage. He went well beyond a defence of the *Treatise* and attacked *Prices and Production* as 'one of the most frightful muddles I have read, with scarcely a sound proposition in it'. Pigou compared Keynes' treatment of Hayek with 'bodyline bowling' – the very aggressive style which the English cricket team adopted in its 1932 tour of Australia to intimidate their hosts.

Both men acted uncharacteristically in this first encounter. Keynes' great charm and courtesy had failed him. Hayek's affability meant that he was almost the only person who could work with von Mises without their relationship souring after violent arguments. Their true selves soon reappeared, and they carried on the debate in private correspondence, although Keynes broke it off to start work on *The General Theory*. When Hayek returned to print with the second half of his review, Keynes delegated the task of replying to Kahn and Sraffa.

In 1936, Hayek stayed out of the debate over *The General Theory*, choosing instead to work on his book, *Pure Theory of Capital*. He expected that this work would explain economic fluctuations and show that Keynes' ideas were largely redundant. When it finally appeared, in 1941, even Hayek had to admit that it was incomplete and unsatisfactory. It had even less effect than Schumpeter's *Business Cycles.*

When the decision was made to evacuate the LSE's staff from London to Cambridge for the duration of the war, Keynes helped Hayek to find rooms in King's College. Then, when Hayek published his great political tract, *The Road to Serfdom* in 1944, Keynes wrote him a strongly appreciative letter. Though they continued to differ substantially about what it meant to be politically liberal, these philosophically inclined economists had become bound by deep mutual respect. Hayek would suggest much later that Keynes and Schumpeter would be his ideal dinner party guests. Most economists would be delighted simply to sit at the table and listen.

With the success of *The Road to Serfdom*, Hayek found himself suddenly propelled into the public gaze. In recommending the book's publication, Jacob Marschak, at the time the director of the Cowles Commission for Research in Economics at the University of Chicago, but who had also been a youthful socialist revolutionary in the Caucuses in 1918, had commended 'the clarity and the passion of a great doctrinaire', who 'warns his fellowmen with loving impatience'.

Where Keynes would have relished the opportunity to engage with the public, Hayek was a rather more conventional academic. He had misgivings about his public profile, and about the risk that the simplification of his ideas would lead to them being appropriated by one side in political debate. That certainly happened after *Readers' Digest* produced a condensed version in 1945. Hayek's forceful arguments against socialism and, more generally, against planning, found a large audience among Americans who were unconvinced by Roosevelt's New Deal.

They lapped up Hayek's argument that economic planning would sooner or later become centralized, so that the economy would descend into socialism. Hayek feared that planners would decide how much of each good should be produced, and where it should be sold. Economic planners would become an intrusive replacement of the invisible hand. Their activities would strip entrepreneurs of any reason to hustle for profits. The economy would become dull and stagnant.

At this imaginary dinner party with Keynes and Schumpeter, Hayek might well have talked with Schumpeter about socialist democracy. In thinking about planning, he would have had a long discussion with Keynes. Through the

Beveridge Report on social insurance, and some of Keynes' subsequent work in the Treasury towards the end of World War II, Britain had committed itself to a form of the economic planning which Hayek feared. He was less concerned about the sudden socialization of the economy after a revolution, than the risk that a sequence of proposals for economic reform might gradually transform the population, so that they would tolerate the loss of their liberty, acquiescing in the rise of a totalitarian government. The suggestion that planning inevitably led to socialism troubled Keynes. Knowing that Hayek agreed that there should be public intervention in the economy, where that did not affect individual liberty, Keynes asked him how 'to draw the line' between beneficial and harmful policies.

It was an important question and much of Hayek's later career was spent answering it. The first step came during the US book tour to promote *Road to Serfdom*. This had originally been planned to involve presentations to academics. Instead, it started with a public address to 3,000 people in New York. During the tour, Hayek met the businessman Harold Luhnow, who controlled his family firm's charitable trust, the Volker Fund. Luhnow then sponsored the initial meeting of a group of 'classical liberal' economists – libertarians to their supporters, neo-liberals to their detractors – at Vévey in Switzerland in 1947. The group took the name of a local feature – Mont Pèlerin – for the society which they founded. As well as Hayek, there were three future winners of the Nobel Memorial Prize in Economics at this meeting – Milton Friedman, George Stigler and Maurice Allais.

The Mont Pèlerin Society's immediate practical achievement was in providing economic arguments for the stabilization of West Germany as a market economy in the early 1950s. It also spawned a network of think-tanks, which together incubated liberal policy ideas until the opportunity came to apply them in the 1970s, when the tools of Keynesian demand management suddenly seemed ineffective during a long period of slow growth and high inflation.

From the 1950s, Hayek's work branched into two parts. In *The Constitution of Liberty*, and subsequently in *Law, Legislation and Liberty*, Hayek set out a detailed account of how a liberal order might emerge and be sustained. The apotheosis of Hayek's career was surely Margaret Thatcher's production of her copy of *The Constitution of Liberty* from her handbag, shortly after she had become the leader of Britain's Conservative Party, announcing, 'This is what we believe', and making it central to her rapidly developing political ideology. Hayek had finally displaced Keynes as the policy adviser of choice.

But before that, Hayek went back to his first love, theoretical psychology, producing *The Sensory Order* in 1952. This was Hayek's considered response to the logical positivism which had developed among the philosophers of the Vienna Circle in the 1920s. That made it a very unusual project for a professional economist. We have seen philosophers thinking deeply about the economy. Here was an economist thinking deeply about philosophy and psychology. To give his political economy what he considered to be an adequate grounding, he explored how we can impose order on all our sensations. That required him to explore the nature of perception and intelligence, and how we can communicate our sensations through language. He argued that there is a physical reality, which is external to all of us, of which the physical sciences enable systematic exploration. Social interactions, on the other hand, are necessarily subjective and will change with our behaviour.

In Hayek's account, our ideas are the building blocks of social structures and institutions. He treated people as autonomous individuals, looking back to Scottish Enlightenment scholars, especially David Hume and Adam Ferguson, and of course

Adam Smith. Their understanding that human action (a preferred term of von Mises) could easily lead to the emergence of social institutions without any process of conscious design became the foundation of his political economy. He went well beyond Smith's argument that there seemed to be an invisible hand ensuring orderly markets, effectively proposing that the invisible hand would first establish markets, or other appropriate ways of managing resources.

To Hayek, such arrangements would be evolutionarily fit. Experimentation and innovation would lead to more effective institutions. The costs of completing transactions would then fall, as well as the costs of production. As examples, think of money replacing barter, or the current digitalization of money. Those innovations have reduced the costs of making payments. In this analysis, a market economy was a very useful way of transmitting information relevant to the management of material resources.

These arguments allowed Hayek to argue that economic planning, with a central authority, was bound to be ineffective. He argued that the information which flows in the economy does not exist separately from people's engagement with markets. That ensures that there is important information in the economy which planners cannot observe. As a self-organizing social order, Hayek's economy was dependent on personal knowledge, distributed among us, and only communicated through our actions. Going back to the dinner party with Keynes and Schumpeter, Hayek would have argued that the impossibility of sufficient knowledge would defeat Keynes' proposals for active government policy. He would also have argued that Schumpeterian creative destruction, with its sudden shifts in economic value, demonstrated how knowledge could flow through an economy.

Given that free exchange was better for society than planning, in *The Constitution of Liberty*, Hayek, who was also an admirer of Mill, started by treating liberty as freedom from coercion by others. He proposed that a liberal government would retain for itself a monopoly of legitimate coercive power, but that it would be scrupulous in restricting use of that power to prevent individuals and organizations from coercing others, ensuring that individuals were, as far as possible, autonomous, with their property rights secure. Liberal governments would exercise coercive powers according to the 'rule of law', applying them impersonally. They would also accept that the law bound their actions, rather than seeking to be above the law.

Since no one can be economically self-sufficient, Hayek's conception of economic liberty was grounded in law. We must all cooperate with other people and organizations, sharing, or exchanging, knowledge and resources. As the set of institutions which permitted resolution of disputes between people and organizations, law was essential, and would also be permissive in a liberal society. In these arguments, Hayek came close to reviving the 'harm principle', with an argument that unless actions cause economic loss to other people, they should be permitted.

As social institutions with their own rules of behaviour, markets and laws allow people to form expectations about how other people will behave. For example, we generally expect that the sellers of goods will be honest in describing their (non-observable) qualities. More generally, how we expect buyers and sellers to behave will depend upon the context. We expect a visit to a supermarket to be a very different experience from buying a used car.

We might then think that a system of markets should have the Walrasian objective of realizing a set of prices. People and organizations will change their behaviour as relative prices change. That will lead to a new set of relative prices, and these changing prices will send messages to market participants which direct further changes. In this evolutionary approach, prices have fitness as the most effective means of disseminating information about the state of the economy as it has so far developed. They enable market participants to abstract from a huge volume of information about how the economy functions and make decisions about how they will adapt their demands for goods.

In making such arguments, Hayek depicted markets as a convenient way for organizing the management of resources. By emphasizing the importance of information flows, and the evolutionary fitness of social institutions, Hayek was pressing against the limits of neo-classical economics. He shared Schumpeter's understanding of the economy as always evolving in response to our innate desire to create new combinations of goods and find new ways of meeting needs.

By the end of his career, Hayek had become critical of the methods of analysis which younger economists had developed. Take the example of general equilibrium theory, which involves complex systems with hundreds of equations, all of which had to be solved at the same time. For Hayek, such structures had very little to do with the functioning of the economy. They were interesting intellectual exercises, whose solutions were largely determined by the assumptions of the model. There was therefore a risk of economics lapsing into what Hayek called 'constructivist' rationality, which made the error of assuming that economic institutions could be designed, rather than emerging through trial and error over time. He argued instead that institutions simply needed to be ecologically rational, so that they met the fitness criteria of being efficient among existing alternatives.

He believed such constructivist rationality had been an important part of European philosophy, and jurisprudence, ever since the work of René Descartes in the seventeenth century. In the efforts to change the distribution of incomes which emerged from free exchange, he saw an example of how a constructively rational approach would lead to the conscious design of institutions to achieve social justice. For Hayek, we could either pursue social justice, or liberty, but not both. Believing liberty to be essential for continued social and economic development therefore meant that he could only accept a very limited role for social programmes in the economy.

Think of the economic system as being like a massive multi-player game. The designers of these games, effectively the government, impose an essential structure – for example, through legislation – but leave it to players to decide how to engage with one another according to their individual objectives, beliefs about the game's structure, and their understanding of how other players will respond to their actions within this environment. In such games, virtual communities emerge. Through patterns of play, these communities develop their own institutions within the underlying structure of the game. As players encounter situations, and they work out their own ways of responding to them, the institutions which they create will generally meet Hayek's standard of ecological rationality. In such an approach, government should not impose order.

When Keynes wrote to Hayek praising *Road to Serfdom*, he had been at the meetings in the USA which agreed to establish the World Bank and the International Monetary Fund. Determined that there should be no repeat of the persistent crises of the inter-war periods, Keynes had argued throughout World War II that it was essential to establish formal institutions which would support the management of national currencies, and the international payments required for trade, while also enabling countries to raise the funding needed for their development.

Keynes was an expert, who trusted the judgement of experts. Asking Hayek where 'to draw the line', he knew that Hayek was not opposed to the possibility of government action in areas which did not involve coercion, such as the legal system and national defence. For Keynes, governments had the ability to undertake investment expenditure to encourage the return of widespread confidence and ensure the return of full employment. Hayek disagreed, arguing that experts could never have the information needed to achieve even that goal, still less to oversee an extensive redistribution of income. In that debate, we see how these two great liberal economists disagreed fundamentally on the nature of liberty. For Keynes, it was a matter of having the resources to enjoy an Aristotelian 'good life', but for Hayek, the good life came from having the freedom to make choices.

12

John von Neumann – The Most Brilliant Mathematician

Defining games to explain economic interactions

As Austria-Hungary fell apart in the early twentieth century, Budapest, like Vienna, had a rich academic culture. A generation of brilliant scientists grew up in Hungary, but almost all of them left the country during the political instability of the 1920s. Often, like the mathematician John von Neumann – perhaps the most brilliant of them all – they eventually became American citizens and played prominent roles in World War II.

Why include von Neumann in a book about thinking like an economist? Among his many achievements, he founded game theory, a branch of mathematics, which he first used to analyse games like poker, in which the interactions between the players are important for the outcome. It is a short leap to start to use game theory to analyse competitive behaviour in an industry which has only a few firms, or in working out the conditions under which there will be cooperation rather than conflict among small groups.

When we go to a doctor or we take a car to a garage, we want to be confident that we can trust the expert whom we are consulting. The mechanic can recommend repairs, knowing that most people will not be able to tell whether they are necessary, or good value, or even if they have been completed properly. Game theory has helped economists to understand why we might trust some experts to act in our best interests, but not others. It has also given them a way of thinking about how economic relationships can be sustained.

Von Neumann, a notably careless driver, who wrote off cars in accidents roughly once per year, never explored the mechanic problem. He simply made it possible for economists to do so. He first developed principles of game theory in 1928. Then, between 1941 and 1944, he wrote *Theory of Games and Economic Behaviour* with the German economist, Oskar Morgenstern. Less than a decade after Keynes had claimed that his *General Theory* was the foundation of a new type of economics, von Neumann and Morgenstern made an even larger claim for their book – that game theory provided the fundamental theory of economics. Perhaps Keynes would have seen the value of game theory. He had argued that a depression was the result of widespread, self-justifying beliefs about the state of the economy. Such consistency of belief and action turns out to be necessary for there to be an equilibrium in a game where the players do not have complete information.

The claim to have established the foundations of economics was bold and speculative. The examples which Von Neumann and Morgenstern used were generally recognizable as games, and not situations like the car repair problem, which involve resource management. But to complete this initial, abstract analysis, they made important contributions to economic theory. In many interesting games, such as poker, players make decisions when they are not certain about the true state of the world. Analysing such games meant that von Neumann and Morgenstern developed the standard approach in economic theory for incorporating uncertainty into decision making.

Coming to economics from outside, von Neumann was well placed to confront economists' hesitancy about using mathematics. Among the economists we have met so far, only Walras, who had emerged from the French tradition of engineers exploring economics, made much use of mathematics in his work on general equilibrium models. Almost incidentally, von Neumann also contributed substantially to this field. In the 1930s, he developed an approach to solving some types of general equilibrium model. In the 1950s, Kenneth Arrow and Gérard Debreu built on those foundations to demonstrate conditions under which such models could be solved. Both won the Nobel Memorial Prize in Economics for their work.

While von Neumann was doubtful that in the 1930s economics had reached the point where his style of mathematics would turn out to be useful, game theory offered an entirely new way of thinking about problems which economics could not previously address. For example, had Marshall been able to use game theory to understand more about the factors which affect the structure of industries, and the implications for business behaviour of having only a few competitors, he might even have found a way of completing the second volume of *Principles of Economics* to his own satisfaction.

Born into an upper middle-class, Jewish family of bankers and merchants in 1903, von Neumann was, by all accounts, a genius. Three generations of his family lived in a set of apartments in the upper floors of a large building, which his grandfather, Jakab Kann, owned. The ground floor housed the offices of Kann's agricultural machinery business. Kann gave his daughter, Margaret, the top floor of the building when she married Max Neumann, a successful banker. Then, when his other daughter, Vilma, married, she moved into the third-floor apartment. Von Neumann, the oldest of Kann's grandchildren, grew up in this extended family.

His family would later tell stories about 'Jansci', known by the diminutive when very young, entertaining adults by memorizing a page of the Budapest telephone directory as quickly as he could read it. That exceptional memory stayed with him throughout his life – he seemed able to recall almost anything which he had read, including literature and poetry, and had an exceptionally deep interest in history. There is also the story of him asking his mother, as she paused for a moment, 'What are you calculating?' His natural talents extended to complex arithmetical calculations.

Enrolling his son in the Lutheran *Gymnasium* at the age of 10, Max Neumann made the decision that the boy would complete his education along with his peers, but that he would provide him with access to private tutoring in mathematics. The result, noted by his friend Eugene Wigner, a year ahead of von Neumann at school, was an almost constant outpouring of ideas about pure mathematics, especially set theory and number theory. That was enough to persuade Wigner, who won the Nobel Prize for Physics, that he himself would never succeed as a mathematician.

Note that von Neumann decided to add the German 'von' to his name after leaving Hungary. In 1913, Max Neumann had bought a noble title. For every upwardly mobile Jewish family in Central Europe, there was always the possibility that violent anti-Semitism would sweep away their comfortable position. With the purchase of a title, the Neumanns may have cemented their position in Hungarian society, but they did so just as the imperial order was about to collapse. After World War I, newly independent Hungary experienced a liberal government, and then a socialist experiment. Both failed quickly, giving way to the repressive, proto-fascist Horthy regime. Max Neumann had moved his family to Austria during the socialist period, but brought them back when his role as a banker appeared secure. That von Neumann reached adulthood during a time of political uncertainty and violence may explain some of his later career. Working with military and government officials both as a scientist and a strategic adviser, he opposed socialism in general and had a visceral dislike of the Soviet Union.

By 1921 von Neumann had graduated from high school. He appears to have come to an agreement with his father that he could become a mathematician – a privately wealthy academic, who could live the life of a gentleman. Enrolling as a graduate student in Budapest, he spent most of his time at the University of Berlin, but he also worked with David Hilbert in Göttingen. (Hilbert, probably the leading mathematician of the 1900s reputedly asked the only question at von Neumann's defence of his doctoral dissertation, 'Who is the candidate's tailor?') By 1926, he had obtained a degree in chemical engineering from Zurich, a doctorate in mathematics from Budapest, was a licensed teacher of mathematics in Berlin and was attached to Hilbert's group in Göttingen. The academic world was spread out in front of him.

And so, to the theory of games. As a title, *A Theory of Parlour Games* is deceptively bland. In this paper from 1928, von Neumann analysed the problem of how to play zero-sum games, of which a very simple example is 'Rock, Paper, Scissors'. The two players in the game must choose one of these outcomes at the same time. If they choose the same action, then neither player wins. But Rock beats Scissors, Scissors beats Paper, and Paper beats Rock. Say that in any of these outcomes, the winner takes a payment from the loser, so that the gain from winning is equal to the cost of losing: a zero-sum game. If we are playing, then if you win, I must lose.

It may seem obvious that the optimal strategy in this game is to choose an action randomly. As a mathematician, von Neumann decided to prove this result. He first needed to derive some important results in pure mathematics, which have been used in many other situations other than in his analysis of zero-sum games. With that groundwork in place, he developed the minimax principle as a general form of the best possible strategy, or decision rule, which a player could adopt.

Von Neumann proposed that players should always maximize the minimum payoff which they received – hence minimax. If we are playing Rock, Paper, Scissors, and you are confident that you can predict the action which I will choose, then it is rational for you to choose the action which will minimize my payoff (because that maximizes your payoff). But I will know that, so I will plan to choose a strategy which maximizes the minimum. And you will do the same.

In some types of the games which von Neumann analysed, this is all that is necessary. Our decision rules would be consistent and our actions would maximize our minimum payoffs. One player might inevitably be the loser but will play the game to suffer the smallest possible loss.

However, given the structure of Rock, Paper, Scissors, applying the minimax principle is a little more complicated. Since every action is associated with the same minimum loss (or maximum gain), von Neumann proposed that players should randomly choose an action every time they play. If you do this, then it will not matter what strategy I choose – my expected payoff from the game will be zero, and so your expected payoff will be zero. I cannot exploit any tendency which you might have to favour one or other of the actions. Of course, for this to be an equilibrium, I must also randomize – otherwise it will be possible for you to exploit the pattern in my play. By choosing our actions randomly, von Neumann's minimax principle is satisfied. We both choose a strategy which gives us the largest possible value of the minimum expected payoff.

His work in the 1920s ensured his international reputation and that led to the possibility of a move to the USA. Princeton was developing its Institute of Advanced Studies and was seeking to recruit the very best European scientists and mathematicians. Where Schumpeter had dithered about moving to the USA, von Neumann was younger and lacked Schumpeter's emotional baggage. Aged 27, he leapt at the chance, pausing only to marry. At Princeton, with his expensive suits, his servants, his beautiful manners, his strongly accented English, and his love of parties, he continued to make substantial advances across mathematics, while being an obviously European transplant. His seminar notes from the 1930s were distributed widely across the USA, since they brought together recent advances from Europe with which the American mathematical community was not yet entirely familiar.

Throughout the 1930s, von Neumann also worked to bring colleagues, and his own family, to the safety of the USA. Convinced of the need to defeat Nazism, he joined the team of scientists at Los Alamos, which developed the atomic bomb. This turned out to be a very congenial experience. As a mathematician with a doctorate in engineering, he developed a roving role as a problem solver, shuttling between the scientific and engineering teams. It turned out that he was a happy warrior. He soon earned the trust of General Leslie Groves, who led the military administration of the Manhattan Project. Groves valued the advice of this politically conservative academic, who thought deeply about strategy and intuitively understood the objectives of the US military. For von Neumann, there was never any question about the value of atomic weapons. His strong dislike of the USSR, stoked by its treatment of Hungary, meant that even before the end of World War II he was already imagining it as the next enemy whom the USA would have to confront.

Set aside his famed charm, and von Neumann was in many ways the coolly rational player assumed in his game theory. With US forces advancing, and on the point of finally defeating

Japan, the USSR was considering whether to enter the conflict. The Americans did not want there to be any opportunity for the USSR to extend its influence in East Asia. Those circumstances led von Neumann to argue that using atomic bombs against civilian targets and compelling the surrender of Japan solely to the USA, was entirely consistent with the achievement of American strategic interests.

His strategic advice reflected his concentration on zero-sum games, in which winning came at other players' expense. It became an important part of his thinking about international relations. He argued that the USA should develop the hydrogen bomb quickly and that it should adopt a strategy of 'preventive' war – planning to use its superior nuclear arsenal and air force to defeat the USSR before it had the capacity to strike against the USA. This element of von Neumann's career is supposed to have fed into the character of Dr Strangelove in Stanley Kubrick's dark comedy about the arms race – it may, for example, just be coincidence that like Strangelove, von Neumann ended up wheelchair bound. His health deteriorated after 1955 and he died, slowly and excruciatingly painfully, from bone cancer caused by exposure to radiation.

While von Neumann was in New Mexico working on the Manhattan Project in the autumn of 1944, Keynes was in New Hampshire at the Bretton Woods Conference, leading the UK delegation in the negotiations to establish the World Bank and the International Monetary Fund. Their careers represent two very different sides of public service. In 1944, Keynes had 30 years' experience in solving problems of international finance, and throughout that time he had worked to increase cooperation between governments, believing that through negotiation and compromise, everyone could be better off. With its emphasis on zero-sum games, von Neumann's game theory had the opposite tendency of naturally emphasizing the competitive elements of economic interactions. Perhaps because of his genius, he often seemed to think that his elegantly logical solution of a problem was the only possible outcome. The mundane stupidity in political processes confused him.

Important as von Neumann's insights were, it would take another mathematical genius, John Nash, to develop his work, and to lay a more general foundation for game theory which could embrace both Keynesian cooperation and von Neumann's competitive framework. In a series of papers written in the late 1940s, Nash developed more general rules for playing games than the minimax principle. He argued that players should choose strategies which mean that the outcome is as good as it can be, given the strategies which other players follow.

As we have seen, in Rock, Paper, Scissors, if I am committed to choosing randomly, it does not matter how you play the game, because you will conclude that what you do will not affect your expected payoff. So, choosing randomly is as good as any other way of playing the game. Then, if we both choose randomly, neither of us would benefit from changing the way that we play. Nash's equilibrium occurs when no single player can change the way they play and expect to be better off as a result. This Nash equilibrium concept, rather than von Neumann's minimax principle, is now considered fundamental. It was perhaps typical of von Neumann's career that he should have established much of the framework for the analysis of games, but that he should now be largely overlooked in favour of someone who only needed to adapt the analysis slightly to generalize the solution substantially.

In this mathematical approach to playing games, players make decisions without communicating with each other. The Prisoner's Dilemma, which is used in almost every social science, is the best-known example of these mathematical games. First described in 1950 by colleagues of von Neumann at the RAND Corporation, a psychologist, Albert Tucker, gave it the name by which it is known. The structure of the game

HOW TO THINK LIKE AN ECONOMIST

is simple. Players must decide whether to collaborate or act selfishly. Together, they are better off collaborating than acting selfishly, but for each player individually, acting selfishly leads to a higher payoff than collaborating. We have a problem which Adam Smith would have relished. The Nash equilibrium is to follow the narrow definition of self-interest, but that makes everyone worse off than if they had collaborated.

Problems with a structure like the Prisoner's Dilemma appear quite often in economics. In the problem of whether it is possible to trust a car mechanic, we know that an unscrupulous mechanic can make immediate profits from offering poor service. However, a trustworthy mechanic will have a good reputation, which will generate repeat business and attract new customers. Taking that long-run view, collaborating with others can easily be justified as self-interested behaviour. Smith would have been unsurprised. The behaviour of the unscrupulous mechanic is neither just, nor temperate. In a society in which such behaviour was common, people would not trust each other and there would be little cooperation. Games such as the Prisoner's Dilemma give us new ways of exploring some of the traditional ethical problems which have long been building blocks for economics.

Further refinements and extensions of the ideas of von Neumann and Nash have extended the reach of economics into areas about which Marshallian economics could say nothing. Mathematicians have given economists new methods of analysis, rather as Ricardo and Walras had done in the nineteenth century, but it took many years for economists to digest their work and make games useful in economics.

13

Ronald Coase – The Placid Observer

*Why orders and negotiation are needed for effective
resource management*

Ronald Coase saw the world as an economist should. As an
undergraduate student at the London School of Economics
in the early 1930s, he travelled around the USA, carefully
observing the behaviour of large businesses and developing a
new explanation of the structure of industry. While Hayek was
arguing with Keynes and trying to perfect capital theory, Coase
had anticipated some of Hayek's later work, and explained why
there are always limits to markets.

He then worked away at his ideas for many years. In middle
age, he analysed the techniques for resolving the disputes
which occur when people are trying to manage their resources.
Almost immediately, George Stigler, who was Coase's colleague
at the University of Chicago, but also a teller of tall tales about
economics, claimed to have found a 'Coase Theorem'. The only
problem was that the theorem was entirely Stigler's invention.
With the term appearing in many textbooks, Stigler's legend has
become fact. Whenever he was asked to explain the theorem,
Coase simply denied all responsibility for it.

In Coase's career, we can see how economics bade farewell
to the long nineteenth century, which began in Paris with the

French Revolution and ended there with the Treaty of Versailles. With Europe exhausted after World War I, an American Century began in the 1920s, although the gradual emergence of the USA as an economic superpower had attracted European economists for many years. Marshall visited it in 1875, and his observations led him to think about the structure of industry in new ways. Schumpeter, always fascinated by the energy of the country, was a regular visitor throughout the 1920s, well before he finally accepted a post at Harvard. Von Neumann arrived when he was still very young. Hayek was also a visitor in the 1920s. He then achieved great fame with *The Road to Serfdom* and worked in Chicago during the 1950s.

Coase continued that trend. Born in London in 1910, he left Britain for the USA in 1950, and spent the last 50 years of his life at the University of Chicago, where he was still working when he died. Since he was 11 years younger than Hayek, he was still a boy during World War I. He grew up during the long economic crisis of the 1920s, which culminated in the Great Depression, while he was a student.

Compared with most of the economists in this book, his family's circumstances were very modest. His father worked in the Post Office as a telegraph clerk. As a child, Coase did not enjoy especially good health and had to have braces fitted to his legs for several years. Lacking ambitious parents to nurture his career, and sent to special schools, it would have been entirely natural if he had not even gone to university. Coase described the process by which he ended up as a student of business law at the LSE as being almost accidental. There, he met Arnold Plant, who ran a final year course on business administration, which discussed how Adam Smith's invisible hand could explain the self-organizing nature of the economy. This inspired Coase, who began to explore linkages between his formal studies which were focused on commercial law, and economics.

He was by no means the first to consider the importance of law when thinking about the economy. The medieval Scholastics had argued that secure property rights were needed for economic justice. Smith treated law, ethics and political economy as the branches of his science of man. The Austrian economic tradition had emerged from within the Faculty of Law in Vienna. Where earlier economics had drawn on general philosophical principles of jurisprudence, Coase's expertise was in business law, and that made it natural for him to think about organization of industry.

With strong support from Plant, Coase applied for the Cassel travelling scholarship which allowed him to travel to the USA in 1931–32. By observing the decisions which American businesses made, Coase concluded that when businesses plan to produce a complex product, they have the choice between making each of the components which go into the final product, or else buying them from other, specialist component producers.

Drawing on an example to which Coase returned repeatedly, he observed that in the USA, automobile manufacturers had mostly integrated the construction of their vehicles within their operations. In the 1920s, with the development of closed body shells, vehicle manufacturers had bought up specialist producers of body shells. Those decisions suggested that manufacturers believed that with complete control, they could design and manufacture the shells to the specification which met their needs at the lowest possible cost. In contrast, they never purchased tyre manufacturers. Buying body shells might be less efficient than making them, but tyres could easily be purchased, since competing brands were largely substitutes and competition kept prices low.

Coase realized that these decisions involved businesses planning how to use their resources. His great insight was to understand that businesses and markets represent two different ways of managing resources. In businesses, entrepreneurs and managers can give instructions, whereas in markets, the price system determines the flow of resources. Economists already knew all of that. Coase simply needed to bring these ideas together and present them in a new way.

With two possible ways of procuring any component needed to produce output, managers would be acting rationally by choosing the more efficient one. They would not need to choose it consciously, but over time, the more efficient arrangement would become dominant through the long-run effects of competition on profits. Coase therefore argued that the boundary of each business should be set so that it would produce components whenever that was more efficient, going to the market to source components whenever that was more efficient. By assuming that the management of resources would become ever more difficult in larger and more complex organizations, Coase quickly concluded that we should never expect to see the sort of mega-corporation familiar from dystopic science fiction taking over the economy and purporting to meet every human need.

Coase returned to the UK and began his academic career, writing up the conclusions he had drawn from his visit to the USA in a short paper on *The Nature of the Firm*, which appeared in print in 1937. More than 50 years later, Coase won the Nobel Memorial Prize. The citation referred to this elegant, but conceptually simple paper, which was little more than an undergraduate dissertation, as the starting point for a new way of thinking about industrial economics.

These ideas complemented Hayek's later claims about the inadequacy of central planning and Schumpeter's thinking about innovation. A central planner might anticipate all needs and act entirely rationally but would still not match the allocative efficiency of markets. With innovation causing changes in production processes, we should expect the structure of industry to change over time. That would change the range of decisions made in firms and in markets. Planners would need to be able to anticipate those evolutionary processes.

It was typical of Coase's style of argument that *The Nature of the Firm* should seem disarmingly simple, with its importance only becoming clear much later. All that he had needed to do was to observe the decisions which businesses made and find a new way of explaining them. Earlier economists had overlooked the structure which Coase saw because their attention was elsewhere.

For example, Marshall had largely ignored the costs of managing production in *Principles of Economics*. That meant treating them as being of no great importance. Of course, such simplifications had made it easier to develop useful theories but limited their ability to explain the changing structure of the economy. Coase's initial argument could easily be adapted to take account of the existing structure of the economy and also the costs of changing that structure, even where such changes will be ultimately beneficial.

His achievement with *The Nature of the Firm* was precocious, but Coase did not have Schumpeter's driving ambition, or Keynes' sense that he would live a great life. His career developed slowly. With economics in turmoil during the Great Depression, the 1930s saw impassioned debates about how to spark a sustained economic recovery, and Coase's ideas about how order might emerge spontaneously in industry seemed peripheral. So he continued to work at the London School of Economics until 1950, when he moved first to the University of Buffalo, and then to the University of Virginia.

At the University of Virginia, he was associated with the group which has come to be known as the Virginia School. James Buchanan and Gordon Tullock were its most prominent members, and their work on public choice theory won Buchanan the Nobel Memorial Prize in Economics in 1986. With many affinities between Coase's thinking about the structure of production and Buchanan's analysis of government as a provider of services, Virginia turned out to be a very congenial home for Coase, and it was there that he completed the work which would seal his reputation as one of the great thinkers of economics.

Where Coase worked at the level of the firm and the industry, Buchanan and Tullock treated government as just another economic agent – although one which inevitably had substantial, ultimately coercive, powers. That made government like a very large corporation, which had the capacity to insist, through taxation, that individuals and organizations made payments to it without directly purchasing goods and services. In some ways, such a theory was a conservative response to Keynesian economics. It could not have emerged before the expansion of the role of government after the Great Depression and World War II. Thinking of government as being like a corporation led Buchanan and Tullock to focus on understanding the sources of government legitimacy, and how to ensure that it would remain responsive to the needs of its citizens.

Earlier economists, such as Pigou, had assumed that government was essentially disinterested, and so would seek the well-being of society. For Buchanan and Tullock, that assumed away the problem of political legitimacy. Like Mill and the nineteenth-century Philosophical Radicals, they emphasized the importance of consent as the basis of citizens accepting the rules which emerged from political decision making. They argued that the social contract implied by those rules should be embedded within a legal constitution. Sharing Hayek's conviction about the importance of individual liberty, Buchanan and Tullock sought first to understand the implications for society of different types of constitutional rules, and then to provide advice about how adapting constitutional rules might support a social order serving the purposes of individuals.

This was the context for Coase's work on how government involvement with broadcasting had affected the structure of the industry. In his 1959 paper *The Federal Communications Commission*, he proposed that the right to use a frequency on the radio spectrum for broadcasts was a well-defined property right. He argued that with the FCC's practice of allocating such rights, competition could only work in the American radio industry through the merger and takeover of businesses, often for much greater prices than the cost of their assets, reflecting the value of the right to broadcast. Coase argued that it should instead be possible to create a market for radio spectrum rights – another idea which has now become commonplace.

In the 1920s, as the radio industry had emerged, the most effective argument against the creation of a market for rights was the possibility that radio signals would interfere with one another. Think of how a pirate radio station can transmit (locally), with its signal swamping the signal of the rights holder wherever it is the stronger one. Coase drew on his knowledge of case law to show that long before the invention of radio, there was a well-established legal principle that the resolution of such conflicts should do the least possible harm to everyone affected by the decision. Coase then remarked that private negotiation over the use of contested assets would be an alternative to court rulings.

To a group of economists at Chicago University, this seemed to be flat-out wrong. They accepted Pigou's argument that it was best to impose taxes on polluters. To explore the matter further, Aaron Director, who was in the process of setting up the *Journal of Law and Economics*, hosted a dinner for Coase – with 20 sceptical Chicago economists in attendance. It was almost inevitable that George Stigler, the Chicago folklorist, should have been there to ensure that the evening's events would be recorded for posterity. According to Stigler, the evening began and ended with indicative votes on the question 'Pigou or

Coase?' with everyone voting for Pigou at the start, and Coase at the end.

That dinner was certainly important for Coase. First, Director invited him to write a follow-up article for the *Journal of Law and Economics*, which appeared in 1960, as *The Problem of Social Cost*. He then moved to the Law School of the University of Chicago in 1964, and in 1965, on Director's retirement, he took over as editor of the *Journal of Law and Economics*. Already in his mid-50s, he spent the second half of his career there, working until shortly before his death, aged 102, in 2013. As the long-term editor of the *Journal of Law and Economics*, he was able to shape the nature of the research which spanned both disciplines.

In *The Problem of Social Cost*, there is an important example of an arable farmer, across whose land there was a right of way on which other farmers moved cattle, which would customarily graze on the crops on either side of the path. The obvious solution might seem to be to allow the arable farmer to put up fencing, but Coase pointed out that this would cause harm to the cattle farmers, whose cattle could no longer forage. Instead, he argued that there are two obvious initial assignments of property rights. In the article, Coase's example is set out to suggest that the cattle farmers have a right to allow their animals to graze. Another version of the story could start with the arable farmer putting up a fence in anticipation of cattle being moved along the right of way for the first time. Then there would not be any established grazing right, and the cattle farmers might agree to pay the arable farmer to remove the fence.

Coase used the example to argue that we should agree to use assets so that they create as much social value as possible. In the example, the land would remain unfenced if the value to the cattle farmer of the grazing right was greater than the loss from crop damage for the arable farmer.

For many years, *The Problem of Social Cost* was one of the most cited papers in economics, partly because its ideas have also been exhaustively debated by legal theorists. That is partly because of Stigler's fanciful interpretation of what Coase had meant to say with his assertion of the 'Coase Theorem'. According to Stigler, Coase had argued that in a perfectly competitive market, where there are no costs of making contracts, the outcome will be independent of the original assignment of property rights. That was much more precise, and much more limited than what Coase had claimed. He had only argued that in situations where there were disputes over how to use resources, it would be possible for people to agree upon a settlement without it being imposed by public authorities.

Coase's ideas led to a new approach to government intervention in markets. Instead of direct regulation, for example, by setting quotas, or minimum prices, or indirect interventions in the market – such as using taxes or setting production standards – a government which takes a property rights approach might set up an auction of (property) rights, and then allow private negotiation over their use. We have seen this approach being used for many years in radio spectrum auctions, as well as auctions for the rights to exploit mineral rights. In the ongoing problems of climate change negotiations, in which questions of compensation for loss or damage are becoming more prominent, there is a Coasean argument that by exploiting an implicitly accepted right to pollute, the richer countries have imposed costs on developing countries without their consent.

Coase's ideas lie behind 'cap and trade' schemes, in which the government sets a ceiling on carbon emissions and auctions time-limited licences to produce them (gradually reducing rights over time). Designing effective schemes has turned out to be technically challenging, but over time, such schemes have become an increasingly effective method of managing the environmental costs of economic activity.

Chicago was especially attractive to Coase because it provided a congenial base for editing the *Journal of Law and*

Economics. That allowed him to establish a critical tradition of the analysis of legal institutions. His observations about the existence of transaction costs as justifying the existence of separate firms led to Oliver Williamson's work, which distinguished between the nature of information flows in markets, and in the hierarchies of institutions. Building on his later observations about social costs (and benefits) in the presence of uncertainty, Oliver Hart argued that organizations would be defined by their competencies. Essential skills and knowledge for the creation of goods and services would cohere in organizations and obtain a share of profits rather than a fixed wage. Think of film stars, who are typically paid a share of revenues as well as a substantial upfront fee. In Hart's analysis, businesses cohere around assets which are valuable within such production processes, and which would have little outside value. That takes us back to car producers making their own body shells but buying tyres from other businesses. That both Williamson and Hart won the Nobel Memorial Prize clearly demonstrates the importance of Coase's ideas for the development of economics. Paul Milgrom's Nobel Memorial Prize for his work on the auction theory needed for successful radio spectrum auctions also built on Coase's initial insights.

As he moved from London, through Virginia, to Chicago, Coase worked in departments within which he could find colleagues who were receptive to his commitment to understanding and strengthening market institutions. In some ways, though, Coase was an old-fashioned political economist. He relied on observation, rather than measurement and the interpretation of data. In Chicago, as well as being dubious about Stigler's 'Coase Theorem' being a reasonable interpretation of his ideas, he was sceptical about Chicago economists' commitment to producing predictive theory, with their predictions being corroborated by statistical analysis. Famously, he dismissed their efforts as 'torturing the data enough, so that nature will confess'.

Originally inspired by Smith's arguments about the self-organizing nature of the economy, law was important for Coase because it provided a framework within which choices could be made. Treating decision makers as being self-interested – again a Smithian insight – he believed that the private coordination of activities would generally be most effective. The law was then a way of managing decision-making processes, which would be overseen by public authorities. All this complemented Hayek's work, providing pathways to greater liberty by developing a richer understanding of the role of institutional structures.

14

Milton Friedman – The Monetarist

Politically conservative, and economically liberal, to undo Keynes' influence

Chicago: the gateway to the Atlantic from the mid-West. Built on meat packing, and famed for its violent gangsters, it is also the home of a great university. The oil magnate, John D. Rockefeller, endowed it lavishly, setting it up as a very different type of institution from the Ivy League universities on the East Coast of the USA. Early in the twentieth century it set out to recruit staff who would espouse personal freedom and work closely with industry, so that their research would have immediate utility.

Hayek spent 12 years in Chicago. Coase settled there. Aaron Director and George Stigler both had important roles in shaping the Chicago economics of the mid-twentieth century. But it was Milton Friedman who ensured that the 'Chicago School' became the world's leading centre of conservative economic thought after World War II. He argued that the economy needed to be free of state intervention in markets. His essentially political commitment to restrained government derived from a strong belief in the Marshallian core of economic theory. For Friedman, prices were very flexible, and that would ensure that supply and demand kept in balance. There was no room in Friedman's thinking for Keynes' ideas about persistent unemployment.

Tracing the origins of the Chicago School we need to go back to Frank Knight, a fierce individualist who arrived in Chicago in 1929. Alongside Knight, we might note the role of the trade theorist and historian of thought, Jacob Viner, who taught the main price theory course to graduate students throughout the 1930s, as well as Henry Simons, who moved to the Law School in the late 1930s, paving the way for Director and Coase. For this generation of scholars, Marshall's *Principles of Economics* was the starting point for economic analysis.

During the Great Depression, even in Chicago, economists recommended radical action. Believing that the accumulation of market power was harming the economy, Simons developed ideas which were intended to reduce the influence of large corporations. The later Chicago School took a very different approach. Director and Stigler argued that market power is essential for economic development and will usually decay quickly as ideas diffuse through the economy. As a result, they claimed that regulation will often cause greater harm than tolerance of market power.

Viner may well have been right in his recollection that there was nothing especially distinctive about the economics taught in Chicago in the 1920s and 1930s. However, many of the leading lights of the Chicago School in the 1950s and 1960s had been postgraduate students in Chicago before World War II – Director in the 1920s, and Friedman and Stigler in the early 1930s.

Director returned to Chicago in 1946, following Simons' suicide, quickly taking over the ongoing discussions with Hayek about joining the university. As a result, when Hayek was putting together the conference which led to the launch of the Mont Pèlerin Society, Director was able to recommend that Friedman and Stigler should be there.

After the success of *Road to Serfdom*, it might have seemed that Hayek was ideally placed to lead a challenge to the suddenly fashionable Keynesian ideas. However, despite being able to match Keynes intellectually, Hayek was never comfortable in the campaigning role which had come so naturally to Keynes – and in which Friedman also excelled. Throughout the 1950s and 1960s, when Keynes' followers had their greatest influence, Friedman engaged tirelessly in public debate. After Keynes' reformation of economics, the Chicago School took on the role of the Jesuits in the counter-reformation, with Friedman its Loyola, shaping a very practical, intellectual response.

Friedman's political message appeared most vividly in two books which he wrote with his wife Rose, who was Aaron Director's sister. Rose and Milton first met in Viner's economic theory class in 1932, when he sat his students in desks in alphabetical order. They married in 1938. Their books, *Capitalism and Freedom*, written in 1962, and *Free to Choose*, which appeared in 1978, were deliberately popular. They first developed the material for lecture tours, (and in the case of *Free to Choose* a TV series). In many ways, they took up the argument for economic liberty which Hayek made in *Road to Serfdom*. Always polemical, they were full of examples about how to escape the dead hand of the state. Early in *Capitalism and Freedom*, the Friedmans set down a list of policy statements which they believed that 'modern liberals' would oppose. Much of the list could have been written by Coase or Hayek. Perhaps it is a measure of their success that almost all of them are now very widely accepted.

The books provided intellectual ballast for the campaigns of two Republican Presidential candidates. *Capitalism and Freedom* fed into Barry Goldwater's policy platform in 1964, and then, to a limited extent, Richard Nixon's in 1968; while in *Free to Choose*, the Friedmans set out the economic arguments which Ronald Reagan made eloquently and effectively in 1980. However, while the political message of the books was consistent with much of Friedman's economics, he deliberately kept his political advice, which was typically given only in election campaigns, separate from his economic research. Instead, he claimed that he ventured into politics purely as an active citizen.

That required him to make a distinction – which would have been entirely foreign to Keynes – between economics as social science, and economic insights as the basis of policy advice. He claimed that his campaigning was based upon observation, to which he applied economic principles, especially what he characterized as Adam Smith's 'flash of genius', that all voluntary exchanges are beneficial to all parties to the transaction and so should be permitted.

A rigorous defence of this position came in his 1953 essay, *The Methodology of Positive Economics*. Many economists have treated the essay as a summary of the purpose and nature of economic research. Presenting economic theory as a prediction engine, Friedman adopted an instrumentalist stance, positioning economics as a close neighbour of the natural sciences. In Friedman's essay, there was an essential role for measurement to determine the accuracy of predictions. However, it does not contain a detailed explanation of how to evaluate predictions, and it also sets to one side the possibility that there is some ultimate truth which might be glimpsed through our insights. It is probably most famous for describing the assumptions of theory as always being unrealistic. Given Friedman's belief that a theory could only be useful if it had substantial predictive power, he did not believe that they were attempts to describe reality, or to abstract from it. Making this argument, Friedman was setting out how the Chicago School's approach to economic analysis would differ from the detailed measurement and detailed description of data which had been characteristic of the American institutionalists of the early twentieth century.

While the *Methodology* essay captured the development of Friedman's own practice as an economist in the preceding 20 years, the book in which it first appeared, *Essays in Positive Economics* was a prospectus for his ultimate objective – the rehabilitation of monetary theories as an alternative to Keynes' use of the savings-investment channel in *The General Theory*.

Friedman's undergraduate studies at Rutgers University in New Jersey had been in mathematics – he had originally intended to become an actuary. While at Rutgers, he had taken economics courses with Arthur Burns (later a chairman of the Federal Reserve Board) and Homer Jones (who introduced him to Chicago style price theory and supported his application to Chicago to continue his studies). After a year in Chicago, in 1932–3, he moved to Columbia University in New York. It took him until 1946 to complete his doctoral dissertation under Harold Hotelling, an excellent mathematical economist, some of whose theoretical models are still widely used.

In the 1930s, young economists were sucked into the New Deal administration in Washington DC. Friedman found a job in the National Resources Committee, where he worked on a consumer budget study, which would become the basis of his later work on the consumption function. That led into work with Simon Kuznets at the National Bureau of Economic Research, on the incomes of private medical practitioners, and the extent to which they were higher because they were able to restrict entry into the profession. During World War II, Friedman worked for the Treasury (on tax policy) and with Hotelling's group at Columbia (on statistical analysis of problems of military effectiveness). He mastered many statistical methods at the time that these were first being applied in economics.

The relationships with Burns and Hotelling at Columbia and the NBER drew Friedman into the orbit of Wesley Clair Mitchell, the foremost institutional economist in the USA. Mitchell had long been concerned with empirical study of business cycles and the changing structure of the economy. Much of this work was summed up in the 1946 study, *Measuring Business Cycles*, written by Burns and Mitchell. The work was descriptive and so did not use the types of statistical analysis which Friedman was beginning to employ.

His essay on method confirms that Friedman was primarily a theorist. Before he returned to Chicago in 1946, he had developed an approach to economic analysis which took Marshall's *Principles of Economics* as the starting point. He taught two courses to almost all graduate students at Chicago for much of the next three decades: Price Theory, and Money. The names themselves are interesting – there was not the division into microeconomics and macroeconomics which has by now been common for many years in other economics departments. Price Theory of course emphasized continuity with Marshall, and Knight, and the application of economic principles to understand the conduct of one market at a time. The course on Money was centred on the implications of the quantity theory of money.

This begins from what is essentially an accounting identity – that the amount of money circulating in the economy will be enough to pay for all transactions which take place. Those payments will depend both on the number and economic value of transactions – the national income of the country – but also the price level. Across any period, the stock of money can cycle around the economy many times to fund payments. In a short period, say a year, we would not expect the rate at which money flows through the economy to change substantially. We would also expect the country's productive capacity to change slowly. It follows that if there is a rapid change in the amount of money in the economy, the price level should also change in much the same way.

Where Keynes thought in terms of the flows of savings and investment, Friedman instead thought about money as the counterpart of bank credit. In lending money, banks debit one account, and credit another one with money. Banks can therefore create money very quickly, and Friedman argued that when this happens too quickly it will lead to increases in prices.

He presented his initial evidence criticizing the Keynesian system in a research study, published in 1957, *A Theory of the Consumption Function*. We can see him implementing the approach of the essay on *Methodology*. He presented theory before the empirical evidence, which largely corroborated the theory.

The theory itself is a rather brief statement, based on the concept that aggregate consumption will be a constant proportion of national income. To do this, Friedman defined income not just as the money which we receive in a period, but as the change in our ability to buy goods and services, not just immediately, but over time. If workers receive a pay increase, that should increase their spending power now and in the future. If they receive a bonus, it will only increase their spending power in future to the extent that they do not spend it now. We can relate Friedman's concept of permanent income to the ability to finance consumption over time.

To give another example, suppose that the value of your house increases. Clearly, you have just become wealthier. You could borrow money now, and spend the increase in value now, repaying the loan from the future sale proceeds of the house, or you could just wait until you have cash in hand to spend the money.

Friedman recognized that some of the statistical evidence was consistent with the Keynesian formulation in which consumption could be divided into the fixed quantity, necessary for subsistence, and a variable quantity, which is proportional to income. He argued that there seemed to be the predicted fixed component in the relationship between consumption and national income when he looked at data during a business cycle of perhaps seven years. However, he also argued that this fixed component vanished when examining the relationship over much longer periods.

He argued that this was exactly the pattern which should be expected if there was unpredictable variation in measured income. A large, one-off, change in measured income would mean a small change in permanent income, and only a small change in consumption. Within a cycle, the proportion of income consumed would be lowest during a boom and highest during a recession, as Keynes had predicted. That was consistent with a trend of consumption increasing in proportion to income across many cycles.

The permanent income theory of consumption treats people as planning for the future when deciding how much to spend now. Friedman argued that the post-war Keynesian economics tended to ignore this desirable element of foresight, or else assumed that prices would not change. In the 1960s, he used these concerns to criticize policy advice based on the assertion of A. W. (Bill) Phillips that there was a stable, inverse relationship between the rate of unemployment and the rate of inflation, which might last for several years. What became known as the Phillips curve extended the Keynesian orthodoxy of planned demand to the idea that it would be possible to contain unemployment by tolerating a small amount of inflation.

To Friedman, this explanation of the Phillips curve had to be wrong. People who expect prices to rise should anticipate that in their behaviour, acting as if prices have risen. Beliefs lead to actions which effectively confirm the beliefs, and that would make inflation very difficult to contain. Again, he presented his arguments in terms of his theory being a better prediction engine than the Keynesian alternative. He accepted that when prices increased suddenly, and unexpectedly, businesses would find that their revenue was increasing. That would lead them to hire staff, so that unemployment would fall.

In contrast, he argued that a widespread belief that there would be substantial inflation would lead to higher wage demands, higher costs for firms, and practices such as the indexing of prices in contracts. That would lead to the Phillips curve shifting upwards. Whatever the level of unemployment, the inflation rate associated with it would increase. Friedman also argued that higher inflation would make the economic environment facing businesses more uncertain. Then, since changes in relative prices give businesses useful information about market conditions, volatile prices would make prices less informative. That suggests that with high inflation, we should expect investment to fall, and unemployment to rise. Friedman concluded that during a period of sustained inflation, as well as drifting upwards, the Phillips curve would shift outwards. The period of stagflation in the 1970s with high inflation, persistent unemployment and slow growth, seemed to confirm this analysis: his prediction engine had worked once again.

The work on the consumption function was intended to show that Keynesian theory was not an effective prediction engine. Completing that task, Friedman turned to monetary theory to argue that economic fluctuations could be explained more effectively in terms of credit cycles. Still treated with reverence by conservatives, *A Monetary History of the United States, 1867–1960*, (published in 1963, with Anna Schwartz) was Friedman's undoubted masterwork. Influenced heavily by Mitchell's earlier work on business cycles (from 1933), the centrepiece of this famous study was a rebuttal of the claim that it was necessary to look to failures of the savings–investment relation to explain the Great Depression. Instead, Friedman and Schwartz argued that from early 1929, the Federal Reserve Board had raised interest rates, and that this had led banks to reduce the amount of new credit which they issued. With a more accommodating policy, the Federal Reserve might have kept control of inflation, and avoided the crisis.

It was entirely consistent with the tenets of Chicago School economics that Friedman explained the Great Depression as a catastrophic failure of government policy. Yet in his understanding of the nature of money, we can also see some of the differences between Friedman's political conservatism and Hayek's liberalism. Hayek argued that since bank deposits are money, and banks create money by advancing credit, there is no need for governments to be involved in the issue of money. All money could be issued privately. He then argued that governments should not be involved in bank regulation, and that there should be no public compensation for depositors if a bank failed. The risk of loss would mean that customers would move their accounts as soon as there was any question about their security. Realizing that, no bank would take exceptional risks. For Hayek, bank runs, in which many depositors rush to withdraw their money from a bank, forcing the bank to close, are a result of government intervention.

Unlike Hayek, Friedman was perfectly content to accept that money should be issued by public authorities. His ideal was for the monetary authority to follow a rule of allowing the nominal money supply to increase modestly every year by about 5 per cent. That would avoid debt financed booms, and the subsequent crises. However, achieving such an objective in an economy in which banks create money by issuing credit has always been very difficult.

Early in his career, Friedman supported the Chicago Plan for banking reform, which Simons had developed during the Great Depression, with support from Knight and the leading US monetary economist of the time, Irving Fisher. The plan would have simplified the financial structure of banks very substantially. To ensure that they were always able to meet depositors' demands, they would have held reserves at the central bank equal to the value of their deposits. Funding for lending would have come from government, but would have been channelled through banks, free of political influence. Simons believed that the adoption of such measures would have restored confidence in the banking system and reduced the risk of future bank crises.

Since the implementation of these ideas would have required very substantial reforms of the banking system, it was probably never politically feasible. Towards the end of the Great Depression, the reforms in the Banking Act of 1935 did just enough to restore the lost public confidence in the banking system. Much as implementing Friedman's 5 per cent money growth rule probably requires a system with public deposits, he concluded that the implicit public guarantee of deposits, which has now become widespread, would achieve many of the benefits of such a scheme.

Hayek wanted to host a dinner party for Keynes and Schumpeter. A party with Keynes and Friedman, the two most eloquent advocates of economic arguments in the last century, would also have been very entertaining. Their discussion would probably have demonstrated that as well as substantial differences about the role of government, they disagreed about the nature of the economy. For Friedman, it was inevitable that prices would be flexible, and that the economy would work best with minimal interference by the government. Keynes' experience of policy advice in the Great Depression had led him to conclude that those recuperative powers could easily fail, and that governments had a duty to supply confidence when no one else would. But Friedman's target was not *The General Theory*. He attacked the followers of Keynes, such as Paul Samuelson, who believed that it was possible to manage the economy.

15

Paul Samuelson – The American Keynes?

Bringing mathematical rigour to economic theory,
and Keynes to the world

Born in Gary, Indiana, in 1915, on the shores of Lake Michigan, completing a degree at the University of Chicago was the obvious choice for Paul Samuelson. He arrived there to study economics in 1932, and quickly fell in with George Stigler who was then a graduate student. There, Jacob Viner used the Socratic method to keep his students' wits sharp in his price theory classes. Samuelson's facility with mathematics allowed him to turn the tables on his instructor and question the gaps in his analysis. Presuming that economic theory should have a mathematical core, through his friendship with Stigler, he quickly learned both what was possible and what had already been done.

On graduating from Chicago, in 1935, he won a national Social Sciences Research Council scholarship for two years of graduate study, conditional on attending a different institution. His teachers were unanimous that he should take the same route as Friedman and go to Columbia. Samuelson, an even more boisterous storyteller than Stigler, claimed that he chose Harvard because he imagined it to be a small village in green, rolling countryside. More practically, at the time, he was attracted by

Edward Chamberlin's work on the economics of imperfectly competitive markets, with its model of monopolistic competition.

That was perhaps a rather unfortunate attraction. During his time at Harvard, Samuelson experienced a degree of institutional anti-Semitism. Shortly after becoming the first American to win the Nobel Memorial Prize, in 1970, he put together a 'roll of dishonor' from that time in a letter to a friend. Topping the list was Harold Burbank, the head of the economics department when it declined to offer Samuelson a permanent position in 1940. Chamberlin's was the second name on it.

When Samuelson arrived in 1935, Harvard was still building its economics department. As well as Schumpeter, it had hired Wassily Leontief, who would remain there for over 30 years as he developed input–output analysis, a way of analysing the behaviour of the whole economy, which breaks it down into many industrial sectors. At a time of very limited computing power, this approach allowed him to think about how the structure of the economy might change in response to sudden changes in economic conditions, such as an increase in global energy prices.

Schumpeter quickly recognized Samuelson's exceptional talents and championed his mathematical explorations. Leontief provided oversight of Samuelson's youthful flourishing, which led to him producing about 25 published papers between 1937 and 1940, while he was a junior fellow at Harvard.

One of the most important of these set out the principle of revealed preference. This was a way of generating the results of the still developing mathematical analysis of choice without relying on the mental, and so unobservable, concept of utility. For this research, Samuelson drew on the same mathematical techniques which Leontief was using, while applying them to a very different area of economics.

Samuelson's work on revealed preference also complemented John Hicks' and Roy Allen's development of indifference curve analysis as a method of explaining choice. They too had effectively dispensed with utility as a measurable concept and assumed that people would be able to rank the available alternatives so that they could identify the best one. Samuelson's revealed preference method instead started from the choices which people made and worked back to the preferences. By eliminating the concept of utility, Samuelson intended to make the theory of choice a set of 'operationally meaningful statements' which would, at least in principle, be testable. Unlike Friedman, with his idea of theory as a prediction engine, Samuelson saw it as describing, and explaining, the underlying reality of the economy.

This reflected the influence on Samuelson of the mathematician Edwin Wilson, who ran graduate courses at Harvard in mathematical statistics and mathematical economics in alternate years. Samuelson completed them both as a graduate student, and Wilson then provided Samuelson with guidance while he was a junior fellow, especially on the choices he faced at the time of his move in 1940 from Harvard to its neighbour, the Massachusetts Institute of Technology.

At the end of Samuelson's term as a junior fellow, he had hoped to stay at Harvard, but MIT had become interested in hiring him and made him an offer. The economics department at Harvard then split over whether to try to match the MIT offer of a permanent position, with Schumpeter's admiration of Samuelson leading him to accuse colleagues who opposed the appointment of being afraid of the young man's ability. (Schumpeter was so dissatisfied with Harvard's handling of Samuelson's position that he had extensive discussions with Yale about a move, even agreeing the salary.) Harold Burbank, as head of the department, eventually decided against the appointment.

Later in life, Samuelson claimed that Burbank had dismissed his mathematical economics, telling him that he should not attempt to work on economic theory until he was 50 – and for Burbank, theory was institutionalist, and inductive, involving mature reflection after years of careful observation. For Samuelson, under Wilson's tutelage, economic theory meant a mathematical framework which generated testable – or operationally meaningful – predictions.

Having worked at MIT earlier in his career, Wilson was strongly supportive of Samuelson going there. He was detached from the tensions within the Harvard economics department and knew that Harvard's leadership was seeking to strengthen its faculty by recruiting leading European academics. Economic forces had already made the USA attractive for Schumpeter, von Neumann and many others. With the outbreak of World War II, the steady flow of academics across the Atlantic became a torrent. That led Wilson to advise Samuelson that he would most likely receive an offer of a five-year teaching fellowship at Harvard in the spring of 1941, but that he could flourish at MIT, not least because he would be working in an engineering school, in which all the students would be capable of understanding a mathematical treatment of economics.

From letters which Wilson wrote in support of Samuelson at this time, we also know that he was concerned that Samuelson's expertise in mathematical economics was too narrow a base for him to become a great economist, and that he believed that teaching (relatively weak students) would be the best way for him to learn how to express his ideas so that they would be easier to understand.

In November 1940, Samuelson left Harvard, while he was working on his doctoral dissertation. At the time, many junior fellows simply moved into academic roles without completing a formal degree, but Samuelson, partly because of anxiety about anti-Semitism affecting his prospects, pulled together work which he had completed as a junior fellow after a few months of hard work, with considerable support from his wife, Marion

Crawford. Like Rose Friedman and Mary Marshall, Crawford had trained as an economist, and she helped Samuelson to express his ideas and clarify arguments. The thesis, completed in 1941, won the David A. Wells prize for the best economics thesis of that year, which guaranteed its publication. This eventually took place in 1947, after Samuelson had completed work on ballistics in the Radiation Laboratory at MIT during World War II.

The thesis appeared as *Foundations of Economic Analysis*. In the book, Samuelson built on the key insight of his doctoral dissertation, that many of the problems of economics had a common mathematical structure, and so could be cast in a consistent approach from which general principles might be deduced. Hicks' *Value and Capital*, published in 1939, anticipated many of the results of *Foundations*, but while that had been a presentation of a consistently mathematical approach to economic theory, it lacked *Foundations'* generality, and applicability to a wide range of problems. With Wilson's continued guidance, Samuelson aimed to develop an approach which would establish economics as a body of operationally meaningful statements.

This meant unifying disparate approaches. Samuelson's tool for doing this was at first Le Châtelier's principle in thermodynamics, that in response to a change in external conditions, a system will respond to minimize the effects of that change. The principle's generality allowed Samuelson to think about how to adapt it to understand conditions for system stability in economics. This process led to the development of Samuelson's correspondence principle.

According to the correspondence principle, so long as certain stability conditions are satisfied within a mathematical model, then even if the equilibrium did not rely upon the optimal choice of actions, the equilibrium of the model would be stable. Remember that in the Keynesian macroeconomic model, equilibrium only requires aggregate income and expenditure to be equal, and this ensures that the circular flow of income can continue. This is a different type of equilibrium from the consumer optimization which Samuelson had developed in his revealed preference approach.

The correspondence principle allowed Samuelson to develop the method of comparative statics, which examines the effects of finite changes in initial conditions. Given that economic data is very often discrete, and collected for a particular time period, this was desirable since it made it much easier to test theoretical results. *Foundations of Economic Analysis* therefore provided a robust basis for treating economic theory as having mathematical form and did so in such a way that the theory conformed to Wilson's, and Samuelson's, operationalism. That allowed Samuelson to dismiss much of what had previously passed as theory in economics as 'mental gymnastics of a particularly depraved type', and to compare academic economists with 'highly trained athletes who never run a race'.

As well as Schumpeter, Leontief and Wilson, Alvin Hansen also had a substantial effect on Samuelson's career during his time at Harvard. Hansen came to Harvard in 1937 from the University of Minnesota, where he had developed a reputation for his work on business cycles. As one of the first reviewers of *The General Theory*, Hansen became the first senior American economist to welcome the book, largely because he could see how to accommodate some of Keynes' thinking into his own understanding of how the economy worked. In 1939, Samuelson wrote a paper which added Hansen's accelerator concept to John Hicks' analytical version of Keynes' theory. By introducing the accelerator, Samuelson started to address the criticism that Keynes' theory was entirely static and did not explain how the state of the economy would change over time. By assuming that investment in any period will be proportional to the growth of consumption, Samuelson demonstrated that it was possible for a Keynesian model to display cyclical effects.

Hansen's promotion of Keynesian ideas throughout the 1940s led to him becoming the first economist to be called the 'American Keynes' – a title which fitted Samuelson better – but he was not simply a disciple. He played an important role in developing policies for the management of aggregate demand to ensure that there would be full employment. Those became important after the end of World War II, with Samuelson becoming one of their best-known advocates.

During World War II, the US government gave its National Resources Planning Board the task of planning for full employment after the war had ended. That allowed Hansen to secure a consultancy role for Samuelson in 1941, which was his introduction to working for government. Assigned tasks which were mostly technical, and which involved statistical analysis, Samuelson led a research team for the first time. Its findings fed into the Board's reports on how to manage the demobilization of the army and, given the demands of fighting the war, the economy. This work led to Samuelson writing articles for newspapers and magazines in support of the Full Employment Bill of 1945, just as he returned to the economics department at MIT.

There, Ralph Freeman, the head of department, asked him to put together a short text which would explain the structure of the US economy to engineering students who had never previously studied economics, and provide them with simple analytical tools so that they could solve elementary problems of theory and policy. His work for the NRPB turned out to be important for this project because it provided him with the applied material which would complement the theoretical analysis.

He now faced almost the opposite problem of writing *Foundations*. Like Marshall writing *Principles*, he wanted to integrate recent developments in economics into a comprehensive introduction to the subject. The sequence of Smith, Ricardo, Mill, Marshall has perhaps ended with Samuelson. *Economics: An Introductory Analysis* will perhaps be the last general economics text to become the standard introduction for a generation. There are now simply too many economists, and perhaps too much economics, for a single book to take on such a role.

The first edition of *Economics* appeared in 1948, the year after *Foundations*. Samuelson revised it 15 times over 50 years, and it was then taken over by another Nobel Prize winner, William Nordhaus, who edited it until the nineteenth edition, published in 2009. About five million copies have been sold. The great theorist also turned out to be a great storyteller. In *Economics*, Samuelson captured what was understood about the economy very clearly, while also introducing undergraduate students to Keynesian economics. He did all this while writing for an audience which had no understanding of the mathematical complexities underlying his research.

The task required Samuelson to tread a careful path. In 1947, the Canadian economist Lorie Tarshis had published *Elements of Economics*. This was the first textbook to embrace Keynesian economics. It quickly became the subject of a national campaign by political conservatives, who, like Hayek, saw demand management policies as a form of socialism. Although many universities had started to use the book, it was soon withdrawn from reading lists.

Samuelson faced a similar challenge from MIT's visiting committee, which reviewed some of the early drafts and criticized the material for being too favourable to 'managed capitalism'. MIT's leaders provided Samuelson with strong support, and it was also useful that the American Economic Association had just made Samuelson its first John Bates Clark medallist, confirming his prestige among professional economists. However, Samuelson also engaged his critics carefully, perhaps aware of how destructive the criticism of Tarshis's work had been. He presented *Economics* as an objective account, which strove to find the 'middle way', as understood by the emerging generation of economists, whose thinking had been shaped by the Depression and the War. Hansen worried that this approach conceded too much ground to those critics. Of course, in presenting his work as objective, and our knowledge of economics as being reliant on data, he was advocating an operationalist approach to economics.

In 1948, Samuelson was still concerned that there would be substantial unemployment during the transition to peacetime. By 1954, preparing the third edition of *Economics*, with the steady expansion of the economy under way, Samuelson's concern started to shift to the management of inflation. It was also in this edition of the book that Samuelson introduced his neo-classical synthesis. With the claim that *The General Theory* complemented the insights of earlier economists, on which he had built with *Foundations*, this quickly became the most famous example of his middle-of-the-road approach. He used it to validate the use of microeconomic analysis under most conditions, while leaving space for Keynesian demand management.

The synthesis was incomplete because the two types of economic analysis would tend to operate under different economic conditions – price theory when there was full employment, and demand management when there was unemployment. That made it impossible to integrate economic theory into a unified whole. The division between macroeconomics, initiated by Keynes, Hicks, Hansen – and Samuelson – and the microeconomics of Marshall's *Principles*, and Samuelson's *Foundations*, was inevitable. It was impossible to move from the determination of prices and quantities in individual markets to the behaviour of economic aggregates, such as national income, unemployment and inflation.

For Samuelson, especially after his work for the NRPB, and the success of full-employment policies to avert a repeat of the challenges of the 1920s, macroeconomic policy tools could reduce fluctuations in the economy, stabilize (the growth of) national income, and control unemployment and inflation. His explanation of income determination was often taken, especially by critics, as being primarily Keynesian, but Samuelson always denied that, emphasizing its pragmatic nature. He was mainly concerned with providing a platform of macroeconomic management, after which it would be possible to determine the efficient application of resources within the economy according to neo-classical principles.

Setting aside methodological differences about the role of theory, Samuelson, like Keynes, rejected Friedman's claim that the technical analysis of economic theory might be kept separate from policy advice. Eloquent, imaginative and highly productive, Samuelson was perhaps most like Keynes in giving policy advice directly to government, and especially to Democratic administrations. Senator John F. Kennedy recruited him as an economic adviser, and he retained that role through the 1960 Presidential election, and into the transition, completing a detailed report on the state of the US economy in January 1961. However, he then chose to remain at MIT, rather than joining the Council of Economic Advisers.

Like Keynes, he turned his hand to journalism. Most famously, *Newsweek* magazine recruited both Samuelson and Friedman in 1966 to write columns on economic analysis. They alternated in a three-weekly cycle with Henry Wallich of Yale University and the Federal Reserve Board. In advertising them, *Newsweek* presented Samuelson as being of the political left, Friedman of the right, and Wallich the centrist. The arrangement lasted for 18 years, running through the time of the Vietnam War, the abandonment of fixed exchange rates, and the linkage of the dollar to gold, then the oil crisis, the

Watergate investigations, the stagflation (high inflation and low growth) in the middle 1970s, and eventually the Reagan revolution. When they began writing, Samuelson's advocacy of Keynesian demand management was seen as entirely orthodox. By the time that they finished, governments were turning to Friedman, and monetarism, for policy advice.

Samuelson described himself as possibly the last of the generalist economists. The discipline was expanding quickly, and that made it almost impossible for anyone to span all of it. Even for Samuelson, this claim to universal coverage does not seem quite true: he was essentially a microeconomist, who turned his hand to the new macroeconomics at the time when it first emerged. Over his long career, he produced a dizzying variety of advances in economic theory, partly because he had systematically developed the tools needed for analysis. This body of work was essential in transforming the discipline from description of complex causal chains of activities into a form of scientific enquiry. While Marshall gave us the shape of modern economic theory, and Keynes' legacy was to turn economics into policy advice, Samuelson moved effortlessly between theory and policy, plumbing new depths, and applying his insights clearly.

16

Herbert Simon – The Social
Scientific Realist

*The impossibility of optimal choices means that we
must understand behaviour*

How do we make decisions? Herbert Simon believed that we typically make them quickly, and well, even when we have very little relevant information. As we have already seen with the work of Keynes, Hayek and Coase, information is an important commodity, which we need to manage well. So, while Simon's work was important enough for him to receive the Nobel Memorial Prize in 1978, he was never a professional economist. After training in political science in the 1930s, he became a professor in that field in the 1940s. With his specialization in the behaviour of public organizations, his move to the Carnegie Institute of Technology as Professor of Organizational Science in 1949 only involved a small shift in emphasis.

However, by the late 1950s he had become one of the first computer scientists. In that role, he laid some of the foundations for research into artificial intelligence through his contributions to the development of the list-processing languages, which are used to obtain computational solutions to non-numerical problems. He enabled computers to replicate the arguments of Bertrand Russell's *Principia Mathematica*. Russell wrote a note congratulating Simon on this achievement, agreeing that it would be good were schoolboys to remain unaware that it was no longer necessary for them to prove results.

Early in his career, Simon developed some general principles of behavioural decision making, and these unified all his activities. In the 1940s, he applied them to organizations, before turning to economics and psychology in the early 1950s to explore how people make decisions. That was the work which won him the Nobel Memorial Prize. In working on artificial intelligence, he applied the same decision-making principles as in his computer programming. Organizations, people, machines: Simon believed that as decision makers, they tended to behave in very similar ways. That made him a true generalist. He was perhaps the most complete social scientist of the twentieth century, making significant contributions across many fields, and achieving a level of eminence in each that would usually be the work of an entire career.

As well as the Economics Nobel, he received substantial honours from the American Psychological Association and the Association for Computer Machinery, which recognized his research in cognitive psychology and artificial intelligence. For Simon, the variety of his achievements was simply a happy accident of timing. Especially in the 1940s and 1950s, he claimed that it was easy to cross disciplinary boundaries repeatedly because he was working on questions which most social scientists agreed were very important, but which had not become central to any specific discipline. Those interests made him one of the originators of what is now called decision science. It is still a multi-disciplinary enterprise, with experts in this area of research scattered through the social sciences.

Herbert Simon was born in 1916, the year after Paul Samuelson. Like Samuelson, he was of Jewish German descent. His father had trained as an engineer in Germany and settled in Milwaukee in 1903. Like Samuelson, he grew up in a city on the shores of Lake Michigan. Again, like Samuelson, it was almost inevitable both that the Depression would influence Simon's politics, especially since it had affected his father's business, and that he should end up arriving at the University of Chicago as a 17-year-old undergraduate. Where Samuelson was immediately drawn to economics, and quickly drew upon his understanding of mathematics and physical sciences to develop his very systematic economic theory, Simon began his study of organizations while he was still an undergraduate student.

Under the leadership of Charles Merriam, the political science department at the University of Chicago had embraced empirical research, based on careful observation. To complete an undergraduate project, Simon returned to his home city, Milwaukee, and studied the behaviour of the city government. He quickly found an interesting problem within its organization. Two departmental heads needed to cooperate to complete a programme. Each managed substantial budgets but they repeatedly failed to agree a spending plan for their joint work.

Simon concluded that the problem stemmed from differences in the managers' thinking about the nature of the service which they should provide, and therefore what resources each department needed to contribute. With each having firm ideas about what needed to be done, they bickered over how to spend their budget. From this, Simon concluded that there was no straightforward way of explaining how resources would be transformed into services. Each manager saw the problem from the perspective of implementing his organizational function, with conflict the natural result. That conflict could be resolved by the decision of a yet more senior manager, applying the city government's decision-making procedures.

In his undergraduate studies, Simon had enough exposure to economic arguments to think of this sort of problem solving in much the same way as Samuelson, or even Friedman. He argued that organizations would identify the set of feasible options, and choose among them, given the constraints which political structures imposed on their decision making. Believing strongly that the investigation of organizational behaviour was amenable to a social scientific approach, he proposed that it should be possible to analyse administrative decision making by using statistical tools which were just emerging. In terms of research methods, then, Simon envisioned the sort of positivist framework, which we have already seen in the applied research which Samuelson and Friedman began at almost the same time.

In studying organizational decision making, Simon found a way of bringing the processes of decision making into economics. He evaded the restrictions which Friedman introduced in *The Methodology of Positive Economics*, of requiring economics only to consider objective, numerically measurable data, which were the result of observable actions. For Friedman, that excluded any use of self-reported attitudes or beliefs, collected through questionnaires, since the responses would not involve any observable actions involving the use of resources. By concentrating on organizations, rather than people, Simon could observe decision making. Not only do managers command resources, but in making decisions about how to use them, they leave rich paper trails. Simon could follow them and understand the process of decision making.

If that sounds familiar, remember that when Coase visited the USA in 1932, he toured businesses and observed their behaviour. That led to his insight that markets and organizations represent different ways of making decisions about the management of resources. For both Coase and Simon, organizations managed information through their internal processes. Well-informed managers would issue orders and direct the activity of other employees.

We might think of Coase and Simon coming to the study of largely complementary problems while they were still in their early 20s. Coase set out to define when it was rational for a firm to manage processes directly, rather than hiring a specialist organization to undertake them. He wanted to work out where an organization should set the boundaries of its direct management of resources. Simon considered the complementary problem in which the boundaries of organizations were given. He then needed to explain what it meant to say that their decisions were rational.

His Chicago training, with its mathematical, orthodox neo-classical economic approach led to him receiving an offer of work from Clarence Ridley, who ran the International City Managers' Association. This was a cross between a research institute and a trade body. With Ridley's mentoring, Simon carried out research involving the measurement of the activities of local government organizations.

On Christmas Day 1937, he married Dorothea Pye, whom he had met while she was working as a secretary in the Chicago Politics Department. Pye had completed postgraduate training in cognitive psychology, and in the 1950s was to be one of Simon's many collaborators in research.

Then, in 1939, still aged 23, he took up a post at the University of California, Berkeley, as the director of administrative measurement studies, in the Bureau of Public Administration. While working in California, and starting a family, Simon was also registered as a research student in politics at Chicago and he completed his dissertation in 1942. By Simon's own assessment, at that point, he had had an excellent training in the research methods in political science, a working knowledge of economics, and enough understanding of mathematics so that it would be possible for him to develop his knowledge further in his later work as he needed it. He also had the experience of running his own research projects in California. In addition, while in California, he had started to experiment with the use of precursors of digital computers for the organization and analysis of data.

He then went back to Chicago and became the head of the politics department at the Illinois Institute of Technology. Developing ideas from his dissertation, in 1943, he published the book which made his public reputation, *Administrative Behaviour*. This was his first attempt to set out a general framework for the behavioural analysis of the decision of organizations which faced an uncertain environment. Rather than a Friedmanite attempt to predict behaviour, Simon wanted to describe, and explain behaviour, using three principles, which he would apply and develop in many contexts throughout his career.

First, he proposed that organizations would avoid trying to achieve very general goals. Instead, they would simplify the problems which they faced, often breaking them down into component parts on which divisions of the organization might work. Divisional managers could then set concrete goals which would be more readily realizable.

Secondly, he argued that since organizations typically devolved authority to semi-autonomous experts, who could then work on parts of problems, effective administration would involve the coordination of these efforts so that teams worked harmoniously. Going back to his early undergraduate study, he was then able to explain that the disagreement between the divisional managers in Milwaukee was caused by the absence of processes which would have enabled joint working.

Lastly, he proposed that organizations would seek to achieve 'good enough' outcomes. They would typically aim to achieve goals in quite general terms, rather than the best possible outcome. Think of a business that is deciding how much output to produce. The firm might reasonably set itself the target of making enough profit to thrive, perhaps so that it could expand its activities. The optimization which had a central place in economic theory would require the business to find the output at which it made the greatest possible profit. For Simon, given all the uncertainties in life, insisting upon optimization would be a counsel of perfection. Doing 'well enough', or, as he later called it, 'satisficing', was as much as an organization should attempt to do.

Given those three principles, Simon then proposed that organizations would make decisions by following procedures, which would have developed from previous experience of making decisions. That would make it likely that outcomes from following the procedure would be satisfactory. For Simon, decisions were rational if they were reached by following a procedure. He argued that this procedural rationality, which aimed only to achieve satisfactory outcomes, captured much more of the behaviour of organizations than what he named substantive rationality, which associates rational action with the optimization of objectives and which is widely used in economics.

Refining his concept of procedural rationality, Simon developed the idea of bounded rationality. He suggested that efficient processes for making decisions might rely upon a few, critical pieces of information. Such economy of information was very different from the assumption that substantively rational organizational procedures would require the use of all available information. Bounded rationality should reduce the cost of making decisions without much effect on the achievement of underlying objectives. He also suggested that bounded rationality could take the form of decision makers reducing attention to a subset of the possible choices open to them. Believing that it was often better to make some decisions quickly than to prevaricate, both methods seemed to Simon to be useful for organizations.

He believed that bounded rationality underpinned much intuitive, but effective decision making.

The economic pedigree of Simon's approach came through the lasting influence of the ideas of Chester Barnard, a retired business executive, who wrote *The Functions of the Executive* in 1938. Simon had first used Barnard's account of how organizations make decisions while he worked at the International City Managers' Association. Barnard's work had been influenced by the ideas of the American institutionalist economist, John Commons, whose theory of business behaviour examined how transactions took place. The influence of Commons and Barnard was especially strong while Simon wrote his doctoral dissertation and *Administrative Behaviour.*

Being in Chicago in the 1940s also brought Simon into contact with an important group of economists, who were associated with the University of Chicago, at the Cowles Commission for Economic Research, which was entirely separate from the university's economics department. A successful investor, Alfred Cowles had a deep interest in economics. At the onset of the Great Depression, he was so concerned by the lack of reliable data available to economists that he supported the founding of the Econometric Society in 1930, and then, from 1932, funded the work of the Commission. Based initially at Colorado Springs, it had moved to Chicago in 1939, where it remained until 1955, when it moved to Yale University.

In the 1940s, the Commission's directors were Jacob Marschak and Tjalling Koopmans. It was engaged in a wide variety of empirical research, but especially the development of general equilibrium models of the whole economy. Marschak quickly recruited Simon to work on macroeconomic research, but he also found an outlet for his interest in computing in research on the input–output models, which Wassily Leontief had developed at Harvard from the 1930s onwards. The Commission also provided Simon with the environment in which he could apply his behavioural decision-making principles of satisficing and bounded rationality to economics.

Once again, we see the importance of participation in networks for the formation and dissemination of ideas in economics. Later in life, asked why someone who was not an economist should have won the Nobel Memorial Prize, Simon was able to list nine other laureates, all of whom won it between 1969 and 1983, whom he had met at Cowles Commission seminars. He also claimed that the Fellows of the Econometric Society formed the global elite of economics research. He calculated that nearly a quarter of the Fellows in 1955, the year in which Simon became one, and who were still alive in 1969, also received the Nobel Memorial Prize. Being a professor of political science, organization science and computer science was no bar to being counted in the intellectual elite of economics.

Simon's understanding of rationality had important similarities with Hayek's. He argued that economic theories, which assumed optimization behaviour, effectively specified the problems so that rational behaviour involved solving logic problems rather than choice. Hayek's preferred 'ecological' rationality for social sciences supported his thinking about decision-making rules emerging within the spontaneous order of social institutions. Like Simon, Hayek recognized that the rules which individual organizations adopted only needed to be 'good enough'. Working in Chicago in the 1950s, they concluded quite separately that rationality involved people and organizations developing suitable rules so that they would not only survive but prosper.

Yet there were also important political differences between them. Hayek considered any type of economic planning to be a risk to liberty. He believed that economic institutions should emerge to support people's achievement of personal objectives through cooperation. Simon was a liberal in much the same way as Keynes and Samuelson. Far from fearing the spread of public organizations, with the dead hand of government stultifying initiative, and sweeping away liberty, Simon thought of them as being important enablers of human creativity, which could enable new possibilities for social development and individual flourishing.

Reaching adulthood during the Great Depression, even into his old age Simon described himself as a 'New Deal' Democrat. Coming from Milwaukee, he had been familiar with trade unions and socialists. As a student and when he worked in California, he was very sympathetic to left-wing causes. Both he and his wife, Dorothea, came under investigation after law enforcement agencies concluded that many of his colleagues at the time had not just been socialists, but communist sympathizers. The FBI's investigation took place about the time that Lorie Tarshis's textbook was denounced as being opposed to free enterprise simply because it contained an unabashed presentation of demand management. Fortunately, the investigation did not turn up enough evidence to proceed, and Simon's career survived.

We have already seen how economics became increasingly concerned with mathematics and measurement. As a Fellow of the Econometric Society, Simon contributed to that movement. But the arc of Simon's career went well beyond such thinking. He may have used similar methods, but the nature of his economics was very different from Friedman's and Samuelson's – indeed, comparing Simon and Samuelson, the deep effect of Samuelson's early Chicago training on his thinking about economics becomes apparent.

Unlike those great economic theorists, Simon, the universal social scientist, built on ideas of the institutionalist economists, and started from observation. In Simon's thinking, decision making is costly, so we have an incentive to try to reduce those costs. Convinced that the presence of uncertainty ensures that decisions cannot be optimal, he demonstrated how decision making can gradually evolve to be more efficient, both in identifying the information needed to make good decisions, and in the process of using information. In Simon's economics, optimization would be a useful theoretical principle if people, or organizations, or even machines, knew everything that could possibly be relevant. Until then, satisficing would be the best that they might do.

17

Thomas Schelling – The Storyteller

*The economist who might have saved
the world with game theory*

Given that economics is the study of resource management, climate catastrophe would be an epic failure. After World War II, when the superpowers teetered on the brink of nuclear war, they found a path which led them towards negotiation and partial disarmament. The career of Thomas Schelling linked those problems. Through his political economy he explained how to foster cooperation between countries, but the hard-headed realism of his analysis could often unsettle his listeners.

While von Neumann, the advocate of overwhelming force against the Soviet Union, was dying in 1957, Schelling was mastering the principles of game theory, which he used throughout his career. He came to game theory after the initial wave of interest, which followed the publication of von Neumann's and Nash's work, had faded away. In the 1950s, he was just one of a group of younger social scientists, mostly very capable mathematicians, who found important applications for game theory in economics, psychology, political science and biology.

Schelling did not quite fit that mould. He was always careful to claim that he was a user of game theory, without being a game theorist. His style was almost always disarming. Reflecting on some knotty problem, which seemed insurmountable, he would distil it into a simple model, and then think how he might best apply principles of game theory to it, so that he could offer policy advice. Like Coase, undergraduate students can understand most of his arguments, but his thinking was so deep that young scholars could build their career by fleshing out the implications of any one of his important ideas. At a time when economics was becoming ever more formal, Schelling never needed to heed Marshall's advice and 'burn the mathematics' before presenting a cogent verbal argument. He had an ability to see so deeply into the essence of economic relationships that he seemed to find mathematics unnecessary.

Much as it is easy to think of von Neumann as having been one of the sources on which Stanley Kubrick drew in creating the character of Dr Strangelove, who revelled in the logical analysis of military strategy, it was Schelling who was an adviser on the film set. We can then think of the film as a justification of the doctrine of Mutually Assured Destruction, which Schelling first proposed in 1960 in his influential book, *The Strategy of Conflict*. Schelling argued that the nuclear powers could achieve a degree of stability in their relations if they both knew that the other one had the capacity to survive an initial barrage of nuclear missiles. That would ensure the destruction of both countries should there be a nuclear war. No country would choose to destroy itself.

The son of a naval officer, Schelling grew up in California between the wars, completing an undergraduate economics degree at University of California, Berkeley. After working briefly for the government, he completed his doctoral studies at Harvard, under Leontief's supervision. He then went into public service, working on Marshall Plan projects in Copenhagen and Paris. This led to his involvement in the negotiations to set up the European Payments Union, which facilitated international payments among European states after World War II. Then, in 1949, as the security of Western Europe came under increasing threat as the Soviet Union succeeded in extending its control of Central Europe, he was assigned to work on the formation of NATO. This work deepened his interest in understanding the strategic behaviour of nations.

In Schelling's career, we see a new type of economic thinking emerging from the observation of behaviour. He realized that in most situations where there was the possibility of competing interests leading to conflict, political leaders managed to find ways of cooperating, which tended to emerge slowly from bargaining and negotiation. He added those to markets and organizations as ways in which we manage information and make decisions.

Concentrating on the interactions between governments, it was natural for him to turn to game theory, and in 1957 he carefully worked through the recently published book, *Games and Decisions*, written by the mathematicians Duncan Luce and Howard Raiffa. While Nash's work on game theory had established that it was possible to treat negotiation as a game in which the players could work together to find a solution, Schelling was interested in problems in which governments could easily breach any agreements which they made. Games such as the Prisoner's Dilemma seemed to be more useful guides. But for Schelling, the standard interpretations of game theory were much less satisfactory. He ended up writing a long critique of the existing use of game theory, which became the whole of one of the first issues of the *Journal of Conflict Resolution*. He called for a 'reorientation' of the field, so that it might be applied more effectively to problems of negotiation.

He then followed in the footsteps of von Neumann and Simon by developing a relationship with the RAND Corporation, a non-profit organization established in 1946 to promote research benefiting the security of the USA. During the Cold War, RAND was the obvious place for Schelling to analyse the relationship between the superpowers as a problem of negotiation. He quickly produced *The Strategy of Conflict*, which launched his public career and his approach to game theory. Setting aside formal modelling, he effectively made a behavioural argument, proposing that negotiations would quickly settle on a 'focal point', which would seem intuitively reasonable to all negotiating parties.

Some of his examples are homely. He suggested that a couple who became separated in a department store might reasonably converge on the 'lost and found' department. He also suggested that if all that you knew was that a friend would meet you in New York, then you might reasonably go to Grand Central Station where she would be most likely to arrive, at a time such as midday. Schelling used examples like these to argue that where there was limited information, and uncertainty about outcomes, people will tend to use the known characteristics of their environment to choose an outcome on which they might converge. Unsurprisingly, Schelling specifically referred to Simon's conception of people as problem solvers and pattern makers. His 'reorientation' involved the development of a behavioural approach to game theory.

When it came to negotiations over nuclear armaments, his proposed focal point was simple: complete disarmament and the abolition of nuclear weaponry. Until that might be achieved, Schelling recognized that both superpowers had a strong interest in deterring the other country from launching an attack. He therefore advocated Mutually Assured Destruction to transform a situation of profound mistrust into one in which cooperation and, eventually, negotiation might be possible.

Imagine that one of the superpowers were to develop the ability to destroy missiles launched by the other country, in flight, using an anti-ballistic missile system. While von Neumann, thinking in terms of zero-sum games, would have encouraged the USA to follow this route so that it could defeat and subdue the Soviet Union, Schelling argued that even the possibility of either country acquiring such a capacity would be destabilizing, and lead to the possibility of sudden attack from the other superpower. Instead, so that the USA and the USSR could build the trust and goodwill needed for sustained arms reduction, he proposed that they should agree formally not to develop any anti-ballistic missile system.

For Schelling, it was important that this problem had many of the characteristics of a Prisoner's Dilemma game. Cooperation and arms reduction benefited both superpowers (and the rest of the world). However, if either superpower defined their self-interest narrowly, or felt under threat, they might conclude that they would benefit from breaking agreements. The purpose of the agreement not to build an anti-ballistic missile system was to build confidence that there was no immediate threat of war. Making credible commitments about their behaviour would engender trust, so that neither would threaten to use their weapons.

As well as focal points and credible commitments, Schelling proposed a rather more chilling idea: that a 'madman', by which he meant a political leader who seemed entirely insouciant about giving the order to use nuclear weapons, would be the most credible leader in bringing about negotiations. We are back to Strangelove, it seems, but also, perhaps, to the hawkish foreign policy of the Nixon administration, under which the USA and the USSR agreed to the Anti-Ballistic Missile Treaty and the Strategic Arms Limitation Treaty, both in 1972. The first treaty prevented both countries from acquiring the ability to win a nuclear war. The second one built on the trust which their commitments created to begin the process of multilateral disarmament.

Repeatedly, Schelling found situations which were too complicated for a formal model, but in which he could explain complex outcomes as the result of self-interested, strategic behaviour. Game theory was the bedrock of most of his work because it allowed him to think about how individual decisions would benefit, or harm other people. He could then explain patterns of behaviour as the result of individual choices. In this approach, he used a form of what is now called agent-based modelling to identify the emergent properties of a complex system in which people would have a range of preferences.

In one very well-known paper, published in 1971, he demonstrated that when people have a strong enough preference to have neighbours who share certain characteristics, their pattern of choices will lead to the formation of uniform communities. However, if that preference about the characteristic of neighbours is weak, communities will reflect the variety of the population. He found that there was a 'tipping point' at which the preference became strong enough for sorting to predominate. There is of course a much more negative way of describing this result. He had found that there is a critical level of discriminatory tendencies at which their effects suddenly become obvious. Small changes in people's preferences could then have very large effects on social outcomes. Discrimination might be present in society, but largely hidden.

In the early 1980s, Schelling turned his attention to the question of how each of us makes complex decisions. He became interested in explaining the emergence of habits and addiction. For economists, addiction is especially difficult to understand. People who describe themselves as addicts claim not to have control over their behaviour. They report that they want to change their pattern of behaviour, but also claim to be unable to do so. That is inconsistent with the assumption that behaviour will be self-interested. We could follow Friedman and pay no attention to these self-reports. In that case the only relevant economic data would relate to the quantities which people consume and the prices which they pay.

Schelling took a different approach. He thought of addiction as a specific example of a class of problems in which people might make a sequence of decisions, which seemed unsatisfying when they viewed their actions with some detachment. In the book, *Choice and Consequence*, he suggested that people might have competing interests, each of which could effectively be treated as a player in a game. Each of our interests could take actions, with the pattern of behaviour which emerged over time reflecting their interaction. In this approach, addictive behaviour was the result of short-run interests causing impulsive behaviour to dominate, while the pursuit of long-run interests would require awareness of the future costs of giving in to impulses.

Schelling then argued that addiction occurs when we become largely unable to control our impulsive behaviour because our short-run interests have come to dominate our thinking. He argued that breaking a pattern of addictive behaviour would often require us to find commitment strategies. These should increase the costs of a relapse into addiction, but also make those costs obvious in our thinking before following them. In this analysis, wise behaviour depends upon self-denial and hard-headed rationality. Smith would surely have approved.

Late in his career, Schelling went back to analysis of the political economy of negotiations among governments. The Carter administration asked him to prepare a report on the effects of greenhouse gas emissions in 1980, and climate change became his main professional preoccupation after he retired from Harvard and moved to the University of Maryland. Able to reflect on half a century of work on cooperation and competition between states, he argued that addressing climate change had substantial similarities with the challenges of the post-war reconstruction which the Organization for European Economic Cooperation had managed, and the 'burden sharing' negotiations of the early years of NATO. In both cases, the

USA made considerable funds available, while the institutions managing those funds invited bids for their use.

Facing the need to reduce carbon emissions, governments have a wide choice of economic tools. Quotas, bans, taxes and regulation are the classic instruments. More recently, following Coase's analysis of property rights, markets for rights to produce emissions have emerged. Schelling was dubious that such methods would be enough. In all these examples, we would manage the activities which cause emissions, rather than underlying emissions. Then there was the very long-term nature of the project and the uncertainties over how events might unfold. Uncertainty about where and when the impact of climate change might be felt added to these problems. All these factors ruled out direct negotiation of a climate change mitigation framework, which governments would then implement in their own jurisdictions.

Instead, Schelling argued for inter-governmental cooperation, which would focus on achieving the essential political objectives without too much consideration of the calculus of costs and benefits. He believed that the financial burden simply had to be taken up by the richer countries of the global north, in North America, Europe, Japan and Australasia, with even large, relatively high-income countries, such as China, effectively being recipients of aid. He thought that there would need to be competition for access to these funds, but that they should be made available wherever they could be used effectively.

Even in this late work – when he died, aged 95, he was still working on two papers – Schelling went well beyond the comfortable consensus. He believed that scientific models indicated clearly that our planned actions would take the planet well beyond the tipping point where the costs of climate change would be very high. Justifiably pessimistic about the possibilities of the necessary agreement to anything like the necessary burden-sharing being enough to solve this problem, he advocated some very unconventional measures, notably experiments into the effects of solar radiation management. The essential concept is simple. The greater the proportion of solar radiation reaching our planet which is reflected into space, rather than becoming trapped within the atmosphere, the less the effects of climate change will be.

In supporting this still rather speculative approach, and especially the scattering of clouds of sulphur particulates into the upper atmosphere, Schelling simply argued that it would allow the time for political negotiations to conclude, so that the transition to a low-carbon economy would take place without being driven by the need to keep ahead of the damaging effects of climate change. Experiments, of the sort which he considered necessary to explore the feasibility of several technologies, only began after his death in 2016.

It is perhaps more obvious in this work on climate change than in his work on nuclear deterrence that Schelling had a strong faith in the capacity of humanity to address problems. The happy warrior of the 1960s turned into the reflective scholar who urged people to be patient and imaginative in developing radical proposals for change.

Much of Schelling's work might seem more suited to political science, but through his career he was a Professor of Economics at Harvard, where, with typical self-deprecation, he styled himself an 'errant economist'. When he finally moved to the University of Maryland, the university's appointment procedure required three reference letters. Schelling obtained them from Nobel prize winners, of which Samuelson's was the briefest: 'Tom Schelling is the best economist I have known.' There is perhaps a touch of Samuelson's own love of storytelling there.

We have seen how Coase took on a leading role in establishing the study of law and economics. Simon has a claim to be the father of behavioural economics, and much else. Schelling simply applied a new approach to political economy. When economics was turning increasingly to mathematics to model the world, Schelling took care to master the mathematical principles underlying game theory, and then used them to analyse situations in which there was no possibility of using formal mathematical modelling. He developed a new type of economic analysis of cooperation and conflict between nation states, becoming one of the most influential policy analysts of the second half of the twentieth century. His academic career started with work intended to stop the Cold War from heating up. It finished with prescient analysis of how to cool the world down.

Uniting the work of Coase, Simon and Schelling, we can see a deep interest in the working of organizations. From careful observation, they made bold inductive leaps to explain something about their behaviour – Coase thinking about capability of managers to command resources, Simon about how they made decisions, and Schelling about the effects of the strategic interdependence of decision makers. Compared with Coase and Simon, Schelling took his time finding the idea which would make his reputation, first using game theory when he was in his mid-30s. But all three of them relied on simple principles, largely derived from close observation, which challenged existing thinking and expanded the sphere of economics. Although all three won the Nobel Memorial Prize, none of them were part of the mainstream of economics. They demonstrate the breadth of economic analysis and the importance of looking at the world in new ways.

18

Robert Solow – Craftsman and Builder

Explaining economic growth and managing the economy

When MIT was planning a new building for its economics department in the 1950s, it reserved the largest office for Paul Samuelson, the department's star. Samuelson insisted upon Robert Solow being given the adjoining office. Over the next four decades, as MIT came to match Harvard and Chicago as a world-leading centre of economic research, Samuelson and Solow remained neighbours. While Samuelson had laid the foundations for the new economics which the department would embrace, Solow, a remarkably tall, genial team-builder, who won the Nobel Memorial Prize in 1987 for his work on long-run economic growth, was the central figure in the department's development.

Solow has defined himself as coming to study economics on the coat-tails of the 'transitional generation', who had been graduate students when *The General Theory* appeared, and who were therefore the first to assimilate Keynes' economic analysis of the Depression. As well as Samuelson, we could add other winners of the Nobel Memorial Prize, such as Franco Modigliani and James Tobin. All were leaders of what Solow has called 'American Keynesianism'. They all believed that it was possible to manage aggregate demand in the economy to limit its fluctuations and encourage steady economic growth. Their best opportunity to put their ideas into practice came with the election of President Kennedy. Solow joined the Council of Economic Advisers, while Samuelson stayed at MIT. The buoyant economy of the 1960s did not require the vast public investment and complex economic planning of the 1930s New Deal, and so Solow and his colleagues were able to analyse the effects of specific changes to the structure of taxation on employment, growth and the distribution of incomes.

Born in 1924 in Brooklyn, Solow has claimed that everyone living there during the Great Depression of the 1930s had been interested in economics. For a Jewish boy in New York, the rise of Fascism ensured that foreign news was both fascinating and horrifying. That background led to his gradual drift towards the social sciences in his first years as an undergraduate student at Harvard, but in 1942, he enlisted in the US Army, serving until the end of the war in 1945. Choosing to remain a non-commissioned officer, he worked as a plane spotter, experiencing battle in a role in which he was an obvious target, serving in campaigns in North Africa, Sicily and Italy. For Solow, this fondly remembered time of service was an important formative experience, in which he worked with the other men in his unit to achieve a common purpose, often in situations in which their individual differences were of no significance at all.

While Solow was serving in Europe, he kept up his correspondence with Barbara Lewis, who completed her academic studies before his return to the USA and their marriage. As was customary, she gave up her work as an economic historian to look after her children, but not before she recommended economics as a discipline to her new husband. (Later in life, she would return to research on the Atlantic slave trade.) Following his return to Harvard, and his incomplete undergraduate studies, Solow's inclination to study economics solidified when he was assigned Wassily Leontief as a personal tutor. We have already met Leontief as a colleague of Schumpeter, and both Samuelson's and Schelling's dissertation supervision. At their weekly meetings, Leontief dropped hints about the range of economics papers which it would be possible for Solow to study if he had a better grounding in mathematics. The result was that Solow turned his attention to the use of mathematics in economics, just as Samuelson published *Foundations of Economic Analysis*.

To develop a deeper understanding of economics, Solow also relied on Hicks' *Value and Capital*, which was in many ways a precursor of *Foundations* and *The General Theory*. He quickly embraced the arguments of *The General Theory*, recognizing that it was the first systematic account of the whole economy. That led him to explore the art of building macroeconomic models while he was a graduate student. However, he put that interest to one side so that he could complete his doctoral dissertation, in which he developed new statistical estimates of the distribution of incomes in the USA.

The delay in completing his training meant that Solow could follow the path, which Samuelson had laid in the 1930s, and become a specialist in mathematical economics and statistics. That extended to MIT deciding that Solow, at the end of his graduate studies and recognized as Leontief's best PhD student, was worth hiring. The Institute wanted to recruit him as a professor of statistics, rather than economics. So that he could fully immerse himself in the mathematical foundations of statistics, MIT sent Solow to work for a year with Abraham Wald at Columbia University. Like von Neumann, Wald was one of the many brilliant Jewish–Hungarian academics who found their way to the USA in the 1930s. While in Germany, he had worked with von Neumann's collaborator, Oskar Morgenstern before finding the safety of a post with the Cowles Commission. He is best known for the argument which he made during

World War II, that to strengthen the airframe of bombers, we should identify where damage was rarely observed on aircraft which had returned from a mission, since we could assume that the aircraft which had suffered damage in those places typically crashed.

When Solow completed his doctoral dissertation in 1951, his thesis won the David A. Wells Prize. Unlike Samuelson, he never accepted the prize, because of the requirement that he publish it, and he thought that 'he could do it better', despite the typescript circulating widely and gaining a substantial reputation.

Although MIT had hired him as a professor of statistics, Solow continued working in economics, resuming work on macroeconomic models when he started teaching a course on business cycles. He reached back to the capital theory of Knut Wicksell, the Swedish economist who had also been an important influence on Keynes' thinking in the 1920s, and who had explained business cycles as resulting from the impact of changing inflation on the level of investment.

In his work, Solow extended capital theory to explain how economic growth might be sustained. At the time that he started this work in the early 1950s, the best-known model of economic growth had been developed separately by Keynes' protégé, Roy Harrod, and by the Russian–American development economist, Evsey Domar. The Harrod–Domar model had the very unsatisfactory characteristic of requiring the savings rate to match the growth in capacity of the economy. A higher rate of saving would feed into higher investment, and runaway economic growth. A lower rate would cause the economy to collapse. For Solow, this was simply implausible. In modern economies, while there had been major depressions, there had never been any explosive collapses, nor runaway growth. He was also concerned with the interpretation of the model for poorer countries, many of which were beginning to acquire their independence. Proponents of the model argued that there should be a strong, sustained demand for capital in these countries, so that increasing the savings rate would naturally lead to higher growth.

For Solow, this approach had the difficulty that its predictions depended far too much upon factors which were determined outside the model. There was plenty of evidence that the aggregate savings rate, which he considered to be determined primarily by social factors, also varied substantially across the business cycle. In contrast, the capital–output ratio would reflect the state of technology, while the growth rate of the labour supply would usually depend on the population. Neither of these would change quickly. Yet somehow, the cyclically variable savings rate was supposed to be equal to the product of the capital–output ratio and the growth rate of the labour supply. For Solow, the equilibrium of the model was not just unstable – it was implausible.

For Solow, a better theory of growth had to explain how there could be a stable equilibrium growth rate, which would be determined within the model. He realized that this would be possible by making different assumptions about the nature of production. The Harrod–Domar model relied upon the type of production functions which Leontief used in his models of the whole economy. That meant that capital and labour had to be used in a fixed proportion. Solow used a different formulation, which allowed for capital and labour to be used in variable proportions. Rather like the change in assumptions about the nature of production in the shift from classical political economy to neo-classical economics, Solow's model could accommodate the substitution of capital for labour in production as part of the development process, so that over time production would become more capital intensive.

While this might seem to be a minor, technical change, it was enough for Solow to produce what he naturally called a neo-classical model of economic growth in 1956. He explained that the Harrod–Domar model had treated equilibrium growth as a process of capital widening, with additional capital being required as the population – and the labour force – increased. When the economy grew, it just got bigger, without any change in its nature. With a steady rate of population growth, Solow's model also predicted a long-run equilibrium with capital widening in which savings would fund the necessary investment capital widening.

Unlike the Harrod–Domar model, though, the Solow model had a stable equilibrium. Since capital was a substitute for labour, a high savings rate would fund more investment than was needed for capital widening. The excess investment would cause capital deepening, in which the quantity of capital per worker would increase over time. In Solow's formulation, the savings rate would then fall as the economy grew, and the rate of capital deepening would gradually fall to zero.

He found that the model has some surprising characteristics. First, since the long-run growth of every country depended on capital widening, this meant that all countries would converge to a unique growth rate over a long period of time. There could still be differences in countries' incomes if savings rates were different. Countries with higher savings rates would experience more capital deepening, and so have higher incomes. It followed that raising the savings rate, as proposed by supporters of the Harrod–Domar approach, would have an immediate effect on growth, and that would lead to higher per capita income in the long-run steady state. However, in the long run, the only way to increase the growth rate would be some form of Schumpeterian innovation, which would increase the productivity of both labour and capital. Solow effectively argued that innovation would lead to creative destruction, since new investments would be more productive than old ones.

Having formulated his neo-classical growth theory, Solow went on to test it in 1957. He used data on the development of the US economy between 1909 and 1949, and found evidence of both capital widening and capital deepening. However, he also found that about half of the growth in national income could not be explained by increasing use of labour and capital in production. This share of growth, which has come to be known as the 'Solow residual' because the model does not account for it, must reflect the changing quality of capital and labour. That allows us to interpret the residual as capturing the effects of technical progress. As well as innovation and invention improving the quality of capital, improved education and training could lead to workers being more productive, while managers could also become more effective in coordinating resources.

The role of the residuals raised the same sort of questions about Solow's model as the structure of the Harrod–Domar model had raised in his mind. Solow had expected to find technical progress, but his model could not accommodate it explicitly. It would take nearly 30 years before another generation of economists would come up with a solution. In those later models, the long-run growth of the economy would depend on the level of knowledge and education, and the extent to which larger businesses would achieve higher levels of efficiency. Until the 1980s, though, Solow's model was the starting point for the economic analysis of growth.

Having landed at MIT as a young academic, Solow found it to be a congenial home and had an affiliation with the Institute after more than 70 years. One of the first academics to take part in what became regular exchanges between MIT and the University of Cambridge, he spent 1957 in England, the year in which a dispute about the nature of capital broke out between Cambridge and MIT economists. Joan Robinson, the intellectual leader of Keynes' Cambridge Circle, had concluded that the way in which Solow and Samuelson had developed an aggregate production function did not measure the use of capital correctly. This Cambridge Capital Controversy lasted nearly a decade, involved detailed exchanges, and ended up having the character of the nineteenth-century Schleswig–Holstein problem. (The British foreign minister, Lord Palmerston, supposedly remarked that it had once been understood by three people – one of whom had died, one who had gone mad, and himself – and he had forgotten the solution.)

By 1966, Samuelson was ready to concede that Robinson was correct, but Solow continued to use aggregate production functions. In Solow's approach to economics, theoretical models were simply tools to assist the development of analysis, rather than being simplified versions of the economy. Over his career, he worked with a wide variety of models, with each one designed to probe very specific problems. In developing his growth theory, he knew that the aggregate production function had unsatisfactory statistical properties, but for understanding what the data suggested about growth, he knew that there was no easy way of avoiding their use.

We can see Solow's problem-solving approach in a paper published in 1960, in which Samuelson and Solow tried to fit American inflation and unemployment data to a Phillips curve. They concluded that there was some evidence of the sort of short-run, negative relationship between the levels of inflation and unemployment which Bill Phillips had found in UK data. While they were very cautious about suggesting that it would be possible to reduce unemployment by tolerating an acceleration in the price level, this was exactly how other people tended to interpret their findings. Years later, Solow ruefully admitted that while they knew such a relationship could only last until people began to anticipate inflation, they did not make enough of that point. Instead, their rather optimistic assessment of the opportunities available to policymakers enabled Friedman to base his criticism of the American Keynesian approach to demand management on the failure of the Phillips relation in the late 1960s as inflation started to increase.

Throughout the 1950s and 1960s, the US government, irrespective of its political affiliation, had adopted many of the American Keynesians' policy proposals. Europe and Japan were rebuilding their economies after World War II, so that there was sustained economic expansion and increasingly widespread prosperity. That sense of permanent well-being did not last into the 1970s. Rapid inflation, especially following the quadrupling of the price of oil after the Yom Kippur War of 1973, and ineffective attempts by governments to control inflation, led to faltering economic growth. Conservative politicians, especially Margaret Thatcher and Ronald Reagan, adopted economic policies which drew on Hayek's libertarian tendencies, Friedman's monetarism and James Buchanan's public choice analysis of the role of the state. Younger economists went even further, arguing that all prices were flexible, including wages. That led them to interpret all unemployment as being entirely voluntary.

Accepting the Nobel Memorial Prize in 1987 for his work on growth theory, Solow noted that in his analysis, there was full employment. He argued that this reflected the intention of understanding the behaviour of the economy in the long run. Having grown up during the Great Depression, he had always considered it entirely possible that short-term fluctuations in the economy might take it away from full employment. The presumption of price flexibility in Chicago School macroeconomics concerned him deeply. That seemed to Solow to be a sign of macroeconomic theory losing touch with reality, so that economic policy advice based on its predictions would be much less effective than it could be. Given that the implications of economic theory were not just intellectual curiosities but could easily affect people's lives, Solow thought it better for policy advice to be approximately right, rather than precisely wrong.

Samuelson once described Solow as being almost the ideal economist, except for a tendency to use humour rather than engage in debate. For example, Solow wrote of Friedman in 1966: 'Everything reminds Milton of the money supply. Well, everything reminds me of sex, but I keep it out of the paper.' His review of John Kenneth Galbraith's *The New Industrial State* outraged the author. Just to take one example of Solow's darts: 'He mingles with the Beautiful People; for all I know, he may actually be a Beautiful Person himself.' He has explained this tendency to joke about disagreements on the basis that it would be pointless to start a serious discussion about tactics at the Battle of Austerlitz with someone claiming to be Napoleon.

He preferred to explain how his opponents had been effective in making their arguments. When Friedman first criticized the Phillips curve relationship, he argued that for any level of anticipated inflation, at a certain level of unemployment, inflation would be constant. That became the 'Natural Rate of Unemployment', which was interpreted as a measure of the long-run capacity of the economy. For Solow, the choice of words was important. 'Natural' suggested that it was desirable, or inevitable. Defining unemployment as 'voluntary' had much the same effect. That choice of language helped political leaders who wanted to move away from the common presumption of the 1950s and 1960s that achieving full employment should be a government's primary economic objective. As a result, in the 1980s, political leaders were able to build much greater support for sustained high unemployment as the cost of crushing inflation.

For Solow, this was much more than an observation about how the acceptability of an economic argument depends upon its formulation. He argued that differences in language would reflect beliefs about the nature of the economy, but also economics. With such fundamental differences among groups of economists, debate was difficult, and humour could soften disagreement.

There are perhaps two ways of assessing Solow's place in economics. In some ways, his growth theory completed what was possible with neo-classical economics. In the marginal revolution, the pioneers had simplified the objects of their analysis as much as possible. They replaced the complex dynamic arguments of classical political economy, concerned with distribution and growth, with a static theory, in which value was derived from the scarcity of resources in meeting needs. Growth theory once again enabled economists to think about the long-run behaviour of the economy.

Solow also built on Keynes' insights in *The General Theory* that there might be long periods when the economy was not at full employment, and that this was because information could not flow through the whole economy quickly enough. That meant that there were opportunities for government to intervene in the economy and to guide behaviour to limit economic fluctuations. Having supervised nearly 100 doctoral students at MIT, four of whom have won the Nobel Memorial Prize, he enabled the next generation of Keynesian macroeconomists to think about how information and behaviour might cause prices to adjust slowly, and unemployment to persist.

19

Gary Becker – The Unwavering Imperialist

Including ourselves among the resources
which we manage

There are no full stops in academic research. Samuelson's formalization of neo-classical economics and Solow's development of a neo-classical theory of economic growth, completed the mining of that seam of knowledge. By the time that they had finished, economists had started to explore the economy and resource management in new ways, for which their work was simply a foundation. For Gary Becker, that meant considering how we are ourselves economic resources. In Becker's approach, our bodies, our minds, our knowledge and our relationships are assets, which we manage.

Becker was born in 1930. By the time that he became an economist in the 1950s, the USA was undeniably the world's leading economic power. Its Declaration of Independence reflected the ways in which the Enlightenment had begun to transform science and philosophy. With its claim that life, liberty and the pursuit of happiness are inalienable rights, we might claim that economics is quintessentially American. Those eighteenth-century ideals seem to underpin Becker's economic analysis. He presented people as being very clear about the nature of their objectives and acting decisively to achieve them.

Relentlessly pursuing well-being, *homo economicus* – rational economic man – is Beckerian, and as American as Uncle Sam.

The mention of liberty takes us back to Hayek, Friedman and of course, Chicago, where Friedman taught the core postgraduate course in price theory for many years. When he stepped aside, Becker took it over. They shared the Chicago belief in the economy as a self-equilibrating system. In some ways, Becker took Friedman's ideas about individual behaviour to their logical conclusion. He believed that since we place a value on everything, we can use the tools of economic analysis to understand all human behaviour. His work encompassed matters as diverse as discrimination, education, crime, addiction, marriage, family life, health care and even suicide, most of which had previously been considered largely as social phenomena about which economists could say nothing.

To expand the scope of economics in this way, his work sometimes reversed the usual structure of the economic analysis of choice. Instead of specifying objectives and resource constraints, and then predicting a pattern of behaviour, Becker would often start from observed behaviour, and then work out what that implied about the form of people's objectives. Take suicide as an example of behaviour which had never really been considered in utilitarian terms before. For Becker, it would be rational to commit suicide when the costs associated with it – at the very least, the pain which we will suffer in dying – are less than the costs of continuing to live. That is simply an application of utilitarian cost-benefit analysis. However, that framing of how people might make the decision also means that we can take the traditional teaching that suicide is a mortal sin, with the soul of a suicide victim being punished after death, as being designed to affect those calculations and reduce the rate of suicide.

Understandably, this approach was always controversial. While he followed in Friedman's footsteps in some ways, Becker never engaged in politics, and so he only became notorious among social scientists. They often treated him as an economic imperialist, who had brought his alien preconceptions and analytical culture to bear on matters where there were already rich traditions of academic enquiry, of which he seemed entirely ignorant. Perhaps their wariness was largely ideological and Becker was simply too much 'of Chicago' for their tastes. But Becker also worried throughout his career that his work was too unconventional to be treated seriously by other economists. His fears finally dissolved only when he won the 1992 Nobel Memorial Prize. Those anxieties relate to the way that he changed what it means to think like an economist.

Becker first encountered economics during his undergraduate studies at Princeton. Even then, he demonstrated the tenacity and single-mindedness which characterized his career by publishing undergraduate projects as papers in the *American Economic Review*. He then went to the University of Chicago for his postgraduate studies. In the mid-1950s, in the early years of the civil rights movement, his doctoral dissertation analysed the economic effects of discrimination. In this work we can see for the first time his characteristic approach of considering a problem, seemingly involving socially determined relationships, and asking how it might be treated as the behaviour of rational, optimizing individuals.

Becker proposed that we might usefully think about some people having a 'taste' for discrimination. In the tradition of neo-classical economics, he defined tastes as shaping our preferences among alternatives from which we make choices. He argued that in the case of racial discrimination against the African American minority by members of other ethnic groups which had economic power, the larger, more privileged groups would tolerate some degree of economic inefficiency. Becker argued that the majority (white) population would choose to give up some consumption possibilities so that they could practise discrimination. For example, if discrimination led to capable workers from the minority group being systematically excluded from some types of jobs, then the overall productivity of the labour force would be reduced. In purely economic terms, society would be worse off when there was discrimination against a minority.

For members of the African American community, which in the 1950s was still subject to widespread discrimination enforced by the law in several Southern states, Becker argued that the effects would be much larger. Anticipating some of his later work on decisions about whether to enter higher education, he argued that since African Americans knew that they were likely to face discrimination after graduation, they would be less likely to go to school or college. That meant that the proportion of the population with the skills and knowledge which would usually lead to being hired into well-paid jobs would be very small.

This was essentially an extension of the standard Marshallian analysis, and wholly in keeping with the Chicago tradition. It predicted that the effects of discrimination would be larger when the taste for discrimination was strong, and the group experiencing discrimination was small. Is also predicted that there would be differences in the nature and effects of different types of discrimination. For example, he argued that the forms which racial discrimination against a small minority might take would be very different to the sex-based discrimination which affected women, who constituted half of the population. It might be better to say that there is an implication in Becker's analysis that we should expect to see countries in which there is extensive discrimination against women struggling to enable economic and social development.

For Becker's critics in other social sciences, even in this early work he demonstrated the weaknesses of viewing social phenomena through the lens of economics. Especially since the 1950s, social movements have been able to address many of the most egregious sources of discrimination. There is plenty of evidence that (at least) in liberal, democratic societies, discriminatory behaviour has become much less socially acceptable. Becker's approach allowed him to measure differences in economic outcomes across groups, and to attribute those differences to the presumed taste for discrimination.

That stopped him from addressing either how discrimination might have emerged, or how it might be overcome. In typical Chicago fashion, he assumed that tastes were given – although he refined what he meant by tastes over the course of his career to allow for the expression of tastes changing over time with experience. The older Becker might well have argued that when people from the majority group start to encounter people from the minority group, then their knowledge of the group will change, and the extent to which they will discriminate will change. Collaboration between Becker and Schelling on discrimination could have had interesting results.

One of Becker's dissertation supervisors was Ted Schultz, who chaired the Chicago Department of Economics through the 1950s. Schultz started his career in the late 1920s as an agricultural economist. By the 1950s, he had moved into development economics, analysing how workers could move from informal, relatively unproductive roles in rural districts into relatively productive, formal roles in urban industry. This was also the process of the Great Migration which took African Americans from the Southern states of the USA to the cities of the Midwest, including Detroit and Chicago. In moving into development economics, Schultz had begun to think in terms of education involving the formation of human capital, a term which we can understand either as one of the most powerful metaphors in economics, or else as evidence of economists' tendency to reduce society to a network of material relationships.

Suppose that we try to classify all activities as either leisure or work. Reading a novel is leisure. Writing one is work. But what about a student reading an economics book? That seems more like work, except that students must often pay to study. Schultz realized that study is like investment and that the knowledge which students acquire is a form of capital: an asset which they might use in their future employment, with the return on capital coming from higher wages.

The idea was ripe for exploration, and in the late 1950s Becker moved from Chicago to work at Columbia with Jacob Mincer, who turned Schultz's concept into the cornerstone of modern labour economics. Working at the National Bureau for Economic Research, Becker produced his own study on the returns to human capital acquired in general education. Rather curiously, while he never seemed to harbour doubts about the economic analysis of discrimination, he worried that critics would decry the reduction of education to greater earning potential, and that likening education to capital formation would suggest that he viewed people as machines.

It had taken economists most of the nineteenth century to understand the nature of capital in an industrial society. Physical capital, in the form of plant and machinery, consists of goods made for the purpose of making other goods. That makes capital a productive asset. For labour economists, the counterpart was to abstract from the complexity of education and simply concentrate upon evidence that education engenders knowledge. If that knowledge is economically useful, it will increase workers' productivity, and employers would reward educated workers by paying them higher wages. In some ways, this idea of human capital is hardly novel. It is part of the practical wisdom of Aristotelian prudence.

Becker took this concept of human capital and made it the cornerstone of his approach to economics. In defining general human capital, he went well beyond thinking about it as the result of education. Observing that in most roles, wages increase with workers' experience, he argued that experience must therefore contribute to human capital, since it appeared to be being rewarded.

He thought that there would be important differences between various types of human capital. University education would typically form general human capital, which would be usable in any type of employment. Workplace experience, which would involve immersion in the routines and practices of a specific workplace, would not be so easily transferrable. Making this distinction, Becker could explain the finding that as workers approached retirement, they tended to be paid a little less than slightly younger workers. While they had greater experience, they had typically spent less time in education and so had less formal training. This justified them being paid lower wages. An additional argument would be that if education and formal training are investments, then older workers will usually have fewer years during which they would be paid higher wages, and so they will be less likely to keep on building human capital. If we also make allowance for the gradual attenuation of skills and knowledge over time, as bodies change and memories fade, then older workers should be less productive quite naturally.

Initially, human capital was a useful shorthand for the accumulation of skills, knowledge and experience, which are valuable in paid work. Over time, Becker generalized from this initial idea. Experience is simply spending time engaged in activity. We acquire experiences all the time, for example, when we go to a new restaurant, or meet new neighbours, or travel as a tourist to a country which we have never visited before. Those experiences will change our behaviour. Holding on to the Chicago assumption that preferences are constant, Becker introduced the idea of 'experience capital' to explain how this might happen. What we call our preferences might largely be the result of forming an idea of what we like from our past experiences.

Such substantial contributions to economic analysis might seem to be enough for any career, but Becker was just getting into his stride. There is a famous story of him falling into the economic analysis of crime at the end of the 1960s when he hurriedly parked his car illegally on the way to examine a doctoral student at Columbia. Supposedly, he started the examination by asking the student to explain why he had just risked receiving a parking ticket.

He also found many ways of extending the work on human capital, one of the most important being studies of health as a form of capital. We can invest in our health by choosing behaviours which will improve our physical and mental well-being now and in the future. Effectively, this treated health as a form of experience capital.

Experience capital was also a necessary concept for work on addiction, which Becker carried out in the 1980s with his former research student, Kevin Murphy. With prior consumption affecting current payoffs, they argued that people will take into account how their current consumption will affect the benefits of future consumption. The formation of harmful habits would occur if two conditions were met. First, current consumption of the addictive substance should be very pleasing. Secondly, through the formation of experience capital, it should reduce the future benefits of consumption of all goods, but especially the alternatives to the addictive good. Addicts would then report diminished satisfaction and dependence on the good.

The commitment to explaining behaviour as the outcome of forward-looking, rational choice meant that Becker and Murphy saw addiction as the best which people could do from a very bad starting point. They saw addicts as being rational within the context of their history of consumption choices. We can compare this with Schelling's approach, in which people could see the environment very differently as their mental state changed.

For Becker, though, the apex of his career and the most demanding work which he ever undertook, was on the economics of the family. To develop his analysis, he attempted to understand the nature of familial relationships in many different cultures. This ended up being his most controversial work because it seemed to reduce complex social relationships to self-interested, economically rational behaviour. In Becker's approach, families coalesce and remain stable when membership provides value, net of contributions to the family group, to all their members. Relationships are therefore essentially transactional and there is no place for love or any of the other complex emotions which we all feel about our families.

In such a transactional approach, families should dissolve – or at the very least some members should leave – if an option outside the family emerges, which is more rewarding. This is just a way of framing the problem before applying the tools of economic analysis. To understand what a family is, how it forms, stays together and splits up, we need to understand much about the society in which these groups have formed.

Becker therefore plunged into lengthy discussions of how specialization of roles within a family might have emerged historically across many societies. For this, he received plenty of criticism for taking an anti-feminist approach with his model in which a *paterfamilias* made all the decisions, including the allocation of resources and work for the whole family. Against that interpretation, social conservatives have criticized the implication of his work that women would be more likely to quit marriages if the labour market opportunities available to them increased, arguing that his work gives a licence for divorce. Overall, the book was a superb attempt to apply economic reasoning to the development of human relationships, and it sits well within the liberal tradition in which people respond imaginatively to the choices which they believe that they have.

Much of *A Treatise on the Family* was devoted to how we raise children. As so often, this now seems to be a standard part of economics, but it was Becker who first thought about it. Whether it is true that at a party in Chicago, Becker announced excitedly to the eminent Chicago labour economist Arnold Harberger that 'children are like refrigerators' hardly matters. It depicts Becker as he was as a young man – intense, driven and imaginative. He was thinking about how to use his favoured tools of economic analysis to understand the allocation of resources in a situation in which there could not be any markets or any prices. In Becker's approach, parents have a choice between immediate consumption and making investments in their children's economic capacity, as a form of transfer of wealth across generations.

The most famous example in *A Treatise on the Family* is the 'rotten kid theorem', which explains parents' ability to affect their children's behaviour through their capacity to make future financial gifts. The theorem states that it is possible that the expectation of future bequests will lead even selfish children to choose the behaviour which maximizes the family income. While it has been easy for other economic theorists to explore situations in which the theorem fails, we must remember that like much of Becker's work, it sets out interesting possibilities for deeper exploration.

Winning a Nobel Memorial Prize typically involves having one simple idea, which transforms the way in which other economists understand a field. Becker's fundamental insight was that whenever there is choice to be made about how to manage the use of resources, we can apply economic insights. We are not restricted to situations in which there are prices and markets. His early work on discrimination naturally led into the analysis of human capital, allowing him to think of people as self-managing resources. From within economics, that initially led to questioning about why he was studying such problems. In other social sciences, his approach seemed at once naïve and threatening.

This economic approach to human behaviour has almost infinite possibilities, even, as with Robert Barro's *The Economics of Brushing Teeth*, parody. Becker's work was a distillation of the Chicago price theory tradition. In the fable of the fox and the hedgehog, Becker was a fox. He knew many things and so kept coming across ways in which he could apply his knowledge differently.

20

Elinor Ostrom – The Political Scientist

*Systems for the collective management of resources
will emerge organically*

At last, a woman.

Over time, as society has changed, roles have become much less gendered. When Marshall opposed the admission of women into Cambridge, he seemed old fashioned. But at that time, women still had limited property rights and could not vote. They could think about the economy – and so Harriet Taylor, Mary Paley, Elizabeth Boody, Lydia Lopokova, Rose Director, Marion Crawford, Dorothea Pye and Barbara Lewis have appeared as wives and supporters of their husbands' careers. But to write about the economy, and to be a professor, was a male privilege for many years.

We have seen that Paley, Boody and even Lopokova took on faithful, caring roles, extending their spouses' careers. Rose Director and Milton Friedman were active collaborators on political economy (publishing as Milton and Rose Director Friedman). Dorothea Pye and Herbert Simon worked together on research in psychology. Barbara Lewis eventually built her own reputation as an economic historian. Social change was gradual. Even in the middle of the twentieth century, many women completed their university education, married, had children, and became the main caregivers in their families.

In economics, Joan Robinson was the obvious exception to this rule. While she married at the age of 22 in 1925 and, quite conventionally, had two daughters, she was also one of the members of Keynes' Cambridge Circle. Widely expected to win the Nobel Memorial Prize in 1975, whether because of her gender, or left-wing political sympathies, that did not happen. Instead, it took until 2009, 40 years after the first award of the prize, for the Swedish Academy to honour a woman, Elinor (Lin) Ostrom.

Born Elinor Awan in Los Angeles in 1933, she grew up in a relatively poor family, but was a pupil at Beverly Hills High School, where many students were much wealthier. That enabled her to imagine going to university and obtaining a degree. She supported herself financially through undergraduate studies at UCLA, and then started down the conventional path. Marriage to a fellow UCLA student took her to Massachusetts, where she found that potential employers expected her to have shorthand. So, she learned that, although she never used it in work. Instead, she became the assistant manager in a personnel department – the first woman employee in the firm other than secretaries. She then started to think about applying to return to university to complete a PhD. Her marriage failed as a result and she returned to California.

At UCLA, the economics department refused to admit her as a postgraduate student. Having been steered away from mathematics while she was at high school, she lacked the necessary background in the subject to become an academic economist. Instead, she was offered a place on the political science program. She later discovered that some staff had been unsettled by the prospect of taking on four women (in a cohort of 40). They had expressed concerns that female students would struggle to find good employment after graduation, and how that would reflect badly on the reputation of the department.

This experience of discrimination continued after her marriage to Vincent Ostrom in 1963, 14 years her senior, and already an Associate Professor. After she completed her doctoral training in 1965, the Ostroms looked for an institution willing to hire them both. The University of Indiana eventually agreed, but Lin Ostrom had to make do initially with the rather precarious position of Visiting Assistant Professor, hired for a year to cover short-term teaching needs. A permanent position followed the following year. Gradually, she built her reputation. In 1973, she and her husband founded the Workshop in Political Theory and Policy Analysis at the University of Indiana. Now known as the Ostrom Workshop, it has operated for more than 50 years and anchors an international network of collaboration in political science.

When the Ostroms married in 1963, Vincent had a substantial reputation for his work on water rights management in Southern California, where the steadily growing population had outstripped supplies. The rapid extraction of water from underground aquifers was causing potentially irreversible damage. For example, in the Western Basin of Los Angeles, whose management became the subject of Lin Ostrom's doctoral dissertation, there was a risk of salt-water ingress, which would make the water unusable. Several cities sat on top of the basin, and all of them had access rights to water. She concluded that smaller cities tended to be highly effective managers. They were able to monitor water use more effectively, but also gave members of their community more opportunities to engage with contractors who managed the water resources. Across the region, there was plenty of evidence of people 'voting with their feet' and moving from cities which managed resources poorly. She argued that diversity of provision had helped to improve outcomes.

The Ostroms' research demonstrated how a network of voluntary agreements had emerged to manage shared resources very effectively. Their findings, like Schelling's arguments about how governments can learn to cooperate, challenged the common belief in the 1950s that effective government would require a single authority. In its place, Vincent Ostrom had begun to develop the concept of polycentric management of resources, in which there could be multiple centres of authority with overlapping responsibilities.

At Indiana, Lin Ostrom took the idea of polycentric management much further. Her early research was on the perceived effectiveness of local government. Aware that people might be biased in their appraisal of the quality of service, whenever possible, Ostrom and her research assistants would obtain objective measures, for example of the intensity of street lighting, or the number and size of potholes – that involved crouching down in roadways with measuring tapes.

Her most important study assessed the quality of police departments. In the USA, there are multiple police jurisdictions and organizations have overlapping authority. Ostrom concluded that across a wide range of service measures, such as patrolling streets, managing traffic, responding to reports of incidents and investigating crimes, the evidence was against larger organizations being more efficient than smaller ones. There was also very little evidence of overlapping jurisdictions being problematic. Polycentric institutions worked well for the public.

Such work was related to Hayek's theories about how spontaneous order might emerge, with institutions for collective action resulting from a shared willingness to cooperate. Where Hayek ended up immersed in legal and philosophical speculation, Ostrom took a much more strongly empirical approach, using laboratory experiments to observe how institutions might emerge, and develop, and comparing the outcomes of those experiments with carefully collected data from the field. That ensured that the results of her research were extremely robust.

ELINOR OSTROM

There were also important parallels with Simon's early work into the efficiency of local government organizations. Where Simon took the institutional structure as being given, and explored the quality of public service administration, Ostrom was interested in understanding the size of community within which specific types of institution might exercise their authority effectively. The success of polycentric structures confirmed that this was not the simple optimization problem which Simon imagined as a student. In relatively large communities, while a single organization might have the capabilities needed to deliver the service, the remoteness of the authority could easily lead to substantial failures in service provision. Such a bureaucracy might act without engaging sufficiently with the community which it is supposed to serve, developing impractical or defective processes, which fail to meet local needs, so that ultimately the public authority would lose some legitimacy.

Ostrom's work also ran contrary to a narrow interpretation of game theory, in which people pursue narrowly defined self-interest, seemingly oblivious to socially desirable objectives. In experimental economics, the equivalent of the Prisoner's Dilemma is the 'voluntary contribution game' in which there are many players, who need to choose between acting cooperatively or selfishly. Among farmers in a developing country, cooperation could involve giving up time to repair a reservoir and clearing irrigation ditches. All the farmers will benefit from the other farmers' efforts, but there will not be any penalty imposed upon shirkers. If only one farmer stays in his fields, while the rest of the community does the work, then he will see almost no reduction in his access to water. Such a 'free-rider' will certainly be better off than if he had joined the communal work. The problem is that what is true for any single farmer is true for all of them. Self-interest should lead to shirking and the gradual loss of the irrigation system.

A related argument had become widely accepted following the publication of Garrett Hardin's 1968 article, *The Tragedy of the Commons*. Hardin claimed that people's selfishness would always prevent cooperation. He defined 'the commons' in much the same way as Ostrom later defined a common pool, as resources which are jointly owned by many people. Hardin's example of grazing rights had the same logic as the irrigation problem. Since any farmer might let her animals loose to graze on common land, they all would. Hardin argued that self-interest would gradually degrade the commons, until it became unusable.

There seemed to be plenty of evidence supporting Hardin's argument. Throughout Europe, over many centuries, land which had been held in common, with everyone having access, gradually became private property. With the formalization of property rights, farmers who wanted to use the land had to lease it. Landlords seemed to have much stronger incentives to husband the resources than the many people who had been able to use it before.

We see similar problems with marine fisheries. Since fish can travel huge distances in the sea, fishing can take place almost anywhere. Hardin argued that no one would have any incentive to maintain these resources, with overfishing the almost inevitable result. The only alternative would be for government to provide the necessary structure to stop rational, but selfish, behaviour, destroying the common pool resource.

Ostrom objected to the claim that property rights could only exist formally, in law, instead of being the result of custom and practice. Building on her doctoral studies of management of water resources in California, she found many examples of stable systems for managing water and grazing rights, all managed by communities which shared access to resources. Often these management systems had persisted for centuries. Those examples demonstrated that at the very least, there was no need for the management of the commons to be flawed. For that reason, Ostrom liked to talk about the 'Drama of the Commons', in which there could be desperate failure but also joyous success.

In laboratory experiments Ostrom set out to understand just what was needed to enable cooperation to be effective. She concluded that there was only one experimental design in which the tragedy of the commons would happen. People needed to be isolated, anonymous users of a resource. That could perhaps be a problem with a marine fishery, in which a boat might travel halfway around the world to exploit a resource in international waters, which had no legal protection.

However, the experimental results showed that simply allowing participants to talk with one another would change their behaviour, by opening channels for cooperation. It turned out that participants in her experiments behaved in much the same way as Schelling had concluded that governments would. If they can see that they share a problem, they will tend to find ways of working together to resolve it. Adam Smith would have been unsurprised. Once again, people turn out to be social animals who tend to truck and barter, working together to solve problems.

For Ostrom, resource management required a set of rules which would limit use of a resource without exhausting it. In many of the agricultural communities in which she found communal land management still being practised, there was a strong connection between farmers and the land, with many farmers expecting the pattern of farming to continue after their deaths. As a result, each generation accepted their responsibility to steward resources and pass them on to subsequent generations. In general, to manage these resources effectively, the number of users had to remain stable and so rules would specify how user rights could be bequeathed on death. In such practices, we see an application of the medieval understanding that ownership of property should be conditional on proper use.

Many of the factors affecting the form and effectiveness of management rules lay outside of the control of the community. These might include the political history of the community, and the nature of the legal system of the country in which the community was located, especially as these affected rights over land. Religious practices and beliefs could also be important. In addition to these social factors, the nature of the resource, the ease with which it could replenish itself, and uncertainty about that ability, would also be important factors in designing a management system.

Ostrom drew together all the strands of her research into her general framework for institutional analysis and development, comprising six principles. While it has been important for economists, this tool for understanding resource management was grounded in political science. Its purpose was to understand better how communities had found a distinctive way of managing resources. It demonstrated that despite the diversity of resource types, and management systems, stable systems had many shared characteristics (which tended to be absent from others).

First, the common pool resource would be well-defined. Typically, that would mean specifying both the area being managed and who would have access rights. Secondly, there would be participatory management, which would give voice to all users. It was important for there to be a process by which users might agree to management arrangements, especially if those needed to adapt to changing external conditions. For example, in the management of a water resource, if there is prior agreement about how additional restrictions can be put in place during a drought, users are more likely to accept them.

That takes us to the question of how best to monitor behaviour. The third principle is that it is likely that there will be extensive monitoring, with the monitors responsible to the whole community. Monitoring almost presumes penalties for breach of rules, but the fourth principle is that such penalties will generally be social, with economic penalties, such as fines, too small to deter breaches of the rules. There also needs to be the opportunity for participants to object to monitors' decisions. That gives the fifth principle, that there will be a forum in which disputes can be aired and resolved – and that, as with rule setting, such a forum should involve the wider community. Lastly, rather than imposing a rigid formal structure for use of the resource, the sixth principle is that participants should be able to work together in informal groups.

In this work, Ostrom complemented Oliver Williamson's adaption of Coase's arguments about the nature of the firm, for which he won the Nobel Memorial Prize with Ostrom. Williamson analysed how economic activity takes place either in markets, through voluntary exchange, or else in hierarchies, allowing the command of resources. Ostrom argued that the emergence of institutions which enable people to cooperate will allow them to achieve outcomes which they could not by themselves. As Schelling had already demonstrated, such cooperation and negotiation are a third type of resource management, which complements Williamson's markets and hierarchies.

More broadly, Ostrom effectively gave us a theory of the emergence of government. Leave aside the question of exactly what services governments should provide. In democratic societies, citizens acquiesce in a loss of autonomy which allows governments to provide many services. The ability of governments to provide services depends on citizens' willingness to pay taxes. That would vanish if people followed the narrowly rational strategy of evading taxes and started to free ride.

We can think of government as satisfying the design principles which Ostrom developed for resource management. Each country has a government and a tax system with unique characteristics, which are the result of their historical development and many other external factors. The boundaries of a country are well-defined and citizenship, or residence, is the basis for people having access to services (and the obligation to pay taxes). Appeals to patriotism within a country – perhaps most obviously where a government is seeking to encourage forced saving to finance a war – emphasize the expectation that the country will outlast the present generation. Governments also establish substantial monitoring of tax compliance and the relative size of sanctions depends on the perceived seriousness of any breach of compliance – although few governments rely purely on social sanctions, rather than fines and even imprisonment, to punish tax evasion. In democratic states, governments are constituted by elected representatives who can be dismissed if they are seen to have failed to manage the common pool resource. We can think of elections as being the process by which the country's population assents to changes to the rules for managing it.

We usually apply the metaphor of the invisible hand to markets, explaining that there does not need to be a central mind which decides how much should be produced and at what price it will be sold. The interactions of many buyers and sellers will be enough to establish order, giving the impression of design. Ostrom's work should remind us that every market is a complex social institution. Buyers and sellers need to be able to find each other, communicate, and decide the terms of their transactions.

Ostrom was interested to find out how people could manage situations in which cooperation would be beneficial for everyone, so long as it could be sustained. Perhaps the most important result for economists is that she found that most people are willing to work together. The principles which she set out seem obvious in many ways. They have the effect of restraining excessive demands, while providing equal rights of access. Relying on temperance, prudence and justice, they allow us to understand more about the process through which Hayek's social institutions might have emerged. They are also consistent with the social philosophy of Smith's *Theory of Moral Sentiments*.

21

Daniel Kahneman and Amos Tversky – Two Psychologists

How the processes which we use to make decisions have predictable failings

In thinking about the economy, two heads are almost always better than one. Great ideas tend to emerge from teamwork. Even so, the partnership between the psychologists Daniel Kahneman and Amos Tversky was exceptional. First, it endured, lasting for more than 25 years and only ending with Tversky's death in 1996. Secondly, it was immensely productive in establishing modern behavioural economics. Their work won Kahneman the Nobel Memorial Prize in 2002. Had Tversky lived, he would undoubtedly have shared the award. The working relationship had been so close that, rather like Lennon and McCartney, it was not always clear who had done what.

In behavioural economics, information is a resource and decision making is costly. Its explanation of decision making has much in common with Herbert Simon's understanding that behaviour is rational when it follows a standardized process and economizes on the use of information. But behavioural economics has diverged from Simon's thinking by arguing that people systematically fail to apply mental processes correctly because of the short-cuts which they take when they process information.

As psychologists, Tversky and Kahneman knew that while our brains are wonderful in many ways, they are still imperfect. We might think of them as having evolved to be very effective in engaging with the environment which our ancestors faced, but much less effective when we start dealing with the typical problems of a modern society. The weaknesses in decision making which psychologists and behavioural economists have identified result from people over-estimating the importance of whatever they can recall or recognize immediately.

When Kahneman and Tversky found evidence that the presentation of information affected decisions, they did not claim to have found evidence that we are irrational. They simply concluded that they had found still more evidence of widespread information-processing biases. Kahneman explained how these biases could arise in his intellectual autobiography, *Thinking, Fast and Slow*. He suggested that we make most decisions using System 1 processes, which are 'always on', and so used by default, but make some using an alternative System 2, in which decision making involves conscious thought.

System 1 thinking is fast, intuitive and uses very little information. It means going with our instincts. This system manages unconscious responses to our environment, like spitting out very hot food which is scalding our mouths, and routine activities such as parking a car. For elite sports players, letting System 2 get involved in their decision making can damage their performance badly. It is too slow, and too demanding of mental resources to be effective in a highly competitive context where speed of decision making is critical. System 2 is much better for a grandmaster playing chess or an engineer calculating the load which a beam will need to bear. That makes System 2 an important part of what it means to be human. But usually, it sits in reserve, and we decide to switch it on when we are alerted to something novel in the decision which we are trying to make which makes us think that it will outperform System 1.

Such a dual decision-making system will have systemic weaknesses. Suppose that you are using System 1, and making quick decisions, of which you are barely conscious. Imagine that there is a subtle change in your environment, and that if you had already engaged System 2, you would now use it. But because you are using System 1, there might not be any cue which alerts you to use System 2, and so you carry on using System 1. That gives us a way of understanding Kahneman and Tversky's early work.

From the early 1970s, they started to use the term 'heuristic' for the decision-making rules which they assumed that people would need to use. Their proposed heuristics were based on the belief that when people encounter information, they will try to fit it to the situation which they think that they are facing, as well as using the information which is easiest for them to use. Then they designed experiments in which using heuristics as part of System 1 thinking might mislead people. When the experiments worked, they had evidence of bias in decision making.

First, they defined the representativeness heuristic as a tendency to look for the expected structure in information. In an early experiment, they asked researchers to make intuitive judgements about problems, all of which were solvable using simple statistical concepts which were widely used in research. The participants in the experiment appeared to expect that the statistical properties of a small group of observations should be very similar to those of the whole population from which they were drawn. For example, think about tossing a coin repeatedly. In a very long sequence, we would expect the number of heads and tails to be approximately equal. But we would be very surprised if heads and tails simply alternated. Such a sequence would not look random.

What about a short sequence of ten tosses of a coin? It might seem that a sequence of five heads followed by five tails (HHHHHTTTTT) is less likely to occur than observing some specific sequence such as HTTHHTHHTT. That intuition is wrong, though. A moment's reflection on the statistical properties of a sequence of coin tosses should have been enough to convince the research scientists participating in the experiment that every possible sequence is equally probable. That is one of the basic results of the theory of probability.

For Tversky and Kahneman the tendency of professionals to expect a small sample to look like the whole population in miniature was the first evidence that reliance on heuristics could cause bias in decision making.

While that result may seem to be of little practical importance, it led Tversky and Kahneman to explain how we can be misled by information. Their classic experiment from 1983 began by providing this information:

Linda is 31 years old, single, outspoken and very bright. She majored in philosophy. As a student, she was deeply concerned with issues of discrimination and social justice, and also participated in anti-nuclear demonstrations.

They then asked this question: Which is more probable?

A. Linda is a bank teller.
B. Linda is a bank teller and is active in the feminist movement.*

---

*It surely says something about the way that our minds work that when I planned to include this experiment, I recalled that Linda was a librarian. My memory had edited the information given to participants so that it was entirely consistent. The information which the participants were given was perhaps intended to make them think that it was unlikely that Linda would have chosen to work in a bank. But, sometimes, needs must and perhaps that turned out to be the best option available to her. To give you some context, 1983 was in the middle of the highest period of unemployment in the USA since 1945, so that there were plenty of young graduates who simply had to make do with almost any job. It is also possible that Linda, on graduating from college in 1974, just as President Nixon resigned, voted for Jimmy Carter in 1976, and then for Ronald Reagan in 1980, as she set aside her youthful concerns. In becoming more conservative while she was in her 20s, she would have followed the same path as Friedman and Hayek.

The problem is that we read the text and we are ready to classify Linda as a feminist activist. We want our description of Linda to be representative of the information which we have been given. Whenever an example like this is used most people, including scientists who regularly use statistics in their research, think that it is probable that Linda is a feminist bank teller. However, there cannot be as many bank tellers who are also feminist activists as there are bank tellers. While it is plausible that Linda is both a bank teller and a feminist activist, the combination cannot be more probable than her simply being a bank teller. Again, our judgement leads us astray, and we see what we want to see.

As well as representativeness, Kahneman and Tversky defined an availability heuristic. They related this to the ease of recall of information given to participants at the start of an experiment. Kahneman has since concluded that it is more useful to think about information being accessible when it is easy to use. Regardless of how we explain their findings, they found plenty of evidence that the form in which people encounter information affects its accessibility. Many good teachers understand this, and so think carefully about how to make materials easily understood, with plenty of memorable examples.

Accessibility is very important in making choices. If you are going to a restaurant, you might choose the first one that you come to, or the one that you went to last week, or one where you recently had an especially good experience. Mentally, they all are accessible, but in different ways. That makes accessibility a very useful, if imperfect, tool for making decisions with minimal information. It builds on Simon's thinking about bounded rationality and Schelling's concept of a focal point. In his Grand Central Station game, he gave people a coordination problem where they were missing important pieces of information. He found that people could solve the problem by identifying information which would be accessible to everyone. Representativeness and accessibility seem to be important in explaining the speed and ease of System 1 thinking.

The presentation of information affects its accessibility and that has many implications for the choices which we tend to make. The optimization approach to rational choice has led us to think about the content, rather than presentation, of information – another legacy of Friedman's essay on *Methodology*. In a series of experiments, Tversky and Kahneman demonstrated how the use of language might affect our willingness to commit resources.

In the best known of these, carried out in 1981, they asked people to think about developing a treatment for a novel disease. In both versions of the problem, they emphasized that without the treatment, 600 people would die, and they described two government programmes designed to tackle the disease.

In the first version, the choice was between a programme which would save 200 lives and one which had a one in three probability of saving all 600 lives. In the second version, the choice was between preventing deaths: either the certain avoidance of 200 deaths or a one in three probability of preventing 600 deaths.

In the first version, a clear majority (72 per cent) preferred the programme which would certainly save 200 lives. In the second version, a larger majority (78 per cent) preferred the programme with a one in three probability of preventing 600 deaths.

The only difference between the two scenarios was in the framing of the problem by using different language. Talking in terms of 'saving lives' or 'preventing deaths' changed the decisions which people made. For many participants, it seemed better to be certain of saving some lives, while to others it seemed better to risk preventing all the deaths. This experiment has been replicated many times – including during the Covid pandemic, where it may even have led to a shift in emphasis from 'saving lives' to 'preventing deaths' in some public messaging. The experiments suggest a tendency for people to prefer certain benefits but tolerate risks to limit losses.

Finding that the framing of problems affected decision making led Kahneman and Tversky to propose that, when facing an uncertain environment, people might try to avoid losses, rather than the uncertainty itself. Together with their understanding of choice heuristics, that insight underpinned the work for which Kahneman won the Nobel Memorial Prize.

To introduce that, we need to go back a dinner held in Paris to 1951. During a symposium on decision theory, the French economist Maurice Allais offered his dinner guests a little entertainment. Effectively, he wanted to test whether the experienced decision makers at the symposium would recognize the pattern between two descriptions of a choice – anticipating the role of framing which Kahneman and Tversky developed 30 years later.

Allais asked his audience to state which one of a pair of situations they would prefer to take part in:

A1 A 100 per cent chance of 100 million francs
A2 An 89 per cent chance of 100 million francs; a
     1 per cent chance of nothing; and a 10 per cent chance
     of 500 million francs.

He then presented a second pair of situations, again asking his guests to say which one they would prefer to take part in:

B1 An 89 per cent chance of nothing; and an 11 per cent
     chance of 100 million francs
B2 A 90 per cent chance of nothing; and a 10 per cent
     chance of 500 million francs.

At the time, 100 million francs was worth about $250,000, so the numbers which Allais chose were very large, perhaps to ensure that everyone took the decisions seriously. Think about those alternatives for a moment before reading on and decide what you would have chosen.

Should you have chosen A1 and B2, then you would have expressed the same preferences as many guests at the symposium. For Allais this was a very pleasing result. He was dealing with people who were familiar with von Neumann's and Morgenstern's mathematical analysis of expected utility, which requires that people concentrate only on differences between the situations which they might face. He had deliberately made that difficult to do.

In the choice between taking part in situation A1 or situation A2, there was an 89 per cent chance of 100 million francs. Across the situations B1 and B2, there is an 89 per cent chance of nothing. Extract those common elements and the differences can be written as

C1 A 100 per cent chance of 100 million francs.
C2 A 9 per cent chance of nothing; and a 91 per cent chance of 500 million francs.

According to the expected utility theory, the common elements in lotteries A1 and A2 should not affect choices. Nor should the common elements in lotteries B1 and B2. If we knew which choice someone would make between lottery C1 and lottery C2, we should be able to predict choices in the other situations. People should either choose lottery one in all three situations, A, B, and C, or else, they should consistently choose lottery two. The most common choice, A1 and B2 was therefore an anomaly, which quickly become known as Allais' paradox. For Kahneman and Tversky, this was more evidence of framing effects affecting decision making. When they came to set out prospect theory (their behavioural explanation of choice under risk), they began from a version of Allais' paradox – we can of course think of that as a form of framing to make the ideas of this pair of psychologists more acceptable to economists.

They emphasized the role of loss aversion and argued that there was experimental evidence of people feeling losses more keenly than gains – as a rule of thumb they suggested that the pain of losing a certain amount is about twice the pleasure of the equivalent gain. They argued that people tend to prefer certain gains to gambles of the same expected value but preferred to gamble to avoid a certain loss. Thinking about losses and gains allowed them to refer to the framing of choices, emphasizing that people would usually be interested in changes relative to some reference level of wealth.

That enabled them to interpret Allais' paradox in terms of the framing of the two problems. There was a certain gain of 100 million francs in alternative A1, and even in alternative A2, the most probable outcome was a gain of 100 million francs. Reading the problem, we might think of participants seeing the gain of 100 million as their reference wealth. They then would have a choice between receiving their reference wealth and a gamble in which they might suffer an avoidable loss, or else enjoy a substantial gain. Many people preferred the certainty of A1.

In alternative B, the natural choice of reference dependent wealth was nothing. That made the choice about different combinations of gains and probabilities. For many people, the small reduction in probability of winning the much larger prize in B2 seemed worth bearing.

They set out prospect theory to explain why people do not always behave according to the principles set out in the mathematical formulation of economic theory. Expected utility theory was one of the high points of this approach. From its development by von Neumann and Morgenstern, it had had many critics, Simon and Hayek among the most prominent of them. With their development of behavioural economics, Kahneman and Tversky gathered together much of that criticism by emphasizing the importance of understanding how we describe choices, and how we make them quickly and intuitively, using the most accessible information. Their theory of decision making was intended to reflect the cognitive abilities with which we have been endowed through processes of evolution and perhaps also socialization.

We will often make mistakes in the way that we manage information. If those mistakes are obvious, then we will correct them. However, there are many situations in which the nature of the mistakes will not be obvious. For example, dietary choices may lead to weight gain and eventually obesity, increasing the probability of health problems in later life. Schelling had explored the problem in terms of competing interests, while for Becker this was a matter of developing our human capital, and so forming habits. Where Schelling believed that it was necessary to develop strategies so that our longer-term interests might predominate, for Becker, habits were difficult to break because of the way that they formed. In behavioural economics, breaking habits was likely to involve System 2 thinking, and a substantial reframing of the problem. Unsurprisingly, the behavioural approach was closer to Schelling's thinking than Becker's.

This leads into the work of Richard Thaler, one of the first economists to realize the importance of Tversky and Kahneman's work, who won the Nobel Memorial Prize in 2017. Thaler built a considerable public reputation with his book *Nudge*. Working with Cass Sunstein, a law professor, Thaler has argued that by making small changes to the ways in which people encounter information, public authorities can help them to make more effective decisions. A very simple example, which Thaler and Sunstein often use, is when a workplace restaurant places salads and vegetarian dishes where they are the first to be seen – and the easiest reached. As people pass through the servery, more people will choose these options. The approach has been very successful in some ways, although debate continues about whether it is acceptable for public authorities to guide decision makers towards the information they might need to have. Arguably, that will reduce individual autonomy in decision making.

In behavioural economics, information is a resource which we must manage. It presumes that intuitive decision-making processes match our cognitive capacities. These allow us to make decisions very quickly, and with very little information, but they have important weaknesses. We can be persuaded not just by a mass of facts but also by their skilful presentation.

22

Robert Lucas – The Idealist

Ridding macroeconomics of all Keynesian tendencies

In building on Milton Friedman's monetary economics, Robert Lucas finally gave macroeconomics a Chicago accent. Convinced that economic behaviour was typically rational, he played a leading role in the development of the New Classical economics. From the early 1970s, this movement successfully challenged what had become the American Keynesian orthodoxy. By the 1980s, the radical ideas of the previous decade had become widely accepted. As a result, Lucas's influence pervades almost all current macroeconomics. With its roots in Chicago, and its commitment to treating behaviour as rational, Lucas's work is a natural complement to Becker's economic analysis of human behaviour.

That commitment to rationality meant that he had little time for Keynes' arguments in *The General Theory* about some prices, notably wages, taking a long time to adjust to changing economic circumstances. His belief in price flexibility also led him to reject the American Keynesian approach to demand management, in which governments would be able to adjust spending and taxation to manage unemployment and inflation, while also encouraging the private investment needed to enable economic growth. A small government conservative, he was very sceptical about economists going into public service. He answered questions about what he would do if he became the Chair of the American President's Council of Economic Advisers very simply: 'Resign.'

Born in Washington state in 1937, Lucas grew up in Seattle. He has written very fondly of his parents, with whom he exchanged letters regularly until middle age. When he was still a baby, his family's business failed. His father went back to work in the shipyards of Seattle but ended up running his own engineering company. His mother also worked, from home, as a commercial artist in the fashion industry while caring for her three children. His parents' experiences had made them New Deal Democrats, and when he was a young man, that seemed perfectly reasonable to their son. His later political conservatism would develop from his economics.

In 1955, Lucas decided that he would leave home to complete his education – and with the University of Chicago offering him a scholarship, he went there. Otherwise, it would have been MIT, and engineering. As in the 1930s, when Samuelson and Simon were undergraduates, the university insisted on most of its students engaging in a broad curriculum based on great books and Lucas became captivated by the arguments of classical philosophy which underpin modern political and social thought. His undergraduate major was in history and, as he put it, while he was at Chicago, he began to imagine the exciting possibilities of a career in which he would pursue 'intellectual interests and writing about them'. At this stage, although he could sense the importance of economics, he had no formal training in it.

Obtaining a Woodrow Wilson Doctoral Fellowship, he went to Berkeley, where he took courses in economic history with Carlo Cipolla and David Landes, who were experts on the role of cultural and social factors in economic development, especially in Europe before the Industrial Revolution. Even with the support of these great scholars, the economists at Berkeley would not accept him as a student – like Ostrom, he lacked mathematical skills. So, in 1960, the year that he voted for Kennedy rather than Nixon in a closely contested US Presidential election, he and his wife went back to Chicago, where he became a graduate student in economics.

As preparation for his studies, he had followed the recommendation in Kenneth Boulding's *Economic Analysis* that Samuelson's *Foundations* was 'the most important book in economics'. After immersion in the first four chapters, as he began to understand the theoretical structure which Samuelson had created, he realized that he was the same age as Samuelson had been when he wrote *Foundations*. There was suddenly the alluring prospect of doing something comparable almost immediately. Of more immediate practical value, that summer reading ensured that Lucas was ready for the intellectual excitement of Friedman's price theory course in his first semester at Chicago.

In the early 1960s, Lucas started to think about how to analyse the changing nature of the whole economy over time. This started during his doctoral studies for which Arnold Harberger was his supervisor, during which he started to think about the processes by which the stock of capital in the economy would grow, increasing the level of economic output. Had he been at MIT, that could easily have led him to follow in Solow's footsteps. But he was in Chicago, where Friedman and Stigler set the tone in debates about the nature of economics. That quickly stripped him of any instinctive Keynesian sympathies. Instead, he would come to epitomize the Chicago idea of the economy as a self-organizing machine which could absorb shocks quickly and effectively.

For his first academic job, Lucas moved to the Graduate School of Industrial Administration at Carnegie Mellon

University in Pittsburgh, where Herbert Simon was the presiding influence. Simon had moved on from active research in economics by the late 1950s, but Lucas found him generous with his time and always willing to talk over a cup of coffee. At Carnegie Mellon, Lucas established a close working relationship with Leonard Rapping. Together, they began to develop the ideas which Lucas championed throughout his career.

He also drew on many of the ideas of John Muth, one of Simon's research team, who had already developed the concept of 'rational expectations'. Muth, working with Simon on understanding organizational decision making, had made the very reasonable proposal that decision makers would use all the information available at the time they had to make choices as efficiently as possible. That meant that their decisions should anticipate the state of the work perfectly accurately if the future was certain. When it was uncertain, only news which broke once decisions had been made would cause them to be inaccurate.

Muth's rational expectations hypothesis was innovative because it concentrated on what might happen in the future – exactly what might be expected in making predictions. In *The General Theory*, Keynes had been vague about how people would think about the future. Some of his arguments required people to believe that the current state of the world would be the best guess as to its future state. At other times, he appeared to suggest that people would expect a gradual adjustment of economic variables, such as interest rates, to their long-run values. Throughout the 1960s, the American Keynesians tended to assume that decision makers would only look back to historic data, so that their predictions would involve extrapolation from recent events.

Lucas and Rapping started by using this approach in their analysis of labour markets, but quickly concluded that it would be better to incorporate rational expectations into their work. Not only did that seem to be a more realistic alternative, but they quickly found that this assumption allowed them to eliminate persistent unemployment in their models, ridding them of what both Lucas and Rapping then considered to be an unpleasant, Keynesian characteristic.

By 1969, Rapping was caught up in protests against the Vietnam War, and had become a radical critic of their work. Their close working relationship over the previous five years had been very important for Lucas. It had lasted long enough for him to have developed a substantial reputation and to be recognized as one of the leaders of a group of young economists, whose inspiration lay in Friedman's critique of the American Keynesian consensus, and the application of Samuelson's optimization approach to economics. Most of its leaders had trained at the leading universities of the US Midwest, especially Chicago and Minnesota. Among them, Lucas, Thomas Sargent, Finn Kydland and Ed Prescott have won the Nobel Memorial Prize. (Colleagues have specifically urged me to include Sargent as an excellent example of the virtue of humility in research.) Together with Robert Barro of Harvard, they were the most important of the New Classical economists. Their rise to prominence in the 1970s reflected the seeming stumbles of American Keynesian analysis.

Through the 1950s and 1960s, governments had found that Keynesian demand management worked well. Friedman had challenged this approach, both in his monetary economics and in his political writings. Lucas was still a postgraduate student when *Capitalism and Freedom* provided Senator Goldwater's 1964 Presidential campaign with an economic blueprint. But by the time that Friedman came to write *Free to Choose* in 1978, he had retired from Chicago. He was still the same persuasively loquacious conservative and a tireless defender of liberty, but the baton of intellectual leadership in macroeconomics had passed to Lucas. Even in the late 1960s, when Friedman dismantled the idea that there could be a stable relationship between inflation and unemployment, which could be useful for government policymakers, he drew on some of Lucas's early ideas about how decision makers predict what will happen in future to make his argument that it was only the unexpected element of inflation which would reduce unemployment.

In the late 1960s, rising inflation and unemployment meant that American Keynesian macroeconomics presented a large target to Lucas and other young economists as they developed their new form of macroeconomics. They replaced the Keynesian approach of thinking about the flow of money between sectors of the economy by trying to understand the behaviour of individual decision makers. That led them first to concentrate on optimization as the objective of rational choice, and then to emphasize that prices could always be flexible. The mix of rational expectations, optimization and price flexibility led them to reject the Keynesian position that wages could be so high that businesses would not hire all the workers looking for jobs.

Lucas argued that whenever there was unemployment, entrepreneurs could start businesses. Their businesses would pay wages which were lower than the market rate, but which were still attractive to the unemployed workers. Able to charge the existing market price for their output, they would then make substantial profits. In typical Chicago style, Lucas argued that there would be 'no money left on the table'. Anyone who could see a chance of making a profit would take it. That meant that flexible prices would ensure that all markets would be in equilibrium, even the labour market. Having ruled out the possibility of involuntary unemployment, Lucas set out to find a new explanation of unemployment and why it might persist.

This came in what is often considered to be his most important paper, in 1972. He emphasized that people do not have complete information and imagined a society which consisted of 'islands' of information. Suppose that you run a restaurant, and you find that your customers are willing to pay higher prices. You could take that as evidence that all prices have gone up, so people simply expect you to raise your prices too. You could also take it as evidence that demand has increased within the economy. Rather than raising prices, you may be able to meet the higher demand by ordering more supplies and asking your staff to work longer hours. Unfortunately, with your limited information, you cannot easily tell whether there has been an increase in all prices, or an increase in demand.

It turns out that this type of limited availability of information is enough to generate a transient relationship between prices and unemployment, as Solow and Samuelson had found in 1960. Lucas then explained that if decision makers predict the future using rational expectations, policymakers can only exploit the relationship between prices and unemployment by doing something which is completely unexpected. If business owners believe that prices are higher because of general inflation, they will not change their production decisions, and policy will be ineffective in raising incomes. The same would be true of any policy which the government announces in advance, or of repeated shocks of the same size. To the extent that policy is predictable, people will anticipate it. Rather than output changing, prices will adjust.

In the 1970s, the leading New Classical economists produced several important papers which predicted similar results in which any attempt to use demand management policy would fail. They shared the common feature that if people have a good understanding of the structure of the economy, and good enough information about what will happen in future, then so long as they are able to agree prices freely, they will anticipate how government actions will affect the economy. Government interventions to reduce unemployment, or increase investment, or increase national income, will fail.

Where Friedman had looked backwards to the monetary theories of Irving Fisher, and the business cycle analysis of Wesley C. Mitchell to argue that Keynesian theory would be ineffective, the New Classical economists relied upon plausible theoretical arguments about the aggregated effects of individual decisions to assert that the analysis of Keynes' *General Theory* had been very weak. That increased the mathematical content of their work. The Islands paper appeared in *Journal of Economic Theory*, after more general journals had rejected it for being too abstract. It was perhaps the enthusiasm of a convert, but Lucas, who had once planned to become a historian, repeatedly suggested that only mathematical models can express ideas interestingly.

He recalled going to meetings in the early 1970s, expecting to be seen as a critic of the mainstream, and instead discovering that many economists were looking for some form of modelling which would generate the results which he was producing. Yet, in some ways New Classical thought can be understood as building on Keynesian foundations. It adopted many of the same techniques and studied similar problems. Relatively small differences in assumptions led to important differences in their results. Solow considered that many of the results which the New Classical economists found were implied in the American Keynesian models of the 1960s.

By 1974, Lucas was back in Chicago, where he developed the 'Lucas critique' of econometric modelling. This built on the results about the limited effects of government policy by posing the problem of how rational, forward-looking decision makers might engage with policy decisions. Suppose that policymakers have a formal model of the economy, which they have calibrated using existing data. Lucas suggested that if they try to use the model to predict the effects of an intervention, they would effectively be assuming that the behaviour of other decision makers would remain unchanged. This seemed implausible to

Lucas, and he argued that policymakers needed to take account of how their policy interventions would affect the underlying structure of the economy.

That was not the novel insight – Lucas specifically acknowledged that the econometricians Jacob Marschak and Jan Tinbergen had foreseen this difficulty; and at the time that Lucas was developing his critique, the English political economist, Charles Goodhart, suggested that as soon as policymakers use the value of any variable as a basis for economic policy, that would be enough to change the behaviour of the variable. Lucas went beyond those widely shared concerns by arguing that when policymakers build models of the economy, they must take account of the way in which policy is made, and implemented, so that the government's policy stance effectively becomes part of the structure of the economic model. Now broadly adopted, the critique has influenced the design of many large economic models. It has driven the development of the real business cycle approach to macroeconomic modelling.

From there, Lucas returned to his very first research interest, capital accumulation. In the 1980s, he was one of the economists who started to extend the growth theory which Solow had first developed in the 1950s. Solow's work predicted that there would be convergence of economic growth. It also presumed that the economy was formed of perfectly competitive firms. In the 1980s, there was clear evidence against convergence. While convergence seemed to be occurring among the advanced economies, the gap between those countries, and many of the poorer countries, was increasing.

To some extent, the first steps on the path of bringing an explanation of increasing productivity into the Solow approach had been taken by Solow's pupil, William Nordhaus, a Nobel Memorial laureate in 2018. In one of his first papers, in 1969, he had developed a growth model in which innovation could be protected by patents, ensuring that firms had transitory market power.

Lucas took a different route, concentrating instead on how the economy can continue to grow when at any time there are only limited opportunities available to firms. His preferred solution was that production depends upon the stock of useful knowledge. Rather like Becker with human capital, we can think of Lucas proposing that we spend time working, as well as time in which we develop our knowledge. Again, this was not an entirely new approach. Marshall's arguments about external economies of scale which would lead to clustering of industries had similar implications within industries.

Such theories build on the important point that economic development may result from decisions which have limited effects at the individual level, but which have substantial aggregate effects because knowledge is freely available, and usable, at least by organizations with some baseline knowledge and capabilities. Such a model of development was entirely consistent with Lucas's earlier approach to the dissemination of information – we know our own local area well, but we do not understand what is happening across the whole of the economy.

Lucas is the last of the Chicago economists whom we shall encounter. He is a fitting culmination of the sequence which ran from Frank Knight, through Milton Friedman. Knight was simply dismissive of *The General Theory* and never sought to engage with it. Friedman set out to illustrate that it was unnecessary by demonstrating that the ultimate cause of the Great Depression was a prolonged tightening of credit supply overseen by the Federal Reserve. Lucas considered the book to be barely coherent. He could see the weaknesses which more sympathetic readers like Samuelson also found. But he could not find any useful theory in all its words.

For Lucas, macroeconomic analysis had to begin from strong behavioural assumptions: that firms would take any opportunity to make profits that they could, that all behaviour was rational, and that decision makers could predict the future quite accurately. The way to express ideas was through mathematics. Famously, Ed Prescott once left him a note, which was simply an equation about the nature of capital formation. Lucas did not ask Prescott to explain it – he put it into a larger system of equations and worked out what the effects would be.

For Lucas, thinking like an economist was to assume that the whole economy was a self-regulating system, through which information would flow freely. That led him to believe that it was impossible for government to manage the economy in the way that had been attempted after World War II. His most important insight was also Abraham Lincoln's. You can't fool all the people all the time.

23

George Akerlof – The Borrower

Bringing behavioural insights, and Keynes,
back into macroeconomics

Since the 1970s, the intellectual nomad, George Akerlof, has tried to establish macroeconomics on a very different basis from Lucas, the economist purist. Ranging across the social sciences, Akerlof has borrowed the ideas which have shaped his economic analysis. The result, recognized in the award of the Nobel Memorial Prize in 2001, has been progress towards behavioural macroeconomics.

Thinking like Akerlof means looking at the world and scouring academia for good stories which can explain what we see happening.

Kahneman and Tversky confirmed that sometimes we see the world that we want to see, and that explains many of the differences among economists. Lucas was committed to the view that unemployment is never forced on people, who are broadly rational. That led the New Classical economists to come up with ideas which explained the high inflation and unemployment of the 1970s better than it seemed the Keynesians could. Their ideas chimed with the times.

However, advances in research always spark off alternative ideas. Lucas made it necessary for all macroeconomists to explain how the ways in which individuals make choices with limited information will affect the whole economy. Economists who were still comfortable with Keynes' idea that the economy might stutter and struggle, rather than being Lucas's well-oiled machine, had to respond to his ideas by thinking about how people would make decisions without always choosing optimally.

There is an important asymmetry between the New Classical approach and the alternatives. If choices are no more than procedurally rational, then there are many possible ways of being rational. In contrast, optimization has a well-defined meaning. Especially in the 1980s. Akerlof's contribution to this debate came through work with his wife, Janet Yellen. They argued that with even tiny differences between the actions of procedurally rational rule followers and optimizing decision makers, they could overturn the New Classical claims about government policy being ineffective.

This was part of what has become known as the New Keynesian response to the New Classical economists. For this group of economists, it was impossible for prices to be completely flexible. Given the structure of Keynesian economics, it was natural for them to concentrate on how wage levels are set. In the mid-1970s, Stanley Fischer and John Taylor developed arguments based on the quite reasonable claim that organizations might be able to change the prices of the goods and services which they produce more frequently than they change the wages which they pay their workers. They accepted the New Classical assumptions of rational expectations and price flexibility, except for these 'sticky' wages. That small change was enough to enable government policy to affect the level of national income.

Then, in the 1980s, Joseph Stiglitz, along with several collaborators, developed the concept of efficiency wages. From the early 1970s, economists had started to think about how easily workers can fool employers about how hard they are working. Since most production processes are complex, teams of workers typically work together, so that there is only a tenuous link between individual effort and team output.

Stiglitz and his collaborators argued that this could compel employers to offer to pay workers more than the value of their observable output. He argued that this would be consistent with organizations aiming to make profits (given the uncertainty about the contribution of individual workers to sales and profits) because the higher wages would reduce other costs. As well as encouraging employees to work harder, they might increase the quality of applicants which the firm could hire and reduce the probability of good workers quitting. Setting efficiency wages was then procedurally rational. Like 'sticky' wages, they ensured policy effectiveness.

Stiglitz could easily have been my chosen representative of the New Keynesian approach, rather than Akerlof. They both completed doctorates at MIT in the 1960s, then spent time in developing countries – Akerlof in India, and Stiglitz in Kenya. Along with Michael Spence, they shared the Nobel Memorial Prize in 2001. Stiglitz has been the Chief Economist of the World Bank, a consultant to many governments and a trenchant critic of neo-liberalism and globalization. He has been rather more prolific than Akerlof and has the greater public reputation. The partnership between Akerlof and Yellen has led to some specialization of roles. Akerlof has stuck closely to academic work, while Yellen has taken on a wide range of public roles, latterly President of the Federal Reserve Board and Secretary of the Treasury. When it comes to thinking like an economist, both Akerlof and Stiglitz have given us a huge amount of material. Akerlof has simply been more imaginative and wide ranging than Stiglitz.

In his most famous paper, published in 1970, Akerlof set out a theory about the difficulties of sharing information which cannot easily be verified by other people. Using the example of 'lemons', (poor quality, second-hand cars) he argued that sellers cannot easily communicate the value of the car which they own. He argued that such knowledge can only come from the experience of driving a car for a long time. In his model, buyers would be willing to pay the average value of a car which is offered for sale. Potential sellers who know that they have cars of very high quality would then decide to keep them, reducing the average value of the cars which are in the market. Buyers who take that into account when deciding how much to offer will set the average value of a car which is being sold below the average value of all cars.

Akerlof set up his model in two ways. In the first one, with cars being either 'peaches' or 'lemons', only the low-quality 'lemons' were traded. In the second one, with the quality of each car being slightly different, the market collapsed, and no cars were bought. That is not the point of the model, although Akerlof, who completed this paper during his time in India, suggested that there are many situations in less developed countries in which there are 'missing markets' because owners of goods cannot easily demonstrate their value.

We see used cars being bought and sold every day – and in the decade afterwards, economists explained how markets could work when buyers did not have as much information as sellers. Michael Spence developed arguments about the seller's ability to do something which the buyer would interpret as a signal of high quality. His most famous example was about education. If employers believe that highly productive workers will be able to complete the problem-solving tasks of sitting exams more efficiently than less productive workers, then they can offer higher wages to anyone with enough education, and only the highly productive workers will choose to complete the necessary education. This is an 'arms race' theory of education in which it has no value, so that highly productive workers waste time and effort in completing pointless tasks to acquire the necessary certification. Even worse, as society becomes wealthier, to ensure that it is possible to identify the highly productive workers, employers will demand that they have more advanced qualifications.

Stiglitz suggested a different method, which works best in financial services. Suppose that a motor insurer sets up a menu of insurance policies, each of which is slightly different. Drivers will choose the one which suits them best. In Stiglitz's analysis, only the highest-risk drivers will be able to obtain full insurance. If lower-risk drivers could obtain full insurance, the policy which had been designed for them will also be more attractive for high-risk drivers than the policy designed for them. Contracts for low-risk drivers in which they will bear part of the losses can stop that happening. Where Spence's signalling requires the owners of high-quality assets to waste resources to make a credible claim about their quality, Stiglitz's screening approach involves asset owners classifying themselves through their choice from a menu of alternatives.

Where New Classical economists believe that assuming rationality is enough to ensure optimal behaviour, the New Keynesian approach emerged from a wide variety of questions about how we can communicate information. The 'Market for Lemons' paper started this line of enquiry. We can think of efficiency wages, signalling and screening as ways of overcoming problems which stem from the challenges of sharing unverifiable information. They establish procedures which allow markets to operate when there is imperfect information. Since there are many ways of specifying such problems, the New Keynesian approach has involved many arguments that small costs of acquiring and managing information can combine to have large effects on the whole economy.

All these ideas go back to the early 1970s, when Kahneman and Tversky were developing the heuristics and biases research programme. However, they published most of their work in psychology journals, and so these strands of research developed together, but almost entirely separately.

These first attempts to explain how behaviour might lead to sticky prices relied on observation of the processes for setting prices and wages. It occurred to Akerlof that around the world, there are many ways of managing resources and making decisions which had already been studied by social scientists in other disciplines. Like the idea that barriers to sharing information might be important in explaining why some countries have low incomes, this idea first occurred to him while he was in India. He tried to understand the caste system and developed a model in which the wage levels for specific jobs resulted from social customs, with set wages for different types of jobs.

Dissatisfied with that first attempt, when he came back to the USA, he set out to understand more about how sociologists, anthropologists and social psychologists had already explained social processes of resource management. That led to a series of papers which justified efficiency wages in many ways. One of those explorations took account of the extent to which workers who are already employed in a firm – the insiders – can tacitly set (and monitor) effort levels, and can influence both the wage level, but also the hiring process. By restraining the hiring of other workers, the insiders could keep wages higher than what would otherwise be the market rate. Such autonomy and self-organization of workers suggests that workplaces rely on something like Ostrom's principles for managing the commons.

Akerlof's challenge was not so much to explain why wages might be sticky, but to turn the insights of other social sciences into economics. This was almost the opposite of Becker's approach, which identified social phenomena and tried to demonstrate that they were the result of optimizing behaviour. Instead, Akerlof used the insights of other social sciences as the starting point of his economic arguments. Where Becker was sometimes seen as applying the logic of economics in contexts in which it could not have any useful role, Akerlof has been seen much more as a borrower, deepening economists' engagement with other social sciences.

For example, in *Labour Contracts as Partial Gift Exchange*, we see Akerlof reintroducing moral sentiments into economic analysis. People form attachments to the group with whom they work and the organization with which they work. In such relationships, there is often reciprocal gift giving. Akerlof suggests that such gift giving goes beyond a staff Christmas party. Instead, teams of employees would collectively make a gift to employers by working together to produce more than is contractually required, while employers would reciprocate by offering contracts with higher wages and better conditions than employees might expect to obtain elsewhere.

Socially determined wages could then easily be higher than the value to the firm of each worker's time, and create the necessary price stickiness for demand management policy to be effective. Reciprocal relationships between employers and workers could also justify the Keynesian assumption that workers will object strongly to reductions in wages by reducing their productivity.

In much of his later work, Akerlof had several regular collaborators, most notably his wife, Janet Yellen. They had met in 1977, when Yellen was on the staff of the Federal Reserve Board and married in the following year. They then moved to the London School of Economics, before returning to Berkeley in 1980. From there, during the 1980s, they explored the concept of 'near rationality', which built on the idea that when organizations rely on decision-making rules, the aggregate effects on the economy of tiny discrepancies between the optimal choice and the outcome of applying the rule in any individual choice, could be very large.

Suppose that the economy begins from equilibrium, but that a change in central bank policy causes a change in the amount of money circulating in the economy. In his islands model, Lucas argued that there could only be an effect on national income if the change in policy was an unobserved shock. Akerlof and Yellen suggested that it would be 'near rational' to maintain wages and prices given that there would not be any immediate evidence of the need to change them, since the cost of not optimizing would be very small.

What was true for each firm could not be true for the whole economy. If prices do not change, money will not just pile up in bank accounts. Some of it will be spent and so the total output of the economy will change. We are back to a Keynesian argument that an increase in the money supply will mean that people will want to buy more goods and, at the given wages, firms will want to hire more workers. Strictly, these results would only hold if the economy consisted of relatively large firms, which did not simply have to accept the market price. Adding the concept of efficiency wages – of which Akerlof's gift exchange concept is one possible formulation – so that workers will exert effort, or quit less frequently, or act loyally to the firm, Akerlof and Yellen established that there will be real effects of a monetary disturbance, and that there can be a short-run equilibrium in which there is unemployment.

More recently, Akerlof has tried to broaden the behavioural basis of economics. Working with Rachel Kranton, he has explored the nature of identity for economic decision making. In their work, identity is an immutable, but socially conditioned, characteristic. Sex and ethnicity are obvious examples. Then people are either men or women, or else white, or African American. They presume that one group is socially superior (men, or whites), and that there will be a range of behaviours (employment, or housework), with which groups tend to be associated. If women are expected to undertake housework, then a woman who chooses to work must overcome feelings of anxiety about making that choice, while a man seeing a woman working may find the dissonance between identity and activity a source of displeasure.

Such work attempts to provide an account based in economic theory in which we see the outcomes of discrimination. Identity becomes a basis for a Beckerian 'taste' for discrimination, but in Akerlof and Kranton's approach, there are more complex responses – for example, the assimilation of a member of the out-group to the standards set by the dominant group may cause upset to other members of the out-group, without achieving acceptance from members of the dominant group.

It would be very easy to dismiss this work because of its relatively simple account of identity. In a society in which there are many ways to express masculinity – in which people can choose to move between sexual identities – we might usefully think of identity as being formed through social interactions, and personal choice, rather than simply being assigned. (Becker treated identity as another form of mental capital, with opportunities for investment to sustain it, while it would also erode over time.) This line of criticism misses the strength of Akerlof's approach, which has always been to visit other disciplines and find concepts which may be fruitfully applied to economic analysis.

Lastly, in work with Robert Shiller, Akerlof has written two books, *Animal Spirits* and *Phishing for Phools*. Together, they defend not just the Keynesian imagining of the economy, but the importance of ethical behaviour as the basis of an economy which functions well. Recognizing that economic analysis is now rarely presented simply as discourse, they argue strongly against the possibility of the equilibrium analysis of the New Classical approach to economics ever capturing the behaviour of the economy because of the assumptions which it makes about rationality.

Instead, Akerlof and Shiller argue that the world is only intelligible through stories. We all extract meaning from accounts which are necessarily embedded within language. That opens the way for misrepresentation of the state of the economy, especially in financial markets, where commodities are little more than promises to pay in the future. Perhaps their most striking claim is that the root cause of the recessions which the USA experienced in 1991, 2001 and 2009 was essentially fraudulent trading, backed by very persuasive stories. Claims to have found new ways of achieving economic growth were soon proven to be empty.

This is not just a Keynesian account. In talking about the importance of fairness in economic relations, and the damage which fraud can cause to entire economies, they are going back to Smith's thinking, in which the pursuit of virtue, specifically temperance, is essential for society to prosper. While they are confident that Keynes was right to emphasize the importance of animal spirits in moving the economy, they also emphasize the importance of narrative in shaping our understanding of it. It is not just that we can end up with many different outcomes from any starting point. We can justify the end point from the story which we tell about how we reach it.

The emphasis on storytelling has been integral to Akerlof's approach to thinking like an economist. He has steadily built up a fund of interesting stories, which seem to be able to explain much of what we can see happening in the world. Central to Akerlof's understanding of economics are: problems about the involuntary nature of much unemployment; the effectiveness of monetary policy (despite the claims of New Classical economists); the lack of evidence that tolerating unemployment is necessary for tame inflation; the extent to which lack of foresight means that governments and public bodies must persuade people to save enough to sustain economic growth; and, most troublingly, the steadfast persistence of an 'underclass' of poor people, who lack opportunities to engage with the economy and broader society.

To address such problems, Akerlof believes that macro-economics needs microfoundations which are much more sophisticated than those deployed in the models of New Classical economics. But there is always the challenge – what microfoundations? The ease with which Akerlof and other New Keynesians have been able to fashion multiple – if closely related – versions of near rationality emphasizes just how challenging it will be to specify good microfoundations, which will become widely adopted in economic analysis.

Does that matter? Perhaps not. If we accept that thinking like an economist means being able to explain the effects of resource management, then having a coherent account, like the New Classical economists is certainly attractive. We come back, again, to Simon's insights that decisions must be made, somehow. The success of *The General Theory* was then in giving economists the freedom to address problems of the existing world. Akerlof, as the most imaginative of the New Keynesians, has given us a way of carrying on with that task.

24

Esther Duflo – The Experimenter

*Running trials to dismantle the traps which keep
people poor*

We end with the first economist to have won the Nobel
Memorial Prize before the age of 50, and the second of the two
women in the first 50 years in which the prize was awarded.
Lucas and Akerlof established their careers in the 1960s. They
had both published papers which the Nobel Committee cited
when recognizing their work before Esther Duflo was born in
1972. By the time that Duflo had completed her doctorate in
1999, Lucas had already won his Nobel Prize, while Akerlof's
turn came two years later. Two decades later, Duflo shared
the Nobel Memorial Prize in 2019 with Abhijit Banerjee and
Michael Kremer – and that was less than a decade after she won
the John Bates Clark medal.

In some ways, the speed of recognition of the importance of
her work confirms the extent to which much of the best research
in economics takes place in networks. Duflo was originally a
student of Banerjee and Kremer – and Banerjee and Duflo are
married. Along with Kremer, and his wife Rachel Glennerster,
they founded the Poverty Action Lab at MIT in 2004 to work out
what types of intervention might allow poor people to achieve
greater well-being and transform their economic prospects.

Rather like the Ostrom Workshop at Michigan, the Lab is today the hub of a vast international network of academic researchers.

Duflo's research is part of development economics, and there is much more to economic development than the sustained growth of national income. A large part of the historical account in *The Wealth of Nations* explored how differences in social and political organization explained why some countries were richer than others. From that starting point, the classical political economists in the nineteenth century put the distribution of incomes at the heart of their theories. They also believed that over-population could easily be a source of economic crisis. Marshall kept the painting of his 'patron saint' close to hand to remind him that his economics should benefit the disadvantaged. It was only in the twentieth century that economists came to think about the creation of value as the purpose of economic processes and invoked optimization as the objective of rational choice. After the Great Depression, the growth of national income became a vitally important economic measure, not least for politicians, whose electoral prospects often depended on it. In trying to understand the lives of the world's poorest people – and how to change them – development economics harks back to the classical tradition.

Since Smith wrote, the experiences of less developed countries and advanced economies have often diverged. During his time in India, Akerlof found that there were many economic opportunities which went unclaimed – a fact that would have appalled Lucas. Where Smith believed that over time, there was a tendency for people living in Europe and North America to become better off, he believed that in China, incomes did not change. China's emergence as an economic superpower since 1980 would have intrigued him.

There is now plenty of evidence against the prediction of countries converging on higher levels of income, as predicted by Solow's growth model. That has led economists to try to explain the conditions which are necessary for growth, and why those conditions might still not have arisen in poorer countries. In growing economies, people can easily acquire skills, knowledge and education. Larger businesses may be more efficient in managing resources and so will have lower costs of production. Such growth theory is one of the areas of economics where Chicago and MIT can happily agree.

Banerjee, Duflo, Glennerster and Kremer are representative of a new generation of development economists, which has built on the capabilities approach of the Nobel laureate, Amartya Sen. In this, development involves people developing the capabilities needed for them to thrive. Nutrition is clearly important, but so are education, access to capital, the ability to transport goods and the rule of law, so that property is secure. All those ideas should be familiar from the economic philosophy of the Middle Ages. Reflecting on more recent history, Sen famously remarked that there has never been a famine in a democracy. He has suggested that the accountability of democratic public institutions prevents such catastrophic failure.

In *Poor Economics*, which Banerjee and Duflo wrote to popularize their ideas after Duflo won the John Bates Clark medal, they start with a famous argument between two leading development economists, Jeffrey Sachs and William Easterly. Sachs has long advocated a 'big push' approach to development, diagnosing poverty as a lack of capital and arguing that if we transfer enough to poor countries, they will jump onto the path of growth. Sachs is essentially arguing for a modified version of growth theory. Easterly has argued that poor countries lack the institutions which are needed for sustained development. Were they to acquire the capabilities for cooperation and investment, which we take for granted in advanced economies, people living in those countries would be able to find their own solutions.

Banerjee and Duflo think that this debate is rather beside the point. They believe that Easterly and Sachs both have a grand over-arching vision of what constitutes development. Both of them can look at exactly the same events and feel vindicated by them. In contrast, Banerjee and Duflo claim that their own approach to research has the much more modest goal of developing ideas, then testing them in relatively small-scale experiments to see if they are likely to work in practice, before scaling them up quickly through partnerships with local governments or charities. The roots of this approach go back to the 1990s, when Banerjee thought about poverty as trapping people in it, and Kremer realized that it should be possible to run economic experiments in communities which suffer from poverty.

Think back to the Malthusian model. An increase in productivity leads to an increase in wages, but also in the birth rate, reducing wages. That takes workers back to the subsistence level. In Banerjee's way of thinking about poverty, that is a trap which prevents development. An increase in income naturally unwinds. Since some societies, but not all, have been able to escape from poverty, there must be a way of breaking free of such traps, but escape is not an automatic process. The right conditions will need to be satisfied.

Banerjee suggested if there could be a large enough increase in productivity, then people's incomes would rise by enough that they could save. Such savings could fund investments. That could take place within the household, with better diet, better health care and better outcomes. Or it could involve organizations, which would buy better machinery and organize production more effectively. Through such channels, labour productivity, wages, incomes, and finally savings and investment would increase further. Development would then become self-sustaining. In terms of the Malthusian model, with high enough wages, people will naturally make use of preventive checks and divert resources away from consumption into investment, so that the population and wages can increase at the same time.

More generally, poverty traps occur whenever the effects of small increases in income are transient. People can escape from traps when larger, though still modest, increases in income cause further increases. Addressing poverty involves the removal of these traps. That is a more complicated process than channelling enough aid or trusting in the inventiveness and imagination of the still poor. Among the many possible causes of poverty traps are lack of access to resources, including clean water; malnutrition, affecting mental and physical capacity; debilitating and disabling illnesses, such as malaria; ineffective schooling; poor health care; lack of transport to markets for farmers; and lack of access to credit. It would be very easy to extend that list.

If we think of persistent poverty as a complex, multi-faceted problem, we should expect that it will take different forms around the world. We should expect to find that the design of effective programmes for tackling poverty will vary substantially across cultures. What works in a city may not be appropriate when dealing with rural communities.

In the mid-1990s, while Banerjee was developing the idea of poverty traps, Kremer was starting to design field experiments. He decided to adopt the methodology of a randomized control trial (RCT). Borrowed from medical science, the idea is that while some participants in the experiment are exposed to a 'treatment', the other participants, who are in the 'control' group, are not. Assigning participants to one or other procedure randomly (and not informing the participants, or the staff running the experiment, who is in which group) should mean that differences in outcomes between the groups can be explained by the process of assignment, rather than the underlying characteristics of the people in each group. Kremer realized that in working with the poorest communities in the world, in which many people live on less than $2 per day, and have very few assets, running such trials need not be enormously expensive.

Go back to the Sachs–Easterly debate for a moment: one of their disagreements involved the value of programmes which distribute free bed nets to protect people from mosquito bites and subsequent serious infections, especially malaria. For Sachs, such programmes have a valuable public health role, but for Easterly, it seemed obvious that people would not value something that they were given for free. They might use them in other ways, perhaps for the veil of a wedding dress, or as a fishing net. However, neither of them had tested the effectiveness of mosquito net programmes systematically.

Kremer's proposal suggested a way of finding out how people might use, and value, nets when they were free or subsidized. When Pascaline Dupas and Jessica Cohen, who are part of the J-PAL network, conducted experiments on bed net use and valuation in Kenya in 2006–07, they found that when they offered them for sale at different prices, demand was quite price elastic. Small increases in the price which they charged reduced take up of the nets. They next obtained evidence that the price which someone pays had little effect on the probability that nets would be used. However, in follow-up visits to participating households, where experimenters offered to sell families a second net, people tended to be willing to pay a higher price if they had previously been given one for free. That seemed to be consistent with people starting to understand how to use a bed net, and what the advantages of one might be.

Thinking like an economist about this, we could argue that as the bed net becomes familiar, people acquire 'bed net capital' which means that they derive greater value from their use. Or, following a behavioural approach, reluctance towards adoption might be the result of difficulties in imagining the benefits until enough people had tried them. Evidence for this latter effect is that after trials, neighbours of users were more willing to purchase bed nets – although we could also extend this example by proposing that there is a form of bed net 'social capital'. Note the references back to the ideas of Becker, Kahneman and Akerlof – and of course Simon. Substantively rational optimizing agents would not need the encouragement of a public intervention to start using bed nets.

This is where the J-PAL approach breaks with Sachs and Easterly. Repeatedly, its field research has started from discussions with partners about simple solutions to poverty traps, which already exist within the community, but which it is easy for people to overlook. Remaining poor may be a question of being in an island of limited information in which many people lack a good enough understanding of how to use resources effectively. One effect of that might be the missing economic institutions which Akerlof noted in India. However, among earlier economists perhaps Mill, with his interest in colonial development, came closest to this, arguing that education was essential for the working class to develop the necessary moral autonomy to live full lives.

Since its founding, the Poverty Action Lab has enjoyed a close relationship with the Abdul Latif Jameel Foundation, which has established a global network of Poverty Action Laboratories, with the MIT team at its heart. The Bill and Melinda Gates Foundation has also been a generous supporter of this work. That funding has enabled a rapid development of the methodology. But that has led to criticism that to satisfy their funders, the results of RCTs claim to offer too much. There is a risk that what works well in a small-scale trial will not be effective in a much larger programme. For example, participants in experiments may engage with independent researchers very differently from the general population when they deal with government administrators.

Overcoming these criticisms has required Duflo and her team to have a very different relationship with policymakers than conventional economists. Traditionally, academics keep a careful distance from politics, perhaps acting as consultants, completing discrete pieces of commissioned work, and then moving on to their next research project, only retaining access to data so that they can complete their analysis. They are often observers without being participants. Duflo considers that well-designed RCTs cannot emerge in such a relationship. Instead, she believes that researchers need to work very closely with public officials, so that they understand fully the environment in which poverty traps have emerged, and then design and test the effects of bespoke interventions intended to avoid those traps.

Duflo's contribution to the development of the RCT approach has largely come through the design of many useful trials. However, the piece of research which made her reputation used statistical theory to show that trials may be better at identifying economic relationships than the complex ways which economists have developed to interrogate data which was collected for other purposes. Economists have often used 'natural' experiments. Say that there is an increase in the minimum wage in one state, but that it remains the same in a neighbouring state. Comparing communities which are close to the border between the states, the minimum wage change should only affect employers' hiring decisions on one side of the border. Otherwise, their decisions should largely be driven by the same factors. That makes a natural experiment a form of trial, but without random assignment of the participants. Duflo and other colleagues demonstrated that there is a tendency for analysis of the results of natural experiments to overstate differences between the 'control' and the 'treatment' groups. RCTs are not just a more direct way of estimating the effects of interventions – they can also be substantially more accurate, and so more useful.

As a result, part of the Poverty Action Lab's work has been to show that some well-supported interventions are not as effective as their proponents have claimed. For example, microcredit became very fashionable in the early years of this century. Muhammad Yunus, who founded the first microcredit organization, the Grameen Bank in Bangladesh in 1976 won the Nobel Peace Prize in 2006. By then, microcredit institutions had spread to many countries and had about 100m clients, all of them poor.

Advocates of this approach argued that poor people struggled to obtain access to formal credit facilities and claimed that a lending institution based in the community it served would be able to provide the small loans that people needed to start new businesses. The first part is undoubtedly true. The second part was the same sort of assertion made by Sachs and Easterly in debating the value of bed nets. In the global wave of public enthusiasm for the idea, a World Bank affiliate, the Consultative Group to Assist the Poor declared that 'there is mounting evidence to show that the availability of financial services for poor households can help achieve the Millennium Development Goals.'

Unfortunately, there was no strong evidence for such claims. Eventually, facing pressure from Indian banks, Spandana, which was the largest microfinance lender in Hyderabad, agreed to become a partner in a randomized control trial exploring the effects of microcredit. The results were decidedly mixed. On the positive side, there was little evidence that money was being wasted, with borrowing being used to fund the purchase of assets, and there was also a modest increase in business start-ups, with some of those businesses surviving and creating substantial wealth. Against that, there was also little evidence of transformative effects, especially through the empowerment of women, which was supposed to be one of the benefits of microcredit. Duflo's team could not find evidence of women who had access to microcredit having greater control of household finances, or of more spending on health and education. After an initial wave of criticism led by the largest microcredit institutions, further research established broadly similar results across microfinance institutions in several countries.

Across all these trials, microcredit's only certain benefit has turned out to be that it enables a small number of people to start up a successful business, and so to exit poverty. That is not their only effect of course – for example, by enabling people to borrow, they allow people to acquire some very useful durable goods (imagine not having a refrigerator in a city in India). They are socially useful institutions and their clients keep on returning for more loans. But on its own, microcredit is not some silver bullet which could substantially reduce poverty.

In describing her work, Duflo is very clear that tackling the challenges of poverty takes time. RCTs often seem like very complex market research undertaken for the public good. Experimenters need to understand how people will respond to a change in service provision, which can then be studied further as the experiment is scaled up. To do that well, experimenters must understand the context in which people make their decisions, to understand better why, if they are not making good use of resources, they might have adopted such a pattern of behaviour. Without that understanding, it is impossible to design an intervention which will have immediate, but lasting effects.

We are finishing this book with a new way of thinking about the role of economics. It is not as if Duflo is the first economist to have a close relationship with policymakers. Schumpeter was a government minister and Keynes, intermittently, a civil servant. The RCT movement is different. In some ways, it does not have any objective, other than improving the quality of decision making. It has nothing to say about the sorts of institutions which might most effectively undertake decision making. Rather like Ostrom's approach to resource management, it does not have strong predictive power, and is concerned with measurable outcomes. Where Ostrom was concerned with the design of institutions, RCTs require a detailed understanding of choice environments, and methods for measuring the potential effects of changes in them. These two approaches complement each other very well, taking our discussion away from the assertions of theory and extending the ways in which economic analysis can effect substantial change.

And with that, we come to the end of the book. It began with Aristotle thinking about household management for the benefit of male citizens of a slave-owning society. We are finishing with economists thinking about how to transform the prospects of the poorest members of our global society. But they are still thinking about how to manage resources within the constraints of the societies in which they live.

AFTERWORD

In every history of economics, the work of great economists inevitably comes to the fore. Compared with the thousands of economists who toil away with very little recognition, the best economists develop ways of thinking which other economists take up, often quickly, although, as with Léon Walras's general equilibrium theory, there might be a long delay in the general acceptance of important ideas. The happy few find new approaches, which relate well to earlier ideas about the economy, and enable other economists to address the challenges of successful resource management.

There are two critical turning points in this history. First, Adam Smith made it possible to think about an economic system when Europe was beginning to industrialize. Then, in the 1930s, as the global economy seemed to be on the verge of collapse, Maynard Keynes argued that there would be times when governments needed to play an active role in Smith's system. To those, we can perhaps add the development of marginal analysis as having been necessary for economics to emerge in its modern form and finally separate it from philosophy, politics and history.

Beyond those essential moments, the rest of this account has set out what it has meant to think like an economist. It was not a comprehensive account of economics – Joseph Schumpeter's *History of Economic Analysis* only covered the first half of this book and ran to about 1,200 pages. That means that there were several economists whose ideas could easily have appeared in this book, but whose contributions ended up being squeezed out in the final selection. For example, Kenneth Arrow was one of the most productive theorists of the 1950s and 1960s. He played an important role in finding the solution of the Walrasian general equilibrium system, and models of collective choice. Possibly the most brilliant economic theorist of the twentieth century, after more than 50 years, he is still the youngest male winner of the Nobel Memorial Prize.

In an early version of the manuscript, a single chapter attempted to discuss the work of both Arrow and Paul Samuelson. Not only were they both brilliant theorists from the time that they were graduate students, but there were important family ties. Samuelson's brother and Arrow's sister trained as professional economists, and later married. Emphasizing the importance of personal connections, their son, Larry Summers, was a leading New Keynesian economist in the 1980s. He then became Chief Economist at the World Bank, US Treasury Secretary and President of Harvard University. It seemed that Samuelson and Arrow both deserved their own chapter, but the question was then who to drop. Perhaps, should this book reach a second edition, Arrow will appear as a substitute – but like a Prime Minister appointing new ministers to a government, some care will be necessary not to affect the balance of the team.

There could also have been much deeper exploration of the variety of ways of thinking about the economy which emerged in the nineteenth century. Concentrating on the British tradition has meant that the ideas of French engineers, the German Historical Schools and the American Institutionalists were scarcely mentioned. Yet, there have always been many ways of thinking about the economy, and the survey of how economics developed in the second half of the twentieth century was deliberately eclectic, showing how the professionalization of economics has not led to it being sealed off from other social sciences.

Thinking like an economist simply means engaging in reflection on the challenges of managing resources. One lesson from this book might be that to affect how other economists think, it is important to develop some deep insight while still young, and to be part of a large network of leading researchers. At any time, the best economic ideas emerge in only a few places around the world.

We can trace the origin of Herbert Simon's and Ronald Coase's greatest contributions to their time as undergraduates. Paul Samuelson started to formalize neo-classical economics while he was in his early 20s. Many great economists completed important work in their 20s, and then developed their insights over the remainder of their career. David Ricardo was perhaps the most obvious exception to this, but he was a gentleman amateur, who only turned to political economy in his retirement. He was then in his early 40s. Keynes, supported by the Cambridge Circle, completed his most influential work while he was in his early 50s – and the effort nearly killed him.

As well as the Cambridge Circle, we have seen how ideas emerged from within the debating clubs of the Scottish Enlightenment in the late eighteenth century, the thinking of the Philosophical Radicals in London in the early nineteenth century, Marshall's Cambridge School in the late nineteenth century, a variety of formal discussion circles in Vienna in the early twentieth century, and the Chicago School in the middle of the twentieth century. After Adam Smith, it would have been perfectly possible to write a book about what it meant to think like an economist concentrating only on work carried out in London and Cambridge, Vienna, Cambridge (Massachusetts) and Chicago.

Those places have been important because the very best economic thinking tends to happen when capable economists talk regularly with each other. The best academic economists attract the very best students and train them to be their successors. The Samuelson–Arrow–Summers nexus was only

HOW TO THINK LIKE AN ECONOMIST

unusual because it involved a family. Between Arrow, Robert Solow, Wassily Leontief and their pupils, we can account for almost one fifth of Nobel laureates.

New economic ideas usually emerge as a response to changes in the economy. Adam Smith wrote at the start of the Industrial Revolution. Maynard Keynes responded to the Great Depression. The marginal revolution might seem to have been largely internal to economics, but it allowed economics to engage with the Second Industrial Revolution in the late nineteenth century. We can be certain that the next major turning point in economics will reflect changes in the economy which economics as it is now simply cannot explain. That makes it almost impossible to predict what it will mean to think like an economist 50 years from now. The obvious possibility is that it will involve the search for ecological sustainability. But perhaps some quite different challenges will turn out to be of greater importance.

It is just possible that there will be an internal revolution in economics like the one at the end of the nineteenth century. Since the time of Alfred Marshall, we have seen economists who have used formal, deductive theory, expressed in mathematical language, which they have tested using statistical analysis. We have also seen economists who have started from detailed observation to generate deep insights, often linked to behavioural explanations. Marshall of course had doubts about the value of formal theory and tried to imagine how economics could take inspiration from biology. The Austrians, such as Joseph Schumpeter, and especially Friedrich Hayek, showed how that might be possible, but neither have ever been part of the mainstream of economics.

If there is a critique of formalism which could give some hint of how thinking like an economist might change, it would be in the approach of Robert Solow, who tended to use models as a way of structuring his thinking, and his pupil, George

Akerlof, who built his models by borrowing from other social sciences. In that case, the new economics would bring together the formality of the optimizing approach with the grounding in observation of behavioural approaches. Economists who think in this way will be able to tell great stories which change our understanding of the economy. They will be a little like Keynes and Friedman, and their ideas will once again grip the public imagination.

ACKNOWLEDGEMENTS

It would have been impossible for me to write this book without the support of family and friends. First, though, I have to thank Tomasz Hoskins, my editor at Bloomsbury for encouragement and direction, and for giving me the space and time to shape the arguments that gradually emerged. The entire team at Bloomsbury have done a superb job in preparing the text for its presentation here, and have always been a pleasure to work with: Sarah Jones for project editing the book, Chris Stone, Guy Holland and Rosemary Dear for copyediting, proofreading and indexing respectively, and also the Publicity and Marketing departments.

Next, my wife Jane Queenan has put up with my vanishing for hours at a time while I wrestled with great thinkers' ideas. Our conversations have been very important in allowing me to work out what was important to include in the book.

To try to list all the people who have encouraged me to think about the history of economics would be difficult. For many stimulating conversations, I am especially grateful to John Sawkins at Heriot-Watt University, Omar Shaikh of the Global Ethical Finance Initiative, Russell Napier, the Keeper of the Library of Mistakes, and to Patrick Schotanus, the research lead on the Market Mind Hypothesis. While writing the book, I ran a seminar for undergraduate students on the history of economic thought at Heriot-Watt University. The participants in that seminar may not have realized that one of their roles was to discipline me to write regularly. Having to deliver weekly two-hour lectures – which invariably finished well after the scheduled time – kept me focused on the overall task. Their enthusiasm for the subject made writing a joy.

Lastly, I need to thank my agent. Jaime Marshall has been unflagging in his insistence that I should express every idea clearly, precisely, persuasively and above all, engagingly. He read far more of my text than I expected, and coached me courteously, but with steely determination, until I became fluent in a style which met his high standards. I never ended a meeting with Jaime without feeling encouraged about what I was doing.

Throughout the process of writing, I have been buoyed up by generous support and encouragement. That has ensured that I have sustained my curiosity as I have sifted the ideas of great economists to discern the threads that link them.

INDEX

Treatise on Law and Justice (Aquinas)   29

Treatise on Money (Keynes)   104, 115, 120, 121–2

Treatise on the Family (Becker)   215

Tucker, Albert   139

Tullock, Gordon   145, 146

Turgot, Anne-Robert-Jacques   40–1

Tversky, Amos   228–9, 230–4, 235–6, 237, 250, 254–5

unemployment   78, 159–60, 171, 202, 203, 204, 239, 243–4, 245, 250, 257

utilitarianism   64, 79, 207
expected utility theory   235–7
marginal utility   92–3, 97

Utilitarianism (Mill)   59

value, theories of   66, 71, 72–3, 74, 78

Value and Capital (Hicks)   167, 197

Veblen, Thorstein   84, 87

Viner, Jacob   153, 154, 163

Virginia School   145

Volker Fund   124

voluntary exchange principle   29

von Mises, Ludwig   121, 122, 126

von Neumann, John   131–9, 142, 188–9, 236

von Wieser, Friedrich   101, 121

wages
efficiency wages   251–2, 254, 255, 257
theory of wage determination   78
wages fund doctrine   65–6, 79

Wald, Abraham   197–8

Wall Street Crash   115

Wallich, Henry   172–3

Walras, Léon   80, 81–2, 85, 86–7, 90, 91, 100, 108, 133, 273

water rights management   219–20, 222–3

Watt, James   42

Wealth of Nations, The (Smith)   9, 36, 38, 40–5, 46, 95, 262

Wesen des Geldes, Das (Money and Currency) (Schumpeter)   104

Whitehead, Alfred North   112

Wicksell, Knut   115, 120, 198

Wigner, Eugene   134

Williamson, Oliver   150, 225

Wilson, Edwin   165, 166, 167

Woolf, Virginia   113

working classes   11, 46, 62–3, 66, 70–1, 72–3, 75–6, 77, 92, 108, 267

World Bank   118, 129

Xenophon   16, 17–18

Yellen, Janet   251, 252, 256–7

Yunus, Muhammad   268